When the Queen was Crowned

When the Queen was Crowned

Brian Barker, OBE

Routledge & Kegan Paul
London and Henley

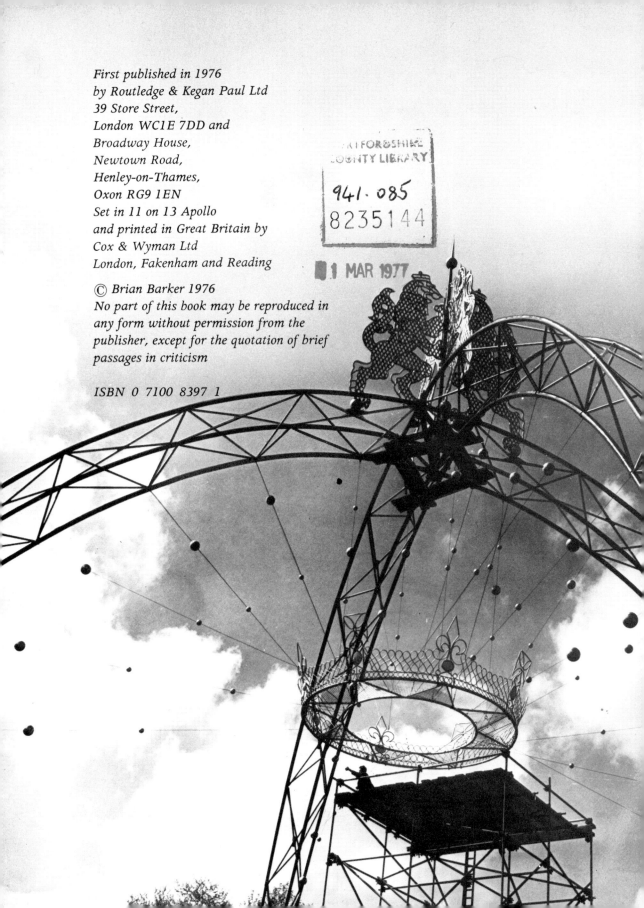

First published in 1976
by Routledge & Kegan Paul Ltd
39 Store Street,
London WC1E 7DD and
Broadway House,
Newtown Road,
Henley-on-Thames,
Oxon RG9 1EN
Set in 11 on 13 Apollo
and printed in Great Britain by
Cox & Wyman Ltd
London, Fakenham and Reading

ISBN 0 7100 8397 1

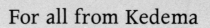

For all from Kedema

First Gent.   God save you, sir! Where have you been broiling?

Third Gent.   Among the crowd i' the abbey; where a finger
                       Could not be wedg'd in more. . . .

Second Gent.   You saw the ceremony?

Third Gent.   That I did.

First Gent.   How was it?

Third Gent.   Well worth the seeing.

Second Gent.   Good sir, speak it to us.

Third Gent.   As well as I am able.

Shakespeare, *Henry VIII*, Act IV, Scene 1

Contents

Illustrations

Acknowledgments

The author and publishers are grateful to the following for kind permission to reproduce illustrations: Times Newspapers 1, 2, 9, 31, 33, 35, 41, 43, 47, 52, 53; Thomson Regional Newspapers 3; Keystone Press 4 and 5; Associated Newspapers 8; Radio Times Hulton Picture Library 19, 21, 22, 24, 25, 26, 29, 30, 32, 34, 38, 39, 40, 42, 45, 48, 49; Fox Photos 28 and 36; The Press Association 44. 6, 7, 10, 11, 12, 13, 14, 15, 16, 18, 27, 46 and colour illustrations I, II, III, IV, V, VI, VII, VIII, IX, X, XI, XII, XIII, XIV are Crown copyright and are reproduced with the permission of the Controller of Her Majesty's Stationery Office. Extracts from the Coronation Service, which is Crown copyright, are also reproduced with permission.

Introduction

'We have had a day', said Winston Churchill, 'which the oldest are proud to have lived to see and which the youngest will remember all their lives.'

The old statesman, himself part of our history, was speaking on the evening of the Coronation of Queen Elizabeth II on 2 June 1953.

Almost every adult in this country will remember what they were doing on Coronation Day. Millions of other people throughout the Commonwealth, in the USA and in other far-off lands will also have their own recollections of that day. It impressed itself significantly on the memory.

On the eve of the Coronation the Gallup Poll estimated that in Britain 17 million people would be taking part in local celebrations, 7 million giving their own parties and 2 million people would be lining the processional route in London.

The huge crowds in London who waited by the kerbside or slept fitfully under ground-sheets in the parks will have their own special recollections of the pelting rain and the cold of the worst June night in living memory. They will remember, too, the voices of all those thousands of people singing together in the rain.

Those who were children will have their own memories. There were children's street parties in every city and town; in the villages there were gatherings on the green and festivities in the gaily festooned village halls. At the end of the day over 2 million children went home clutching their own special souvenir of a Coronation mug.

The wave of happiness and goodwill seemed to spread round the world. Every city and big town throughout the vast territories of the Commonwealth had their streets decorated and their own festivities and parades. Crowds waited through the night as they were doing in London. In Melbourne after the broadcast, the empty streets were suddenly filled with 600,000 people singing and dancing. In the Canadian Arctic Eskimos had gathered in the grey, cold dawn to hear the Abbey service. In Cape Town immense crowds, flocking into the centre of the city to see the decorations and illuminations, brought all the traffic to a halt. In Hong Kong the Chinese population took to the streets to see a quarter-mile-long dragon which symbolised the monarchy leading a procession of stilt walkers and banners with pictures of the Queen. A ring of bonfires on the kopjes around Salisbury in Rhodesia marked the beginning of twenty-four hours of festivities, parades and celebrations. In Colombo, Ceylon, there was a great children's festival of song and dance before the night sky over the crowded city was lit by fireworks and illuminations. Far away in Korea the Commonwealth troops sent salvos of red, white and blue smoke shells into no-man's-land. Millions of people throughout the Commonwealth and in countries which have since sought their independence will remember that day.

So, too, will many in countries which owed no allegiance to the Crown. The streets of beleaguered Berlin were crowded to watch the British troops march by in ceremonial parade. In Paris, thousands of French people jostled outside the shops with TV sets specially placed to show the ceremony. British flags flew all over Copenhagen and they stopped the traffic in the centre of Santiago to let the crowds hear the broadcast without interruption.

At the height of the Cold War, the Soviet Premier Malenkov with Molotov the Foreign Minister came that evening to the British Embassy and smilingly toasted the Queen. In Peking the Chinese ministers also came to the British party, although their battalions, a million strong, were still confronting the Commonwealth and UN troops in Korea. For one day, across the frontiers and ideologies, the nations seemed united in a common sentiment. It is something which many people may also remember about that day.

This book is about what I remember. I was privileged as a Gold Staff Commander to be only a few paces away from the Queen as she was crowned. I was also close to the arrangements which had to be made before the Coronation could take place – the preparation of the ancient Abbey, the decorations of the route, the building of the stands for thousands of people and the many other tasks which had to be done.

During the months leading up to the Coronation I was fortunate to be working close to two remarkable men at the centre of the Coronation, the Duke of Norfolk, Premier Duke and Earl Marshal of England, and Dr Fisher, Archbishop of Canterbury.

I was in 1952 a senior civil servant in the Ministry which, under many different names, had been responsible for the upkeep of the Royal Palaces and for making the preparations for the coronations for many centuries. In my time it was called the Ministry of Works and Public Buildings. It has since been swallowed by the gargantuan Department of the Environment – like Jonah inside the behemoth. I am sure it will emerge intact to discharge its ancient duties on some distant future occasion.

I believe that this is the first time that some account has been given in one book of the work of all those concerned with a coronation – the Earl Marshal and the College of Arms, the Archbishop of Canterbury and the Dean and Clergy of Westminster, the Ministry as well as the other organisations, artists, craftsmen and firms who were concerned during the months of preparation. The tasks they all had to do were within a pattern which had come down to us through the centuries.

The Coronation of Queen Elizabeth II derived its form deep in the past, it summoned up many ancient traditions and was a living proof of how much we had inherited from past generations. I have tried, therefore, to set the Coronation within this historical context.

The monarchy has not always been popular, nor has every coronation day been great and glorious. The first William was crowned in the Abbey with the ancient rites of the conquered people, while outside his Norman troops in a sudden panic drove their horses and drew their swords on the Saxon people around them. King John sat through the ceremony with a sneer on his face and refused to receive the Communion. The coronation of Richard I, the gallant Crusader, was marked by the massacre of the Jews in London and in York. Usurpers have climbed on to the Throne. The monarchy has, however, survived the worst that autocratic kings and self-indulgent Hanoverian princes could do to it. The monarchy seems to have deep roots and an enduring quality in Britain.

Mr Emrys Hughes, MP, published a pamphlet in 1952 criticising the expenditure for the Coronation. It did cost money. The Civil Estimates in 1953 provided a gross sum of £1,206,000 in addition to the £367,000 allocated in the previous year's estimates. The figure was reduced by £648,000 from the sale of seats and other things; the net cost of the Coronation to the public purse was, therefore, less than £1,000,000. It is perhaps worth mentioning that the election and inauguration of President Eisenhower in 1952–3 had cost the equivalent of £25,000,000!

I do not know how to evaluate the credit side of the Coronation accounts. How do you quantify the happiness and rejoicing which spread through the country as the flags and bunting went up? How does one estimate the happiness of millions of children at their Coronation parties? How does one measure the way everyone suddenly seemed to shake off the drabness of the war years and come out to festoon their houses and their little streets and to join hands with their neighbours around the bonfires, the firework displays, the regattas, the roasted oxen and in the crowded and swirling happiness of a thousand ballrooms?

I put the happiness of people first but there were also material benefits. The world focus was turned on Britain – on her industries, her products, her arts and services. There were substantial orders and enquiries which would not have come but for the light that the Coronation had suddenly turned on Britain.

The Coronation also forced the pace of development in many technical fields. The electronics and communication industries certainly felt the impetus. It accelerated the growth of television and lifted it from a junior partner of the media into the dominant position it has since held. The vice-president of one of the TV networks told me that the Coronation had forced television to 'leap forward ten years in ten hours'. Colour television moved a big step forward and behind this progress were the technical developments which spread into other industries.

Overseas visitors came in greater numbers than ever before. The airlines, the shipping lines, the railways and the hotels did very big business. I was reluctant to mention those hundreds of thousands of tourists who came to share the infectious gaiety of London and to see the young Queen drive past in her golden coach. Year by year since then the tourists have come to watch the Changing of the Guard and to stare at the outside of Buckingham Palace. They may indeed come to do just that, but their presence here is not the reason why the monarchy exists, or any justification for it. I am sure the Queen would abdicate if she felt that she exists only as a tourist attraction.

The monarchy is there because it is part of our history. It is there because both the monarchy and the people have been able over the centuries to adjust to the changing needs of the times. It is there, above all, because it meets some deep unexpressed need of the British people.

I am not delving into the psychology involved in that statement. It goes into the depth of our feelings. Mostly we are not even conscious that it exists. It is like the unacknowledged sentiments which often exist between members of the same family. It is a feeling which rejoices at weddings, is saddened at bereavements and joins the members tightly together when threatened from without. Particularly when threatened.

Our attitude to the Queen and the Duke of Edinburgh partakes of that customary family feeling. We are interested, amused, sometimes mildly critical and not prepared to indulge in great shouts of loyalty. We may cheer respectfully on appropriate occasions, but on the great national family occasions all the strong emotions suddenly rise to the surface.

I have seen that happen. An older generation will recall their feelings when the radio kept repeating that the life of King George V was 'drawing peacefully to its close'. I can remember vividly the feelings of sadness and the sense of bereavement as the King's life ebbed away.

I remember, too, the sudden shock at the news of the death of his son, King George VI. Business in shops and offices came to a stop as people gathered together. The lines in London were blocked as people telephoned their families and their friends as though they were seeking mutual consolation.

I was on duty in Westminster Hall during the days when the long lines of people slowly passed the catafalque of the King. The sadness on those multitude of faces was deep and personal. Thousands of those mourners had stood in the bitter cold and driving snow of the long February nights to pay their tribute. They had not endured those hours of waiting to see a spectacle; they came to mourn the death of their King, to pay their last respects of affection and loyalty.

What had been given to the father was also bestowed on his daughter. The 'family circle' closed around her in affection and loyalty. The Coronation was a great event for all her people, not only because she was young and dedicated like her father, but because she was Queen. There was magic in those days leading up to the Coronation.

I was described as a propagandist for the monarchy. It is true that I was the civil servant responsible for the information policy of the Ministry and for its media services. There was in 1952–3 no need for propaganda. I did not send invitations to all the journalists, cameramen and broadcasters who came pouring into London from all over the world. We made no attempt to slant the news or provide any privileged priorities. There were never any special briefings of editors, nor any 'off the record' conferences. We gave the facts as we got them and we kept the record straight.

Nearly a quarter of a century later, I have still tried to keep the record straight in this account of the Coronation. The account can only be given in the context of our history. The event which took place in Westminster Abbey on 2 June 1953 was the perpetuation of a rite of regal inauguration of which the antecedents are far beyond our recall. The 'mists of antiquity' is a fitting phrase to describe the obscurity which surrounds the origins of the ceremony. The mists began to clear about one thousand years ago. Many of the acts, words and anthems in Westminster Abbey in 1953 were seen and heard on the feast of Pentecost in St Peter's church at Bath in 973 when King Edgar was crowned the first King of all England.

I apologise for any errors or omissions in this account. It may have been difficult to avoid them. The history of coronations is a field strewn with errors. Some spectators at past coronations imagined they saw more than they did. There were times, too, when even the experienced officers of the College of Arms, so to speak, tripped badly over their tabards. There was a distinguished historian who brought back by name an Archbishop of Canterbury 100 years after he was dead to consecrate another king! There were even learned liturgists who for over 200 years were unable to distinguish between a stole and a bracelet.

I acknowledge my debt to many people and organisations. I was grateful to the Duke of Norfolk, the Earl Marshal, for his confidence and his hospitality. I recall with respect and affection the patience of Dr Fisher, Archbishop of Canterbury, beneath the non-canonical lights which I had fixed above his head and for his lucid explanations of the liturgy of the Service. I am grateful to the whim of Winston Churchill which brought David Eccles, later Lord Eccles, as Minister of the Department – he brought his great good taste and inspiration to many of the civil aspects of the Coronation.

I have an enduring debt to many of my colleagues in the Ministry, particularly to Auriol Barker, the able Ceremonial Officer who placed his wide knowledge at my disposal. I am most grateful to my own officers who supported me through the strenuous months of the preparations. I must also express my gratitude for our predecessors who had made the preparations for the coronations of other kings and queens. Their meticulous records were valuable sources of guidance and information. I hope that the records which we, in our turn, have left will prove as useful to those who come hereafter.

I am grateful to those to whom I turned for information in writing this book. The Hon. Sir George Rothe Bellew, KCB, KCVO, who, as Garter King of Arms, shared with the Earl Marshal much of the responsibility for the civil aspects of the Coronation, read the chapters on the rehearsals and the Service and made valuable suggestions. The Queen's Press Secretary, Mr Ronald Allison, provided useful information, and the Dean of Westminster, Rev. Edward Carpenter, and the Abbey Librarian, Mr Howard Nixon, gave me the opportunity of checking my recollections of the liturgical aspects. I gratefully acknowledge their co-operation while accepting personal responsibility for the facts and opinions I have written. Finally, I express my deep debt to my wife for her encouragement and suggestions. Her influence is on many of the pages.

The Ministry's photographers recorded each stage of the preparations on the processional route and in the Abbey for our official archives. I am grateful to the Department of the Environment for permission to use many of these photographs. The Central Office of Information also recorded the events and they have given me permission to use their photographs. The colour pictures of the Regalia are Crown Copyright and are published by permission of the Controller of Her Majesty's Stationery Office. The Times Library and the Radio Times Hulton Picture Library provided other illustrations. They are a few of the tens of thousands of pictures which were sent around the world on 2 June 1953.

1 Flight to the Throne

On a cold and grey February day the young Queen, Elizabeth II, came home to begin her reign.

The silver BOAC airliner broke through the thin cloud cover over London Airport, precisely on schedule at 4.18 p.m. on 7 February 1952. Watched by hundreds of anxious eyes it came down gently on the runway and taxied slowly round the perimeter track to No. 1 bay. The BOAC officer standing beside me gave a long sigh of relief. The Queen was safely home.

Princess Elizabeth's accession was undoubtedly the strangest in the long history of the British Throne. At some moment during the early hours of 6 February King George VI had died quietly in his sleep at his home in Sandringham House, where the life of his father King George V had also passed peacefully to its close.

The theory of the British monarchy is that it continues from one heart-beat to the next. Three thousand miles away in tropical Africa, without intermission, the young Princess had become Queen. At the moment of her accession she was in an observation hut, perched among the branches of a giant fig tree overlooking a water hole in an African game reserve. The night had been filled with the sounds of the bush – the trumpeting of elephants, the snorting of rhinoceros, the trampling of fighting water bucks and the noisy chattering of baboons. A place very remote from St James's Palace where the resplendent heralds and the long silver trumpets would shortly come with the ancient sound and ceremony to proclaim her Queen.

Princess Elizabeth and the Duke of Edinburgh were at the start of a tour of Australia and New Zealand by way of Kenya and Colombo. They were deputising for King George VI whose serious illness had forced him to withdraw. They had flown out from London Airport on 31 January 1952 where they had said their public goodbyes to the King. The next morning millions of people had seen the press pictures of that farewell, the tired face of the King, the brave tremulous smile, his right hand raised in a last salute.

Kenya was to be an interlude before an arduous tour. It had been the King's idea, the wish of a parent to have his daughter visit a place where, in the early years of his own marriage, he and his wife had spent happy and exciting days. He had remembered the vast country with affection and had often spoken to the Princess of its teeming wild life, the great trackless bush, the picturesque slopes of Mount Kenya and, above all, of its colourful and varied peoples.

A further inducement to the visit for the Princess was the wish to see Sagana Lodge, the hunting lodge on the banks of the Sagana River which had been presented to her and her

1   The Last Farewell. King George VI waves goodbye to his daughter Princess Elizabeth, as she leaves Heathrow with the Duke of Edinburgh on her Commonwealth tour.

husband as a wedding present from the people of Kenya.

Furthermore, a few miles from the Lodge was 'Treetops', the observation house among the branches overlooking the water hole and salt lick where the wild animals came out of the African night to quench their thirst, attracted by the artificial 'moonlight' around the pool – an irresistible place for a young woman with a flair for cine-photography.

Less than twenty-four hours after leaving London Airport the Princess and the Duke of Edinburgh stepped out of the Argonaut aircraft into the brilliant tropical sunshine at Eastleigh Airport, Nairobi. As the royal visitors were greeted by the Governor of Kenya, Sir Philip Mitchell, the huge African crowd strained forward to see the Princess. There was a great roar of greeting and a wild waving of hands, flags and coloured head bands.

From a high dais the Princess looked down on the excited crowd whose voices were almost drowning the thunder of the twenty-one gun salute. It was a brilliant and exotic scene. Below her were ranged 400 chiefs and headmen who had come from the remotest parts of that vast country – the warriors of the Turkana tribe with towering head-dresses of ostrich feathers and leopard-skin capes, wearing ivory ornaments through their lower lips; beside them were the chiefs of the fierce Masai with tossing plumes of lions' manes, and alongside the sober blue of the RAF guard of honour were the ebony-faced Askari troops in tropical shorts, broad scarlet belts and tall red tarbushes. The strong reds, yellows and magentas of the Africans' robes mingled with the delicate pinks and other shades of the Indian women's saris. It was a flamboyant, tumultuous welcome by the peoples of Kenya. The grey, chill streets of London must have seemed very far away.

There were two days of official events in Nairobi. The Princess relaxed, responding with laughter to the infectious gaiety around her. At the Pumwani Hospital for African Women, newly opened that morning, the smiling mothers proudly held up their babies for the Princess to see. The laughter and eager talk followed her through the wards.

In the afternoon there was a garden party on the sunlit lawns of Government House, surrounded by some of the world's most brilliant shrubs and flowers – a riot of scarlet poinsettias and purple bougainvilleas, sweet scented frangipani and pink oleanders. On that sunny day Africans of many tribes, as well as Indians and Europeans, gathered round the Princess in amity and equality. A reporter wrote that 'fellows in leopard skins were eating cream buns next to women dressed for Ascot'.

The next morning the Princess stepped on to the portico to be greeted by 12,000 children waving a forest of flags, shouting and cheering, in their brilliant dresses looking like some vast herbaceous border. The Princess laughed with happiness at the animated scene.

It was the beginning of another morning of crowded engagements which included a visit to the European Hospital, the opening of the new headquarters of the Kenya Regiment and then on to the Cathedral of the Highlands before returning for a civic reception at City Hall.

That was the end of the official round. In the afternoon the Princess and the Duke drove out to the Nairobi National Park to film and photograph the abundant wild life of that great reserve. The game put on what might almost be described as a 'royal performance'. The Princess was able to film giraffes and zebras, the graceful leaping flight of Thomson's gazelles, the strange gambolling of wildebeeste and at the end of the day their car edged close to a magnificent male lion busy about his supper of wildebeeste. Later as the royal photographers were driving back through the warm, tropical dusk they met a lioness with her four cubs. It must have been a happy and enthralling day.

Early the next morning, 3 February, the royal party drove along the rough, dry Kenya roads up into the Highlands. They were covered in red dust when they arrived at Sagana Lodge, their wedding present house, where it was intended they should spend four carefree and relaxing days. The Princess was delighted by the appearance of the long single-storey building of wood and stone, with its veranda giving a magnificent view of Mount Kenya across the Sagana River. In her eagerness to get inside the Princess fumbled with the key in the lock until Sir Philip Mitchell came to her assistance.

When she was very young the Princess had told a friend that she wished she could live in a small house instead of big palaces, and the Lodge was indeed, by her standards, a small house.

2 Princess Elizabeth opens the door of Sagana Lodge, the gift of the people of Kenya, where she learned of her Accession to the Throne.

There was one sitting-room which ran the width of the house. It had a big bay window overlooking the gay tropical garden. There was a wide stone fireplace and the big armchairs were covered in bright chintz. It was the room in which the Princess was to learn that her hour of destiny had come.

The rest of the house was soon seen. There was the bedroom with chintz curtains and bedspreads. The simple wooden table of the dining-room with tall chairs of untanned leather set out for eight people. Only the Princess's lady-in-waiting, Lady Pamela Mountbatten, and her maid Miss Margaret MacDonald could be found accommodation in the house. Major Charteris, her secretary, and Commander Parker, private secretary to the Duke, as well as Mr Clarke, the detective, had to sleep under canvas in the garden.

The garden itself was a delight. There were English roses planted alongside the exotic African shrubs and flowers and a long winding path shaded by tall trees went down to a rustic bridge across the Sagana River. When she had seen it all the Princess clapped her hands and exclaimed, 'It's a lovely home.'

That Sunday evening they went to evensong in the tiny stone church of Naro Moru and met the Kikuyu tribesman who had built it. Life, it seemed, could be simple and serene.

Monday was another delightful day, riding in the morning, a hasty snatching up of cameras to photograph from a distance a herd of wild elephants moving down the forest road, a game of polo for the Duke at the Nyeri club, an evening fishing for trout on the Sagana River. That evening the Princess told the Lodge caretaker, Mr J. L. Richardson, that they intended to 'come back again and again and would bring Prince Charles and Princess Anne for a holiday too'.

It was now Tuesday 5 February. It was the day for the visit to 'Treetops' where the night would be spent high among the branches of the huge fig tree in the Aberdare forest. The Princess put on brown slacks and a bright yellow shirt. The car stopped at the local primary school in Nyeri where 2,000 children, European, African and Indian, raced out to mob the royal car, wild with enthusiasm. They went on down the dusty road until they had to leave their car at the edge of the forest and begin walking in single file along the narrow pathway through the tall trees. A white hunter with a rifle went ahead and the Duke also carried a rifle in case an elephant or rhino should suddenly come charging down the trail. About every fifty yards rough escape ladders were fixed to convenient trees.

Where the trail broke into the clearing they came to an abrupt halt. The space around 'Treetops' was occupied by a herd of elephants including a large bull elephant. The danger signal of a white pillowcase was fluttering from the hut as the bull elephant circled about ten yards from the access ladder. There was a whispered consultation; the Princess was determined that she would not delay or abandon the long-planned visit to that unique place. The Duke and the white hunter covered the restless animals with their rifles while the Princess stepped out quietly into the clearing, passed the elephants and climbed up the ladder to 'Treetops', thirty feet above. A few moments later she was on the balcony filming the herd which was milling about below her. The white hunter, Colonel Jim Corbett, who watched her cross the clearing, described it as an act of great and cool courage.

In all its twenty years of existence 'Treetops' had never seen such a record show of animals as those which came to the clearing that afternoon and night. Princess Elizabeth was full of delight as the pageant of African wild life trooped, charged and struggled around the pool which filled most of the clearing. The film slipped through the camera, reel after reel.

The cow elephants suckled their young before lumbering away into the forest. The 'resident' party of baboons swarmed back into the clearing, eager for the customary gifts of sweet potatoes. Kraa, the leader of the troop, climbed up to the balcony where the Princess was able to film him in close-up. Two male waterbuck raced out of the forest to clash in combat in the midst of the lake. Five warthogs and a dainty doe bushbuck trotted down to drink.

The long evening shadows lengthened, the night noises of the forest grew, the frogs became vocal and the rhinos came lumbering down to drink. Mr Sherbrooke Walker, the

3   Treetops. The observation hut in the Aberdare Forest where some time during the night of
6 February 1952, Princess Elizabeth became Queen.

owner of 'Treetops', switched on the artificial moonlight. They watched the great beasts snort and splash in the pool until Nderito, the African cook, came to announce that dinner was ready.

Over the simple meal the Princess told Col. Corbett how her father would enjoy the film she was making. She was sure that he had been out shooting at Sandringham that very day. Col. Corbett recorded that 'The young Princess spoke of her father that night with such affection and pride and never had the least suspicion that she would not see him again.'

After dinner they stayed a long time looking down into the strange excitements of the African night. Down below the rhinos circled, splashed and fought in the light of the artificial moon.

It must have been about that time that, 3,000 miles away, King George VI, pleasantly tired after his day's shooting among the wintry woodlands and frosty pastures of Norfolk, leaned back on his pillows and turned off the light.

Several times during the night the royal couple got up from their camp beds as new groups of animals came trooping down to the pool. As the new day broke over the teeming forest, the baboons came swarming up to collect the sweet potatoes placed for them on the window sills.

Their departure was delayed for a short time by two rhinos who were suspiciously investigating the ladder. When they had lumbered away, the Princess said her reluctant good-byes. 'It was one of my most thrilling experiences,' she said.

They climbed down from the tree and went silently along the forest path to the waiting car. Along the dusty road groups of Africans were waiting to see them pass. They did not know that the young girl in the bright yellow shirt, who laughed and waved to them, was already their Queen.

Soon after 10 a.m. the royal party were back at Sagana Lodge. There was still to be another whole day before they left to join the *Gothic* at Mombasa on the next stage of their journey. They went trout fishing again in the Sagana River until lunch time. During the meal, with tropical suddenness, the peak of Mount Kenya was hidden in swirling cloud and a fierce thunderstorm began.

At the Outspan Hotel, 17 miles away, the private secretary to the Princess, Major the Hon. Martin Charteris, had finished his luncheon. It was about 1.30 p.m. local time. He was walking out of the hotel to his car when he was told that he was wanted at the telephone booth near the hotel reception desk.

He knew the man who was waiting for him there. It was Grenville Roberts, a reporter on the *East African Standard*. The journalist was white with shock and blindly turning over and over a cigarette packet in one hand. He looked at Charteris and blurted out his news without any preliminaries.

'The King is dead.'

Charteris looked at him for a long moment in silence.

'How do you know?' he asked quietly.

'I've just had a call from my office in Nairobi,' Roberts replied. 'They have received a message from Reuters.'

Charteris went into the telephone booth and rang Sagana Lodge. He spoke to the Duke's private secretary, Lt Cdr Michael Parker.

'Mike, I've heard what may be bad news about our employer. Do not alarm the lady until I can get confirmation.'

He telephoned Government House in Nairobi but could not get positive confirmation. The Governor of Kenya and almost all his staff were on the train to Mombasa and there was no one to deal with the incoming cipher telegrams. Charteris told John Irving Bell, the Governor's secretary, to put through an immediate priority call to Buckingham Palace and rang off. Telephone calls from the hotel were almost inaudible owing to the storm. Charteris drove to the little wood and corrugated iron post office at Nyeri. Here he was able to get a call through to Sir Frederick Browning, the Queen's Comptroller, on the *Gothic*. Browning had not heard the news. They talked about what to do.

It was not until 2.45 p.m. local time and 11.45 a.m. Greenwich Mean Time that the official confirmation came.

Cdr Parker went round the house to the bay window overlooking the gay tropical garden and managed to attract the attention of the Duke. Cdr Parker beckoned urgently. The Duke came out and the news was broken. They looked at each other in silence before the Duke turned away and went in to tell his wife that the King, her father, had died peacefully in his sleep.

The storm had passed. The sun shone on the wide lawn with its English roses and African trees. There was the harsh calling of an African bird in the podocarpus trees. From far away in the forest across the valley there came the distant trumpeting of an elephant. The Lodge itself was wrapped in silence. In the garden the Askari soldiers were standing dumbly by their tents. In the strangest setting in all our history, far from the customary courts and palaces, a sovereign had learned of her accession to the Throne.

The Queen was the forty-second Sovereign of England since the Norman Conquest. She was the third monarch to succeed while absent from the kingdom; Edward I in 1272 was away on a crusade and George I had been waiting expectantly in Hanover.

She was the sixth Sovereign Queen and the one who was undoubtedly the least prepared for the news of her succession. The first Queen Mary knew that the death of her half-brother, Edward VI, was imminent. The first Elizabeth, secretly forewarned, prepared for the dramatic moment when the Privy Council arrived at Hatfield. Apparently over-whelmed by their tidings, she sank to her knees, exclaiming, *'Domino factum est istud, et est mirabile in oculis nostris'* – 'This is the Lord's doing, and it is marvellous in our eyes'.

The third Queen Regnant, Mary II, like her husband William of Orange, was fully aware that the throne was within their joint possession from the moment of James II's panic-stricken flight to France.

Queen Anne in 1702 had waited at St James's Palace reading the scribbled notes which told of the passing hours of her brother-in-law, William III. Even the young Victoria was not wholly unprepared for her accession. As she hurriedly threw on her dressing gown on that early morning in 1837 she must have known only too well why the Archbishop of Canterbury and the Lord Chamberlain had so urgently ridden through the night from Windsor Castle.

Maybe Princess Elizabeth should have been better prepared, but it is sometimes those who are closest who are the least expectant. They very often do not see what others can see so clearly. The burdens of the monarchy had rested heavily on a good and conscientious King. After fifteen years of incessant strain, including the long war years, he seemed to be a very tired man during the times I saw him in 1951, the year of the Festival of Britain. After the opening of the Festival on 3 May, the King's health began to deteriorate. There was an attack of influenza from which he was slow to recover, a persistent cough, and on 15 September 1951 he had to fly back from his holiday at Balmoral to undergo lung surgery.

The King seemed to make a rapid recovery and by the end of the year he was out and about on the Sandringham estate. On New Year's Day he went out shooting at Heath Farm. The Royal Family were delighted with his progress. On the evening of 30 January 1952 there was a happy theatre party with the King and Queen, the Princess and her husband and Princess Margaret at the Drury Lane performance of *South Pacific*, with its nostalgic and very appropriate songs of faraway places. The audience rose to give them a prolonged ovation. The next morning from the top step of the BOAC Argonaut, *Atalanta*, a smiling young woman turned to wave good-bye to her father.

The blow which fell upon the new Sovereign offered little respite for sorrow. The step from one happy carefree moment to the immense responsibilities of the next had to be taken almost immediately. There was a desk between the window and the big stone fireplace. The Queen sat down to begin the first tasks of her reign. She wrote messages to her mother and her sister, to Queen Mary and the Duke of Gloucester. Then she began writing out the telegrams to her hosts in the Dominions, not cancelling but indefinitely postponing her visits to them.

She was asked how she wished to sign her name. The Queen had been christened Elizabeth Alexandra Mary, and she could have chosen to be known by any of those names. Her father who had been christened Albert Frederick Arthur George had taken the last of those names. But the Queen replied at once, 'Oh my own name – what else!'

Major Charteris had been decoding a telegram from London which requested permission to call a meeting of the Accession Council. The few people who had rallied around their Queen in that remote place were far from the experienced and constitutional advice which would have been available in London. It was correctly assumed that the request implied an affirmative answer. There was a brief discussion on whether the Queen should sign 'Elizabeth R' (Regina) before the Accession Council had met to proclaim her Queen. Again, as it later proved, the correct constitutional decision was made. The Queen for the first time wrote the signature of her reign, 'Elizabeth R'.

The Duke of Edinburgh had been busy on the telephone about the Queen's return to England. He learned that much had already been arranged.

Before the news of the King's death was known to the world, Sir Miles Thomas, chairman of BOAC, had been in touch with his deputy director, Captain Jack Hawkins. They began what Miles Thomas later called a 'frenzy of activity'.

The Argonaut *Atalanta*, which had flown the Queen to Nairobi, had made a second journey with members of the Household to Mombasa, where they had joined the *Gothic* ready for the next stage of the journey. The nearest airfield to Sagana Lodge was at Nanyuki on the Equator, about forty-five miles from the Lodge. It was little more than a landing strip surrounded by bush which was dangerously dry. It was impossible for a large four-engined aircraft to put down at Nanyuki, so it had already been arranged that a Dakota of East African Airways would fly the Queen from the landing strip to Mombasa.

The Argonaut was ordered to fly to the big airport at Entebbe in Uganda and a message was got through to East African Airways to begin tuning the Dakota for a linking flight to Entebbe instead of Mombasa as soon as possible. There were no means of lighting the runway at Nanyuki other than flares, which might set the dry bush alight. The short tropical day would bring darkness before 7 p.m. The Queen had to be flown out of Nanyuki before the night closed down.

In a few hours everything was planned. Instructions were radioed to places thousands of miles apart. Reports on weather and sea conditions over the whole 4,000-mile route were secured and collated. RAF Lancasters with land and sea rescue equipment were put in readiness along the route. Three destroyers – *Saintes*, *Armada* and *Vigo* – were detached from the naval squadron off Egypt to act as sea escort for the Mediterranean crossing. Planes, destroyers and ground stations were allocated a special wavelength for continuous watch. A chain of stations down that long route began to check the efficiency of their radar screens. Within a few hours hitherto routine jobs from Nanyuki to Heathrow were filled with a new and very emotional significance, as thousands of her subjects began to work with speed and concern to ensure the safe return of their Queen.

At Sagana Lodge the time was passing in quiet preparation for the journey. Even on that occasion the royal courtesies were not forgotten. The Queen sat down at her desk again to sign a photograph for each member of the household staff at the Lodge. She gave the photograph and a present with a word of thanks to each one of them. They were overwhelmed with emotion, shaking, tearful, only able to mumble their gratitude. I got their names later in an official report and I think they are worthy of a place in this account. It has usually been chancellors, chamberlains, statesmen, soldiers and archbishops who have surrounded a sovereign on the day of accession. The attendants of the new Queen were more humble folk and they were also possibly more representative of the Common-wealth of which she was now Head. In addition to J. L. Richardson, the caretaker, there was the chief steward, Tom Johnson, who was born in Madras; Paul Fernandes, the cook, was from Goa and the head houseboy was Martin of the Luo tribe; Waithaka of the Kikuyu was the butler; Juma, a Swahili, was a houseboy, and Hussein, a Somali, the table boy. These were the men, so strangely diverse in birth and appearance, who on that historic occasion stood in the sitting-room around their Queen.

As the Queen came out of the door the waiting ranks of Askari troops brought down their rifles in the first Royal Salute to the new Sovereign. Before she entered the car the Queen turned and looked for a long moment at the low building. It was then a few minutes after five o'clock. It must have seemed to her that only a little over two hours ago she had been living in an entirely different world.

The car sped along the red dusty roads where little groups of Africans stood to watch it pass. The town of Nanyuki was beflagged for what should have been the morrow's celebrations, but its streets were filled with silent crowds. So very different from the exuberance of the other days in Kenya.

At the airstrip the Queen was met by Lt Gen. Alexander Cameron, GOC East Africa Command, and the District Commissioner, Mr Glen Lockhart. A group of reporters and press photographers were also waiting on the edge of the airstrip. The Queen was wearing a flowered dress with a white hat and gloves; the mourning clothes which are always in the luggage of royalty on long journeys would be flown in the Argonaut to Entebbe. The press photographers were asked, therefore, not to take any photographs. Every camera was put away. The purple shadows were beginning to fill the low scrub. The Queen turned to enter the plane, and then the instinctive result of her long training made her turn back for a moment to wave and smile. The Dakota was swiftly airborne, just minutes before it would have been necessary to light the flares.

As the Dakota droned along on its 500-mile flight to Entebbe the lightning flickered across the sky and bush fires were burning in places far below. The radio began to crackle. It was a message from Winston Churchill expressing sorrow and allegiance on behalf of the Cabinet. It ended, 'The Cabinet in all things awaits your Majesty's Command.'

The Dakota arrived at Entebbe just before the Argonaut from Mombasa. The Queen was met by Sir Andrew Cohen, Governor of Uganda. The Argonaut landed shortly afterwards just as a violent tropical storm broke over the airport. Departure was delayed for three hours, while the Queen and her party waited in the airport building.

Then at 11.47 p.m. local time and 8.47 p.m. Greenwich Mean Time, the Queen, with the Duke beside her, walked across the shining wet tarmac to board the aircraft from which she had waved good-bye to her father only a week before.

On board the royal couple retired to their private sleeping quarters in the rear cabin. The flight continued under star-bright skies, passing down the Sudan over Khartoum and Wadi Halfa. A refuelling stop was made at El Adem in the Libyan desert. This RAF airfield was still ringed by the bombed German and Italian hangars of the Desert War. The Queen had passed the half-way mark on her 4,200-mile journey.

Soon after the take-off from El Adem, the Radio Officer, J. Miller, in the *Atalanta* reported that they were 168 miles north-west of Tobruk. The bad weather conditions forecast for the Mediterranean had improved. 'Conditions are good, flying at 16,000 feet, speed 240 miles an hour.' In London BOAC again confirmed estimated time of arrival of 4.30 p.m.

From Malta, the naval Commander in Chief, Admiral Sir John Edelsten, signalled to the *Atalanta* over the Mediterranean. 'With humble duty I offer your Majesty the deepest sympathy of all under my command, and the assurance of our unbounded loyalty.'

At every hour, on the hour, Captain R. C. Parker reported height, speed and progress. Rome passed far below and the *Atalanta* began to gain altitude for the crossing of the Alps. The Queen came forward to sit in the second pilot's seat to watch the immense panorama of the mountains passing below. Mont Blanc was crossed in clear skies.

At 2 p.m. Captain Parker reported that the plane was 31 miles from Dijon and heading for Paris. England was coming closer; the long confined hours in the aircraft must have given the tragic flight at times an unreal and dreamlike feeling for all on board.

4   The Queen Returns. The arrival of the young Queen at Heathrow where the Prime Minister, Winston Churchill, and senior Ministers and Privy Councillors wait to receive her.

Approaching Paris the Argonaut began to fly in along the 'Amber Airway N 2'. The coast was crossed at Dungeness and then it began to follow the radar beam from Ashford to Heathrow. Below, with startling suddenness, was the reality of the green fields, the towns and villages and the road patterns of England until the low clouds nearer London pulled a screen across the landscape.

Two motor cycle police escorted the plane as it taxied to Bay 1. Captain Parker cut his engines. The long flight had ended.

As the steps were wheeled across to the big silver and grey aircraft, a small group of black coated and bare headed men appeared on the tarmac. They lined up below the steps.

The Prime Minister, Winston Churchill, and other senior members of the Privy Council were waiting to receive the Queen. In addition to Winston Churchill there was Anthony Eden, Secretary of State for Foreign Affairs, Sir David Maxwell Fyfe, the Home Secretary, Lord Woolton, Lord President of the Council, Mr Clement Attlee, a former Prime Minister, and Mr Clement Davies, Leader of the Liberal Party. As they stood in that wide space, dwarfed by the big aircraft, they looked strangely small, hunched and old as they waited with bowed heads for the young woman to whom they now owed their allegiance.

The Duke of Gloucester went aboard with messages from the other members of the Royal Family. There was a few moments' pause. Then the Queen appeared in the doorway. She stood for a moment looking down at her Privy Councillors. She was wearing a small black hat and a black coat over a dark blue dress. In her left lapel sparkled the flame-lily brooch which had been given to her by the children of Southern Rhodesia.

She walked slowly and firmly down the steps to take up the lifetime of responsibilities which now awaited her. As she stepped on to English soil the waiting Councillors bowed their heads.

She gave her hand to Winston Churchill. 'This is a very tragic homecoming,' she said. She went slowly along the waiting line of statesmen, saying a few words to each.

Lord Woolton later recalled, 'The sight of the young Queen coming, unattended, down the gangway from her plane was one that will never be forgotten. . . . It was a period of deep emotion for everyone – and most certainly for the Queen, and yet, having shaken hands with each member of the Council she went along and spoke to the air crew – royal courtesy took precedence over private grief.'

The great windy space of the airport seemed strangely deserted as the Queen walked to her car. In conformity with the wish expressed by Winston Churchill there were no crowds at Heathrow to greet her. It was a strange contrast to the thousands who had given her a tumultuous send-off exactly one week ago.

In London all traffic halted as the royal cars approached. Little groups of people moved to the edges of the pavements, men took off their hats.

It was shortly after five o'clock when the royal Daimler turned into the entrance of Clarence House. A guardsman was waiting to run up the Royal Standard for the first time. One of the strangest and longest journeys to the British Throne was over. The Queen was home.

2 'The King is Dead . . .'

The Queen returned to a country which was shocked and subdued by the death of the King.

All over Britain, on hearing the news, the churchwardens and sextons came hurrying to the small stone churches, some of whose bells had been cast in the great foundries of the Middle Ages at London, York and Gloucester. They had tolled for the passing of many kings. The bells were also awakened in tall cathedral spires and in the square towers of the minsters.

The people of Windsor listened to the leaden sounding of the Sevastopol Bell in the Round Tower which is tolled only for the death of a sovereign. The Great George in the new cathedral at Liverpool carried its deep message down to the rushing ferry boats at Pier Head. In Oxford, the bell in Christ Church Tower echoed with solemn emphasis over the quadrangles of the medieval colleges and the long congested lines of traffic at Carfax. The bell of Westminster Abbey was heard in the subdued chamber of the Houses of Parliament. The tolling of the bell of St Paul's reverberated over the City of London.

At noon the deep sound of guns added their ceremonial emphasis to the tolling of the bells. The slow crash of the twenty-five-pounders of the Honourable Artillery Company from the Tower echoed over the grey river and the shipping of the Pool of London, firing fifty-six times at minute intervals, one round for each year of the King's life.

In Hyde Park a small crowd gathered in the rain to watch the King's Troop of the Royal Horse Artillery lining up their guns. At Dover the gunfire sent the seagulls clamouring over the white cliffs and at the same minute the harsh vibrations from the old Castle towering over Edinburgh filled the narrow wynds of the Royal Mile and echoed over the Royal Palace of Holyrood. The first solemn ritual for the passing of a king had begun.

Death had come quietly to King George VI at Sandringham, on the estate where he was born and in the house where his father had died. His passing was discovered at 7.30 a.m. when his valet brought him his morning tea. The Queen Elizabeth and Princess Margaret who were also at Sandringham were quietly told.

Sir Alan Lascelles, the private secretary to the late King, began to inform all those who by reason of ties of blood, custom or courtesy must be told before the world heard the news.

Queen Mary was at Marlborough House. She was 81 and the first Queen to see a grand-child ascend the Throne. She was in her sitting-room when her Woman of the Bedchamber, Lady Cynthia Colville, asked to speak with her. The old Queen looked at her with her direct gaze. 'It is the King,' she said.

The Duke of Gloucester, who was at his home, Barnwell Manor, Northamptonshire, prepared to go immediately to Sandringham. The Princess Royal was told at St James's Palace. The Duchess of Kent arranged to return by the first available flight from a visit to Germany. In a suite in the Waldorf Astoria in New York the telephone awakened the man who might still have been King. It must have been poignant news for the Duke of Windsor.

After the members of the Royal Family had been told, the more official business of the King's death was begun. The Prime Minister, Winston Churchill, as was his custom in the morning, was sitting up in his bed surrounded by official papers. The deep emotion of the moment when he received the news was still evident in his voice when he broadcast that evening.

The Archbishop of Canterbury, who was ill with bronchitis at Lambeth Palace, was informed at about the same time as the Home Secretary, Sir David Maxwell Fyfe.

The Lord Chancellor, the Speaker and Lord Chamberlain began to prepare the business of state which they would have to transact that day.

At Arundel, the Duke of Norfolk, the hereditary Earl Marshal of England, interrupted his breakfast for the urgent call to the telephone. When he had last received a similar call on the death of King George V in 1936, he had been a young man of 28. The funeral of the King's father and the coronation of George VI and Queen Elizabeth had been among the first of his hereditary duties.

The Foreign Office began to cable in cipher the news of the King's death to the embassies and ministries. The message flashed round the world instructed ambassadors and other British representatives to inform the governments to which they were accredited and to pass the news to all consular posts. The Accession Council had not met so there was not any reference in the messages to the new Queen.

The communication centre at the Admiralty in Whitehall began to send out the message to all commands, ships and shore stations of the Royal Navy. The signal lights in the long grey or white ships began to flash from Portsmouth to the great harbour of Hong Kong. At that time there were Royal Navy ships on every ocean of the world from the cruisers and destroyers still on active service off the coast of Korea to the frigate *Burghhead Boy* off the bleak Falklands. At the Royal Gunnery School at Whale Island, Portsmouth, the captain of HMS *Excellent* was ordered to make ready the gun carriage on the quarter deck which had been used for the funerals of Queen Victoria, King Edward VII and King George V.

All Army commands around the world were informed by priority signal. It was a time when the British Army was stretched very far around the turbulent globe – in Cyprus, Aden, Malaya, Singapore and in far-away Korea. In Korea the bitter truce discussions were still going on at Panmunjom. There was a strange episode when the North Korean delegates were informed that the artillery of the Commonwealth Division would fire a ceremonial salute!

The King's Company, First Battalion of the Grenadier Guards was ordered to leave Victoria Barracks at Windsor for Sandringham immediately. Since the reign of Charles II this company of the Grenadiers had provided the bearer party at the funeral of every sovereign.

My own Ministry was among the first to be informed because of the duties it would have to put in hand immediately. Early on the morning of 6 February I was telephoned by the Ministry with the request to get to Lambeth Bridge House as soon as possible. The duty officer told me he could not be more specific on the open line.

We had been called together by Sir Eric de Norman, the Deputy Secretary in charge of the 'traditional' side of the Ministry. We were joined by my namesake, Auriol Barker, MVO, who was Assistant Secretary of the Ancient Monuments Division and also the Ceremonial Officer of the Ministry. During the coming months I was to be very grateful for his wide experience. With us also was Sir Charles Mole, the Director-General of Works, responsible for the architects, surveyors, engineers and other technical staff, and Eric Bedford, the Chief Architect who was to have an important place in the planning of the Coronation.

That day the Coronation was not mentioned. The Minister, David Eccles, would meet the Earl Marshal and the Lord Chamberlain before midday to discuss the King's funeral. He had to be given a short brief – in the meantime there was much to be done.

The Jewel House in the Tower must be closed to the public to remove the Imperial Crown, the Orb and the Sceptre for the Lying-in-State. C. V. Mann, the Crown Jeweller, would have to check the setting of the jewels. At the funeral of King George V, the new King Edward VIII, walking behind the gun carriage, had seen a 'flash of light dancing along the roadway', as the Maltese Cross on the Imperial Crown had fallen from the coffin. It was snatched up, scarcely missing a step, by the alert Company Sergeant Major. The new King had walked on, wondering, so he later said, if it had been a bad omen.

Westminster Hall had to be closed for the building of the catafalque and arranging the carpeting and lighting. Crush doors had to be erected at St Stephen's Entrance, and provision made for medical services for people who might come to wait during the long cold hours. Special arrangements were made for the entry of royal mourners, foreign royalties, High Commissioners and other VIPs. The custodians of all Crown buildings had to be instructed to put flags at half-mast as soon as the public announcement was made.

When I returned to my office I turned on the radio. The interminable *Mrs Dale's Diary* was chattering along. The voices faded slowly away. There was a long silence before I heard the voice of John Snagge, the BBC's senior announcer.

'It is with the greatest regret that we make the following announcement.' He paused for a few seconds and went on. 'The King, who retired to rest last night in his usual health, passed peacefully away in his sleep early this morning.' He paused once more before he added, 'The BBC offer profound sympathy to Her Majesty the Queen and all the Royal Family.'

I looked across the grey river and watched the flag being slowly lowered on the Victoria Tower of the Houses of Parliament. I knew that the flags were also being lowered over all the territories of 500 million people to whom George VI had been King. Later in the official press summaries I read how flags had come down in nearly every country in the world. In the USA the flags were at half-mast not only in New York and Washington but also on state capitol buildings and little red schoolhouses right across the continent. At a bitter time of the Cold War the tribute of the flags was paid in the Soviet Union, and even on the Soviet HQ in beleaguered Berlin.

The reaction to the news passed round the world. The legislatures of Commonwealth nations were adjourned, as was the Congress of the United States. Across Europe senates and legislative chambers interrupted their business while the deputies rose to stand in silence. The world paid tribute to a good and sincere man who had served his peoples with quiet devotion.

The British Parliament met at 2.30 p.m. that afternoon. The proceedings lasted only a few minutes. Usually they began with a prayer which had included the reference to 'His Majesty King George'. The formalities for the Accession had not been completed so there could not be a reference to 'Queen Elizabeth' and prayers were omitted. Shortly before 2.30 the subdued murmur of conversation stopped as the doorkeeper called 'Speaker'. The assembly rose at the entry of the Speaker, Mr W. S. Morrison, who was wearing the white lawn bands of mourning, and the Serjeant-at-Arms, black-gloved with the Mace.

The Prime Minister, Winston Churchill, waited until the Speaker was seated, then he rose in his place. He was wearing the Edwardian frock coat and black cravat of his usual formal attire. It was a strange destiny which, time and again during his long lifetime, had called upon him to assume the principal part at some moment of historical significance. When Edward VII had died in May 1910, both Houses were in recess, and the Prime Minister, Asquith, was abroad. Parliament was recalled and it fell to Winston Churchill as Home Secretary to make the announcement. He was 35 years old. Forty-two years later he rose again to make a similar statement.

'Mr Speaker – the House will have learned with deep sorrow of the death of His Majesty King George VI. We cannot at this moment do more than record the spontaneous expression of our grief.'

'The Accession Council will meet at five this evening.' He glanced towards the Speaker. 'I now ask you, sir, to guide the House as to our duties.'

The Speaker replied that he would suspend the sitting until seven that evening. At that hour he would take and subscribe the oath and give an opportunity for members to do the same.

In the House of Lords the same simple formality was carried out. The Lord Privy Seal, the Marquess of Salisbury, made the announcement, and he too referred to the five o'clock meeting of the Accession Council.

The Lords and Commons had suspended their sittings. The supreme legislative assembly of the United Kingdom – Parliament itself – had passed the authority for the inauguration of the new Sovereign to a body which most people knew nothing about and which they hear mentioned only once in the lifetime of a sovereign – the Accession Council.

3 'God Save the Queen'

The Accession Council is much older than Parliament. Constitutional historians trace its beginnings to the great Council of Elders, the Witan of the Anglo-Saxon peoples. It was the Witan which in those distant and often troubled times selected the man most fitted to be king.

After the Conquest, the Witan was replaced by the Great Council of the Norman Kings, composed of the great officers of state and other notables. It did not always hold fast to the feudal principle of primogeniture. When Richard Coeur de Lion died childless, for example, the throne by strict hereditary descent should have passed to Arthur, son of Geoffrey the King's next brother. Instead the Council, unwisely as it proved, elected John to be King.

The Council was not superseded by the growth of Parliament. The Council was constantly meeting: Parliament often did not meet for long periods. Furthermore until 1867 Parliament itself was dissolved immediately on the death of the king. Only the Council was able to act with the speed which the times often required. In those days the king made haste to be crowned.

As Parliament grew in influence, it slowly came to have a more powerful voice in matters affecting the Crown. Kings went beyond the Council for confirmation. The founders of the new dynasties in particular were careful to have their royal title confirmed by Acts of Parliament. When Henry IV deposed Richard II his title to the crown was confirmed by statute. Again, the crown which was picked up by Henry VII on Bosworth Field was also confirmed in his possession by Act of Parliament. The issue of the 'divine' right of the Stuart kings was decisively settled by the Revolution of 1688. James II believed he had become king by hereditary and divine right. William III and Mary II could have had no such illusions. The crown was conferred by Parliament conditional on their acceptance of statutory obligations – the Declaration of Rights, the Coronation Oath and the principle of the Protestant succession.

In every reign since 1689 Parliament has legislated to define the relationship between State and Crown. An Act in 1701 'for the further limitation of the Crown and for the better securing of the Rights and Liberties of the Subject' enacted that 'whosoever shall Hereafter come to the possession of the Crown shall join in the Communion of the Church of England'. That is still the position.

The post-war years brought great changes to the new nations and the territories of the British Empire. The India Independence Act of 1947 removed the title 'Emperor of India' from the royal titles, and the reference to 'Dominions' also disappeared. The title 'Head of the Commonwealth' appeared for the first time in the Proclamation of Queen Elizabeth II.

It was within this complicated context of law and custom, ancient rights and solemn obligations that the Queen had come to the throne. Despite all the changes of the centuries, the passing of kings and even dynasties, the revolutions and the constitutional upheavals, the Accession Council was still there and once more was moving into its traditional place at the centre of events. Parliament was quietly leaving the centre of the stage to a body which, so it seemed, was being summoned out of the remote past for its single brief appearance.

An old form of words, used again on this occasion, summoned an assembly of 'the Lords Spiritual and Temporal of the Realm assisted by the members of his late Majesty's Privy Council with numbers of other gentlemen of quality with the Lord Mayor of London and the aldermen and citizens of London.'

Over 300 members were summoned as soon as the death of the King was announced. The summons also included the Great Officers of State like the Lord Chamberlain and the Earl Marshal, the Duke of Norfolk, whose ancestors had attended many such Councils of the Realm. In keeping with the new status of the Commonwealth nations all their High Commissioners in London were invited. The Deputy Prime Minister of Australia chartered a plane from Paris and arrived in time to sign the Proclamation.

A small crowd had collected in the darkness and the rain to see the members of the Accession Council arrive at St James's Palace before the five o'clock meeting. The City provided the only touch of colour and pageantry with the liveries of the Sheriffs and Aldermen.

At the meeting the Clerk to the Privy Council, Francis Fernau, read the Proclamation which was signed by the 191 persons present. It was published the same evening in the London Gazette.

It was the traditional practice after the reading and signing of the Proclamation that those who were not Privy Councillors should withdraw; the second part of the Accession Council was, therefore, a meeting of the Privy Council at which the Sovereign entered to make the formal Declaration and to sign the necessary statutory documents. At that moment in February 1952 the Sovereign was over 4,000 miles away being driven along the red dusty roads to Nanyuki airstrip. It was arranged, therefore, that this second part of the Council should be held on 8 February 1952, two days later, at 10 o'clock on the morning after the Queen's return to London, when 170 Privy Councillors gathered. They were joined by the Duke of Gloucester and the Duke of Edinburgh.

A few minutes after 10 o'clock the Lord Chamberlain, the Earl of Clarendon, came to indicate that the Queen was ready. Then the double doors of the Throne Room were opened wide and the Queen entered. For everyone there it must have been an unforgettable moment. She was wearing black from her shoes to her close-fitting felt hat. She walked alone to the table. She looked composed, dignified and very young, as she took up the text of her Declaration and began to read in a clear voice.

'Your Royal Highnesses, My Lords, Ladies and Gentlemen: By the sudden death of my dear father I am called to assume the duties and responsibilities of sovereignty.

'At this time of deep sorrow it is a profound consolation to me to be assured of the sympathy which you and all my peoples feel towards me, to my mother, and my sister, and to the other members of my family.

'My father was our revered and beloved head as he was of the wider family of his subjects: the grief which his loss brings is shared among us all.

'My heart is too full for me to say more to you today than that I shall always work, as my father did throughout his reign, to uphold constitutional government and to advance the happiness and prosperity of my peoples, spread as they are all the world over.

'I know that in my resolve to follow his shining example of service and devotion, I shall be inspired by the loyalty and affection of those whose Queen I have been called to be, and by the counsel of their elected Parliaments.

'I pray that God will help me to discharge worthily this heavy task that has been laid upon me so early in life.'

The Queen placed the text of her Declaration again on the table and taking up a pen she signed the two copies of the first official document of her reign. It was the traditional Oath to 'preserve the settlement of the true Protestant religion as established by laws made in Scotland'.

The first copy of that document was immediately sent by messenger to Edinburgh where the Lord President of the Court of Session would direct that the appropriate record should be made in the Books of Sederunt of the Court and that the document should be lodged in the Public Register of Scotland.

The Queen completed the meeting by signing a few official documents which had arisen from her father's death. Then, still alone, she walked back to the Throne Room, while the standing Councillors bowed deeply once again.

The constitutional formalities of the Accession were completed. The way had been prepared for the King of Arms and the Heralds to appear on the scene.

That morning when I had walked through St James's Park the grass was still crisp with the snow which had fallen during the night. The wind from the lake had a knife edge. The Guardsmen in their heavy greatcoats and bearskins had already lined the Mall and the approaches to Friary Court, on the east side of St James's Palace. A great crowd of spectators were tightly packed along the pavements.

The winter sun glowed on the rose- and honey-coloured bricks of the Palace; the hands of Henry VIII's clock on the tower were just visible above the battlements. Shortly before 11 o'clock a window in the north-west corner was discreetly opened, inside I would see the square-set figure of Winston Churchill, here to witness another episode in our history.

As the old clock moved to the hour a blaze of brilliant colour began to spread out along the parapet. The State Trumpeters in their magnificent plum-coloured coats heavily laced with gold moved to each side of the balcony. Behind the trumpeters came Garter King of Arms and the Heralds and Pursuivants of England. Their tabards were brilliant in shades of red, blue and gold. The Duke of Norfolk was in plumed hat and gold-braided uniform.

The trumpets pealed. The old clock began melodiously to sound the hour. The troops presented arms. Sir George Bellew, the Garter King of Arms, stepped forward to read the

PROCLAMATION OF ACCESSION

Whereas it has pleased Almighty God to call to His mercy our late Sovereign Lord King George VI, of blessed and glorious memory, by whose Decease the Crown is solely and rightfully come to THE HIGH AND MIGHTY PRINCESS ELIZABETH ALEXANDRA MARY:

We, therefore, the Lords Spiritual and Temporal of this Realm, being here assisted with these His late Majesty's Privy Council, with representatives of other Members of the Commonwealth, with other Principal Gentleman of Quality, with the Lord Mayor, Aldermen and Citizens of London, do now hereby with one Voice and Consent of Tongue and Heart publish and proclaim, THAT THE HIGH AND MIGHTY PRINCESS ELIZABETH ALEXANDRA MARY is now, by the death of our late Sovereign of happy memory, become Queen Elizabeth II by the Grace of God, Queen of this Realm, and of Her other Realms and Territories, Head of the Commonwealth, Defender of the Faith, to whom Her Lieges do acknowledge all Faith and constant Obedience with hearty and humble Affection, beseeching God by whom Kings and Queens do reign, to bless the Royal Princess, Elizabeth II, with long and happy years to reign over us.

GOD SAVE THE QUEEN

Proclamation. His clear modulated voice carried effortlessly far beyond the Court.

'Whereas', said Garter King of Arms, reading from the parchment roll, 'it has pleased Almighty God. . . .' The ancient form of words rolled smoothly on.

'The Crown is solely and rightly come to the High and Mighty Princess. . . .'

The Tudor battlements of St James's Palace were looking down on a scene which they had witnessed many times before.

'. . . to whom her liege do acknowledge all faith and constant obedience with hearty and humble affection, beseeching God, by whom Kings and Queens do reign to Bless the Royal Princess Elizabeth the Second with long and happy years to reign over us.'

Garter looked up from the parchment, raised his plumed hat high and cried, 'God Save the Queen.'

The trumpets began to sound with peal rising upon peal until their fanfares were merged in the rising notes of the National Anthem from the Coldstream Guards' band. When the last note faded away everyone stood in silence as though reluctant to leave the moment behind. Then the glittering pageantry on the balcony began to filter away through the open window. In the silence we could hear the distant crash of the guns firing the salute in Hyde Park.

I looked up at the window in the north-west corner. Winston Churchill was standing looking down into the Court. He had lived in six reigns. He was 77 years old. His glance seemed sombre.

We walked swiftly down the Mall with the crowds towards Admiralty Arch. The flags were again flying at full mast, as they would this day to sunset. Trafalgar Square was a densely packed concourse of thousands of people. The 'Blues' of the Household Cavalry clattered through the Arch, plumes dancing. They were followed by the College of Arms in four closed landaus, the coachmen and footmen wearing red cloaks and black silk hats with gold and black cockades. Behind were four State Trumpeters and another escort of red-coated and white-plumed cavalry.

The carriages and escort halted before the statue of King Charles I. The hood of the first carriage was lowered and the Lancaster Herald, Archibald Russell, stood up to read the Proclamation. Once again the trumpets pealed, the Corps of Drums of the Brigade of Guards began to roll and the band began the National Anthem. Immediately the huge crowds in the square took up the words, singing with intensity and fervour. It was the first time in most of their lives that the familiar words rose with a great swelling of emphasis to 'the Queen'.

The procession clattered away towards Temple Bar where the traditional red silken cord barred the entrance to the City. The Marshal of the City would ride forward with a curt challenge, 'Who comes?' and the trumpets would sound the notes of the medieval parley. A Pursuivant would advance to the barrier, 'Her Majesty's Officers of Arms who demand entry into the City of London in order to proclaim Her Royal Majesty Queen Elizabeth II.'

The Pursuivant would present an Order in Council requiring the Proclamation to be made. The Lord Mayor would receive it and reply, 'I have attended to perform my duties in accordance with the ancient usages and customs of the City of London.'

When the ancient usages had been thus asserted, the barrier would be removed and Norroy and Ulster King of Arms, Sir Gerald Wollaston, would read the Proclamation at Temple Bar, and it would be read again before immense crowds waiting at the Royal Exchange.

With less splendour but with similar formality the Proclamation was being read in the cities, towns and ancient boroughs of the United Kingdom.

Along the Royal Mile in Edinburgh a long procession walked in state to the ancient Mercat Cross – the scarlet-robed judges of the Court of Session, the Lord Provost, the Hereditary Keeper of the Palace of Holyrood, the Duke of Hamilton and Branden, and other uniformed officers of the Queen's household in Scotland and of the Armed Services. The members of the Court of the Lord Lyon King of Arms were waiting in their gold and scarlet tabards.

Edinburgh, like London, also has its ancient customs. The Proclamation was read first by the Lord Provost, James Miller, to his own citizens of Edinburgh. Only then was it read to all the peoples of Scotland by the Lord Lyon, Sir Thomas Innes of Learney. The guns from the Castle ramparts roared out across the city. It was then read again at the gate of the Castle, at Holyrood Palace and at the shore of Leith. At Leith, the Albany Herald, Sir Francis Grant, had read the Proclamation for the fifth time, having proclaimed Edward VII, George V, Edward VIII and George VI.

The ancient city of York had also its own customs. The Lord Mayor, Alderman J. H. Kaye, surrounded by the Esquires of the Sword and Mace, having read the Proclamation, raised to his lips the ancient gold cup from the City Treasury. 'I drink to the health of her Majesty the Queen.'

In Cardiff, thousands of children were among the crowds gathered before the City Hall to hear the Queen proclaimed. At Caernarvon the words were read in Welsh and English.

At Plymouth the silver bugles of the Royal Marines sounded the fanfares before the guns of the warships in the harbour thundered across the Sound.

Later, in press summaries and official reports I learned how the Queen had been proclaimed throughout the nations, colonies and territories of the British Commonwealth.

Canada was the first of the Commonwealth nations to proclaim the Queen, without waiting for the Accession Council in London. She was proclaimed as 'Queen of Canada and Head of the Commonwealth'. It was only in the United Kingdom that the title 'Defender of the Faith' conferred on Henry VIII by the Pope was used in the Proclamation.

In Australia, in drizzling rain a huge crowd gathered to hear the Governor-General, Sir William McKell, read the Proclamation from the steps of Government House in Canberra. Beside him stood the Prime Minister, R. G. Menzies. In Australia the Queen's titles included 'Supreme Liege Lady in and over the Commonwealth of Australia'.

In New Zealand the Proclamation was read on the steps of Parliament House and telegraphed to the mayors of towns and cities throughout the country for 'public acclamation'.

In Ceylon the Proclamation was read in three languages, English, Sinhalese and Tamil, to the large crowds outside Parliament House. The Royal Title was 'Queen of Ceylon'.

In Nairobi, the Queen was proclaimed from the steps of Government House where a few days before she had been greeted by the gay and excited gathering of thousands of children. The Queen had cabled the Governor, 'Our sorrow at this time will not erase the happy memories which my husband and I will always keep of our visit to Kenya.'

The Queen was proclaimed as 'Sovereign in and over the Union of South Africa' in ceremonies from end to end of that vast country. In Southern Rhodesia, the African chiefs and thousands of their tribesmen came hurrying to Salisbury for the Proclamation.

In Pakistan the Proclamation was surrounded by some of the old splendours of the former Imperial times.

Round the world in all the British realms and territories – Malta, Gibraltar, Cyprus, Hong Kong – the same words were spoken with the traditional ceremonies.

The reports spoke of the great crowds of many races in many lands who gathered, often in the rain, to hear the Proclamation. In a world full of brilliant spectacles there should not have been anything of great interest in seeing a man in a plumed hat reading from a piece of paper. Yet in every state and provincial capital throughout the vast territories of the Commonwealth there had been large gatherings of people to witness a simple ceremony, which most of them could have heard on the radio.

Even more impressive were the reports from the local papers. What motivated the population of a small town in Alberta, Canada, to shut up their shops and stand in freezing temperatures to hear the local store owner, their civic head, proclaim the Queen? Why did such big crowds gather around the residence of a District Commissioner in Tanganyika so that he had to climb on to the roof of the bungalow to be seen and heard?

On that day there was a remarkable similarity between the behaviour of the people in an African kraal, a Sinhalese village, a small town in the Australian outback, a sheep-farming community in New Zealand and a village in the Cotswolds.

In many languages, the peoples of many lands 'with one voice and consent of tongue' were also proclaiming at that time their own unity beneath the Crown.

Winston Churchill, in a broadcast on the evening of the Queen's return, had found memorable and eloquent words of tribute to the late King and of allegiance to the new Queen. His broadcast was heard throughout the Commonwealth and the next day's events were reflected in his concluding sentences. 'Tomorrow the proclamation of her sovereignty will command the loyalty of her native land and of all other parts of the British Commonwealth and Empire.

'I, whose youth was passed in the august, unchallenged and tranquil glories of the Victorian era, may well feel a thrill in invoking once more, the prayer and the Anthem.'

His voice rose in a powerful acclamation in which the millions who were listening to him must have also joined in the loyal invocation: 'GOD SAVE THE QUEEN.'

4   The Royal Book of Kings

Winston Churchill was standing at the top of the steps from St Stephen's entrance, looking down into Westminster Hall. I paused behind him so as not to cross his line of vision. He was wearing a black overcoat with a blue scarf wrapped closely around his throat; his skin was like pale wax. He was watching the preparations going on below. He turned his head, saw me and gestured towards the big floodlights which had been placed at the side of the Hall.

'Those lights?' he questioned briefly.

'They are temporary, Prime Minister – to help with the sewing of the carpets.' He nodded, satisfied.

He turned to look at the flags of the Commonwealth which were fixed below the great window. He stumped away, his gait like that of a man climbing a mountain.

Westminster Hall is a place of echoes, every footfall on the old flagstones is magnified by the vast hammer-beam roof. Hundreds of yards of felt and carpets were needed to hush the footfalls of the thousands who would come this way during the Lying-in-State. Six sewing women were moving slowly forward on their knees.

The carpenters were busy with deal and Columbia pine making the pedestal for the catafalque. The old roof caught the sound of tools which were still very like those which had shaped its timbers over 600 years ago.

The evenings I spent there were the coldest I can remember. The old stone walls seemed to magnify the freezing temperatures outside. The lights in the roof were diffused by a pale mist. The place had the depression and chill of a tomb.

King Edward VII had been brought here for his Lying-in-State in 1901. King George V had lain in this Hall, and, in his turn, his son, King George VI, would be carried here. His catafalque was being built on the exact spot where his father had rested. In a subdued atmosphere the work went forward.

On the late afternoon of Monday 11 February all was prepared and we were waiting. The subdued lights from the dark roof were falling on the crimson carpet on the steps leading up to the purple catafalque.

Four Yeomen of the Guard came down the steps from the north-west corner and took up their positions as silently as Tudor ghosts. There was a shuffling of feet on St Stephen's steps as the long lines of the peers and the commons came down into the Hall on each side, to stand in silence. In their brilliant tabards, in two lines, the heralds and pursuivants paced down the Hall to the great north door. Behind them went the Earl Marshal and the Lord Chamberlain in scarlet uniforms and David Eccles, the Minister, in morning dress.

Two Yeomen were slowly drawing open the great door. There were brisk words of command, the grating of wheels, the tramp of feet in New Palace Yard.

In a moment, behind the heralds came the eight Grenadiers, their arms linked, moving in the unison of six-inch paces. They moved without sound on the heavy carpeting. Above the dull grey of their white-belted greatcoats was the conspicuous yellow-gold of the Royal Standard draped around the coffin. The diamonds in the Imperial Crown sparkled with a hundred points of light as they moved towards the catafalque.

Behind the coffin the Queen walked alone, heavily veiled and in deep mourning. The Queen Mother and Queen Mary walked behind her. A few moments before a press photographer had taken the historic picture reproduced on page 32. The camera had recorded a unique moment in English history: three Queens, together at one time, in a common unity of sorrow.

The service, conducted by the Archbishop of York, Dr Garbett, was short and simple – the Lord's Prayer, a prayer of remembrance and thankfulness for the King's reign and for his 'unwearied devotion to duty; for his steadfast courage in years of war; and for the love and loyalty borne to him by a vast family of people in every part of the world'.

The choirs of the Chapel Royal and Westminster Abbey sang the sweet and melancholy cadences of 'Abide with Me'. The Archbishop gave the blessing. It was over. The Queen turned slowly and walked quietly to the great door; the heralds moved alongside the royal mourners. The late King was left in the care of his soldiers and his servants.

The jewelled Orb and the glittering Sceptre were brought down and placed beside the Imperial Crown, the Orb on the right and the Sceptre on the left. Never for a second during the next three days and nights of the Lying-in-State was the guard around the catafalque relaxed. The Yeomen of the Guard were on the outflank, the reversed points of their partizans touching the floor. Then, on the first step, the Gentlemen at Arms, axes reversed, in their dark cloaks with scarlet collars, their plumed helmets towering above everyone; and one step higher, the four officers of the Household Cavalry, their arms resting on their reversed swords. They were all so still that it was difficult to believe that they were breathing men until at the signal of a sword hilt moving in its scabbard, they came into slow ceremonial life. Later the breastplates and plumed helmets of the Household Cavalry were replaced by the scarlet tunics and bearskins of the officers of the Foot-guards.

For two hours the High Commissioners, the Ambassadors and other privileged people passed through the Hall. After them came the people. In daylight and in darkness, in bitter frost and swirling snow the people waited outside the Hall, moved forward a few feet, and waited again. Hundreds waited all through the night and thousands more came at first light. At times the line of people, four deep, stretched away down Millbank and over Lambeth Bridge for a distance of three miles.

Inside the Hall the two-fold column moved endlessly past. Women curtsied to the catafalque; men paused to bow. Now and then a woman or a child dropped a posy of violets or primroses at the feet of the Yeomen. They were representative of every age, type and class of the British people; among them were people from the Commonwealth, Americans and Europeans. There were crippled people who were carried past by the ambulance men we had provided.

5   The Tragic Queens. Outside Westminster Hall the three Queens, Queen Mary, Queen Elizabeth the Queen Mother and Queen Elizabeth II await the arrival of the funeral cortège.

6   The Lying in State. The sombre scene in the ancient Hall.

One by one the kings and heads of state came to the Star Court entrance on the west side of the Hall and stood in the archway opposite the catafalque. There was Queen Juliana of the Netherlands, King Haakon of Norway, King Frederick of Denmark, King Gustaf of Sweden.

I was standing near the archway when the Duke of Windsor came with his mother, Queen Mary, and the Princess Royal. I bowed to the man who might have been King and to the old Queen and her daughter. The Duke's face was grey and deeply lined. His feelings were beyond my imagination. I went away.

By day and by night, the ordinary people came to pay their last tribute to the King. More than 300,000 people waited in the bitter winds and snow by day and through the long nights to pass silently through that ancient Hall.

After three days the doors were finally closed. Tens of thousands of people lined the funeral route through London. The last guard was mounted at the catafalque before the Grenadiers linked arms again to bear the King away. To those of us left standing in the Hall it seemed that there was a strange feeling of emptiness around us. The long vigil was over.

The preparations for the Coronation pressed in upon us immediately. The Ministry's Coronation Committee held the first of the weekly meetings which would continue until the ceremonial events were finally over in the late autumn of 1953. We met under the chairmanship of the Permanent Secretary, Sir Harold Emerson, a very capable and experienced administrator, and we were the heads of the divisions which would be responsible for the thousand jobs which had to be done – Sir Charles Mole, Director-General of Works; Eric Bedford, the Chief Architect; H. L. Raybould, the Controller of Supplies; the Ceremonial Officer, Auriol Barker, and myself. The heads of other divisions such as Contracts, Engineering Services and the Bailiff of the Royal Parks attended when their work came up for discussion. Through its personnel the warrants of the Earl Marshal, and later the decisions of the Coronation Commission and the Joint Coronation Committee were carried out so far as they fell to the Ministry to perform. The Ministry's Committee provided not only a forum for decision, but also gave a broad view of the progress of the whole Coronation arrangements.

Immediately after the Accession the press speculation on the possible date of the Coronation began. They read like facts and were copied as such in Commonwealth papers. R. A. McMullen, the Agent-General for Alberta, Canada, telephoned to say he had heard from people in the Province who wanted to know if they should book their hotels for the 'Coronation in August'.

I looked at the press cuttings. The *Empire News* had big headlines – 'Coronation on August 7'. The *News of the World* also had on its front page – 'Early Coronation Prospect'. The Monday morning papers were following their Sunday companions in forecasting an early date.

By then I knew that these speculations were not feasible. In past centuries the new sovereign had been hurried off to the security of the Tower of London while hasty preparations were made for the coronation. Those were the times when 'good swords were more important to a king's coronation than the preparing of long clothes'.

As the centuries passed the interval between the accession and the coronation had grown longer and the arrangements had become more complex. Queen Victoria had been crowned fifty-three weeks after her accession and since then the interval had been at least one year. There were many reasons for this.

The coronation was no longer the personal business of the sovereign and a tight little band of court officials and statesmen, with a piece of pageantry for the worthy citizens of London. It had become a world-wide affair which could affect many interests in Britain and in the many countries and territories under the Crown.

As in 1937, all these interests would be brought together in the Coronation Commission under the Chairmanship of the Duke of Edinburgh. Its members included the Prime Minister and Cabinet Ministers, Privy Councillors, the Archbishop of Canterbury, the Earl Marshal, the Lord Chancellor and the Scottish Law Lords. The Commonwealth countries were represented by their Prime Ministers, when they could attend, but more continuously by their High Commissioners in London.

The Coronation Commission at its first meeting in May appointed the Coronation Joint Committee to examine the various problems which might arise. There were also two committees to deal with matters relating to the United Kingdom. These were the Coronation Committee of the Privy Council which made any necessary Orders in Council and the Coronation Executive Committee of the Privy Council which comprised the United Kingdom delegation to the Coronation Joint Committee. It was through this hierarchy of committees that the main decisions would be made and recommendations submitted to the Queen.

This set-up was cumbersome in practice. It took a long time for decisions and recommendations to reach the top and the delays made difficulties. In spite of the wide range of experience represented on the Commission and its committees some unwise decisions were made. The decision to restrict the televising of the ceremony was perhaps the most conspicuous lack of collective judgment; it created such a popular clamour of protest that the decision had to be reversed.

That was, however, in the future. In the meantime the Ministry had to get on with all the tasks which were, in theory, dependent on the decisions of the hierarchy of committees. Many months of work would be necessary. In deciding the date of the Coronation account had also to be taken of the weather. Multitudes would pour into London for the Coronation. Tens of thousands would line up along the route for the whole night to get a good place. There would be outdoor fêtes and festivals everywhere. The prospect of warm summer weather was, therefore, a very important consideration. These events needed long hours of daylight. These factors ruled out the period from September to April. July and August are holiday months. That left May and June.

At the first meeting of the Departmental Coronation Committee we made the informal estimate that the Coronation would be in the last week in May or the first week in June in 1953.

The date of 2 June was within our forecast. It was also, alas, one of the coldest June days of the century!

In the meantime press speculation had focused on an early Coronation in August 1952, and the lead of the British press was being followed by newspapers all round the world. A lot of premature plans would be made by thousands of organisations and people unless something was done. I got in touch with my colleagues in other Government Departments. The War Office estimated that 20,000 troops would be needed for lining the route, and the Commonwealth countries and the Colonies would want to send their own contingents. Transport and quarters would take months to arrange. Furthermore British troops were fully stretched from the cold front in Germany to the troubled areas of Malaya and Korea. In a year things might be better.

The Admiralty would have its own problems in staging the Naval Review which had become a regular event in coronation years. The RAF saw great difficulties in assembling its own presentation. The Commonwealth Relations Office estimated that at least 200,000 people would come from the Commonwealth and the Foreign Office spoke of even larger numbers from the USA and other countries. This meant the organisation of ships and aeroplanes to meet the demand. The Board of Trade stressed the need for new hotel accommodation where so much had been destroyed during the war.

All these views and many other considerations confirmed my own Ministry estimate that the Coronation could not take place for at least a year. In the meantime something had to be done about the press speculation which was growing into a firm editorial commitment to the coming August. At that time no one was in the position to make a firm official announcement. The Coronation Commission had not even been appointed. A very unofficial finger had, therefore, to be placed in the leaking dyke of speculation. My colleagues in other Ministries and myself began, very informally, to tell our friends in Fleet Street why, in our personal opinions, there was unlikely to be an early Coronation. Newspapers usually respond when they have the facts – it is secrecy and silence which create the problems. The speculations died away. *The Times* and the *Daily Mail* quoted 'reliable sources' as stating that speculation about the date of the Coronation was premature at this stage. The *Manchester Guardian* reported that the Ministry had not yet begun its preparations and could not do so until the 'ceremonial framework' had been established.

While I was thus concerned with the complexities of the modern world a far more remote past caught up with me. A messenger wheeled into my office a trolley loaded with files. My personal assistant, Miss Sheila Bell, came with them.

'Did you send for all these files?' she asked with astonishment.

I looked at the top files. 'No,' I replied, 'they have come from the Ceremonial Officer.'

'You have papers from the Building Research Station, and Mr Roberts wants you to approve the format of the new Housing Manual.'

'I think we can deal with that this afternoon.'

I began to take the files from the trolley. 'Arrangements for the Coronation of Her Gracious Majesty Queen Victoria.' Inside were pages of the beautiful penmanship of an early Victorian civil servant.

'Matters Consequent upon the Postponement of the Coronation of His Majesty King Edward VII.'

'Decorations of the Royal Processional Route for the Coronation of His Majesty King George V.'

'Design and Construction of the Annexe for the Coronation of His Majesty King George VI.'

With the files had come a note from Auriol and a small book, beautifully bound in red leather. He wrote: 'You might like to borrow this book from my personal library. Expert opinion is that it was prepared about 1307, with the longer rubrics introduced about 1377. Religious and dynastic changes have brought some amendments, but the arrangements will still be the same for the coming Coronation of Her Majesty. We shall certainly be following the same fourteenth-century directions for the preparation of the Abbey.'

I looked at the book of directions which were still extant after 600 years. The gold lettering on the soft red leather read – *Liber Regalis* – The Royal Book. I opened the book to read:

This is the Order according to which a King must be crowned and anointed.

First, there is to be prepared a stage somewhat raised between the high altar and the choir of the Church of St Peter near the four high pillars in the cross of the said Church. At the ascent of the stage there are to be steps from the middle of the stage in the west side by which the Prince to be crowned can ascend the said stage at his approach, going through the midst of the choir. In the midst of the said stage shall be prepared a lofty throne, that the Prince may sit upon it and be seen by all the people. . . .

There were pages of instruction for the crowning and anointing of an English king. The preparation of this order of the ceremony was, I read, attributed to Nicholas Lytlington, Abbot of Westminster in the fourteenth century. Even he, so it also seemed, was collating the form of a service which had been used at least as early as the coronation of King Edgar at Bath in AD 973. Now after all these centuries the old churchman was still prescribing the order of the ceremony by which Queen Elizabeth II would be crowned in 1953!

5 'The Earl Marshal's Handyman'

The Minister was looking at the faded illustrations of other coronations. A senior architect pointed to the Annexe built on to the Abbey for the coronation of William IV.

'You will notice, Minister,' he said, 'that the style has always been pseudo-gothic.'

David Eccles looked up from the drawing. There was a moment of icy silence. Then he said, very quietly, 'There will be nothing pseudo about this coronation.'

He was referring to more than the design for the Annexe.

David Eccles's appointment as Minister of Works had taken the Civil Service and his parliamentary colleagues by surprise. There was a rush for the reference books. They did not tell us much. The Member for Chippenham was the son of a Harley Street doctor. He had been adopted as Conservative candidate for a by-election at Chippenham in 1943, and had scraped in with a mere 195 votes. He was 48 and had been at Winchester and New College, Oxford. In 1926 he had begun work at the Central Mining and Investment Corporation and, thirteen years later, at 35, he was managing the £4,000,000 business.

We looked at our new master with curiosity. He had bright brown eyes, greying hair streaked thickly back at the sides, a pink complexion and a deeply dimpled chin. Sitting behind his work desk he looked completely self-possessed, remote and very determined.

He needed every scrap of that determination. The building industry had been enmeshed in a web of post-war licensing and other restrictions; bricks, timber, cement, drain pipes and even nails were in short supply. Housing drives had been repeatedly started and had lumbered to a halt.

The '300,000 houses' announced by Harold Macmillan seemed an impossible task. Eccles tackled his part with confidence. There was nothing gentle about his methods. He punctured the fumbling excuses, trod heavily on reluctant toes; his arrogant determination was often furiously resented. But things began to move – brick kilns were opened up again, cement works raised their targets, other materials began to move forward. He showed the impact which a resolute Minister can make on an industry.

Across the river at the Ministry of Housing, Macmillan was introducing, in his own words, 'some unorthodox methods to win success', often to the dismay of some of his senior civil servants. Regional Housing Boards were set up. Ernest Marples with his great drive and knowledge of the industry was pursuing unorthodox methods of building houses. By January 1952 over half a million houses were on order or already in the programme. The impossible was becoming the attainable.

Harold Macmillan got the houses, but in my opinion it was David Eccles who gave him the bricks to do the job.

Then suddenly, Eccles found himself responsible for the preparations for the Coronation. The man and the moment had come together. He had taste, style and imagination. He felt that this was a great opportunity to lift people out of the bleakness of a post-war era where meat, eggs and sweets were still rationed and where the bomb sites in London were still showing the broken teeth of bricks and rubble.

'The Ministry of Works is the builder, decorator, electrician and stage hand of the world's most glorious and moving pageant,' David Eccles told journalists. 'I am the Earl Marshal's handyman. My job is to set the stage, to build a Theatre inside Westminster Abbey; to provide seats and standing room, decorations along the path of the processional route which is Crown property; to arrange flowers, floodlighting, fireworks and other expressions of public rejoicing; and to take care of press broadcasters and cameramen.

'In due course I shall receive a warrant to take control of the Abbey from the Dean and Chapter and to carry out all the work necessary to provide the setting for the Coronation ceremony itself. The transformation of the most historic church in the Commonwealth has to be carried out with minute care. Some of the monuments and tablets will be muffled in felt and boarded up. We must return the Abbey to the Dean exactly as it was when we took over.

'The Coronation Theatre, the Sanctuary and St Edward's Chapel have to be prepared in accordance with the tradition which has come down to us over the centuries.

'We are already busy on the designs for the fabrics and carpets with which the Abbey will be decorated. The finest embroideries will cover the Altar frontal and the Regalia table. The Throne Chair, the Faldstool and the Homage Stool will be made for the occasion.

'I shall also have a warrant to build and furnish an Annexe at the West End of the Abbey. . . . Its design will give an opportunity to harmonise a modern structure with the ancient grandeur of the Abbey.

'The tradition and ceremony are inherited from the past and must be scrupulously preserved, but it is our duty to express in colour and design the age we live in and the Queen who is to be crowned.'

The final sentence remained his keynote for the Coronation.

The Ministry had a huge shopping list; and a big task of building, decorating, craftsmanship and designing. We required steel scaffolding and timber for the Abbey and for twenty-seven miles of seats in the public stands. We had to place contracts for miles of cotton, nylon and silk draping, thousands of yards of carpets; eleven acres of flowers had to be grown to come into bloom on a single day. We required coats of arms, tapestries, Commonwealth emblems, cloth of gold, tons of fireworks and a thousand other requirements.

This meant the prospect of much work for architects, designers and craftsmen. Several of them suddenly remembered our distant acquaintance. I had pressing invitations to lunch, particularly if I could bring the Minister. The Minister himself received similar indications of goodwill. Eccles would have none of it.

'There is plenty of talent in this Ministry,' he said. 'The men who can build atomic plants, furnish embassies and design public buildings have the capacity to do this task. It is only fair to let them get on with what is a gay and colourful job.'

Eccles brought only three outsiders into the creative team which worked for the Coronation – Constance Spry for the floral arrangements, Professor Robert Gooden, who designed the blue and gold frontals in the Abbey, and James Woodford the sculptor.

My closest working contacts were with the talented and charming Constance Spry. She had the splendid idea of flying flowers in from the Commonwealth to decorate the Annexe and the Commonwealth stands in Parliament Square. For that moment of inspiration she paid with months of panic-stricken anxiety. 'They must not arrive too early or too late,' she pleaded. I had struggles with airlines and officials all round the world to achieve that result. Many strange and exotic flowers arrived in the peak of perfection on the coldest June day of the century. Constance Spry was the only woman in the history of the Coronation who kept a rare Malay orchid alive through a cold night with a hot water bottle!

The first speech of the Minister about the Coronation was, appropriately, to the Federation of Painting Contractors.

'Let us have a return to gaiety in colour,' he said. 'London for the past hundred years has been painted in sombre greens, drab greys and browns. Let's brighten up our buildings. Dip your paint brushes in the new and brighter colours. Let's make London and our other cities gayer. There is no better time than the Coronation. The Ministry will do its part. We haven't a lot of money to spend. We will have to make this a great Coronation out of very little. We are going to do it. It is going to be a better Coronation than ever before.'

He was out next morning, striding round Parliament Square and Whitehall, looking at the frontages of the buildings for which he was responsible. They were black with the grime of the war years. They had, he said, to be bright and beautiful before June 1953.

The Victoria Tower of the House of Lords was swathed in an ugly web of scaffolding. A few workmen scraped and replaced the bomb- and grime-scarred stones. He wanted to know when the scaffolding would come down. It was a big job said the surveyor, and would not be finished until the autumn of 1953. The Minister went to see for himself, ascending the 392 feet of the Tower in a windy builder's hoist. The work was remarkably speeded up.

It had to be the 'best possible Coronation' but there was not going to be any rush to spend public money. With the Contracts Division, Eccles began to work out ways to get some of the expenditure back. The timber for the Abbey and the stands was cut to lengths which would enable it to be sold again for other building work. In 1937 the Government had subsidised the seats in the public stands at half their cost price. Not this time. 'They are a bargain at their full cost price. The ticket agencies are selling places in shop windows along the route for five times the price.'

During the months of preparation Britain came back into the focus of the world in a way which had not happened since Dunkirk. A young Queen on an ancient throne had a compelling interest for the media. Here was romance, colour, pageantry and glittering ceremonial. Here was an enchanting relief from a world divided by the menace of the Cold War, weary from the agony of Korea, beset with monetary problems, plagued with shortages and darkened with doubts about the future. Pressmen, film-makers and

7   Coronation Press Conference. David Eccles, the Minister of Works, describes the Ministry's preparations to hundreds of journalists, film and TV cameramen. The author is seated on the left of the Minister.

broadcasters turned to Britain as though a warm bright light had been suddenly lit in a darkened world.

I told the Minister how the world was knocking on our door. He saw the implication at once.

'We must look after everyone who comes,' he said. 'For every thousand who will watch the events in London in June next year, there will be a million who will watch through the eyes of the press, the film and TV screen. We must do all we can to see that those eyes are not obstructed and that what they see brings credit and dignity to our Queen and to our country.'

These were sentiments which he repeated on more public occasions. We unfolded our part in the Coronation story as we went along. It was often a strenuous task.

David Eccles made his own contributions to the effective telling of the story. He went carefully through the photographs of previous coronations to see how the placing of the press and film cameras could be improved.

We went to a screening of the black and white film of the 1937 coronation. He noticed that when the King arrived at the Annexe his face was in deep shadow. He told the Chief Architect to use a transparent canopy which could let in the maximum light.

He said to me, 'That is a superb place for recording the Queen's arrival and departure from the Abbey. Can we fit in a press photographer and a film camera behind the fascia?'

We did. The chosen two nearly died from cramp and exhaustion. The photographs through the canopy were reproduced all round the world.

I arranged another screening, this time of the colour films which were made of the royal funeral. From that moment he was determined to get colour films of the Coronation, inside and outside the Abbey.

He told the film producers: 'It should be the best colour film ever made. Even Cecil B. de Mille can't put on a background like our Coronation.'

From then on, much of the colour planning for the Mall and other parts of the royal route were looked at as they would appear to the eye of the camera. He brought his own good taste and very prolific ideas to the architects. He encouraged them to break away from traditional designs for buildings and for decorations. He wanted high arches, brilliant plaques of heraldic designs, surfaces filled with colour.

During all this he did not relax his drive on the housing problem. He divided his days and often his nights to keep both fronts moving. As his later career was to show, once he was committed to a course, he followed it with inflexible determination even at the expense of his ambitions. He was outstanding in those fields in which his personal interests and taste could march with his political ideas. He was acknowledged by all parties later to have been, for example, a first-rate Minister of Education.

He did put his personal interests, his tastes, his ideas and his political ambition into the preparations for the Coronation. His influence was felt in nearly every aspect of these preparations. I think he succeeded in his aim to make the setting for the Coronation one that was fitting for 'a young Queen and for the age we live in'.

6 The Master of Ceremony

The coronation was a muddle from beginning to end.

The workmen in the Abbey had come out on strike for more pay and delayed the preparations for two days. On the morning of the coronation it was found that the deputy Earl Marshal had forgotten to order the canopy and the chairs of state. He had also mislaid the Sword of State and the Lord Mayor of London came forward to offer his own sword as substitute. The start of the whole Service was delayed for more than an hour, and even when it began the continuing blunders and confusion caused titters of amusement from the congregation in the Abbey. The solemn service was in danger of becoming a coronation comedy.

These events happened at the coronation of George III in September 1761. The blunders and confusion did not end with the service in the Abbey. Chaos reigned at the Banquet in Westminster Hall. The service in the Abbey had blundered on for six hours until darkness fell; the attendants in Westminster Hall had not dared to light the candles in case they burned out before the end of the Banquet. The head of the returning procession stumbled into the Hall in the dark; swords got tangled with legs, robes were torn, coronets lost. The Hall resounded with the jangling of metal and the shouts and curses of the noble Knights of the Bath. The candles were lit just in time for the arrival of the King.

But worse was still to come. In the confusion of the entry many guests had hurriedly seated themselves without regard to order or precedence. The Barons of the Cinque Ports lost their traditional places, but so also had the Knights of the Bath and the powerful Aldermen of the City of London. They all surrounded Lord Talbot, the High Steward, with shouts and threats. The Aldermen, believing that money talks, shouted that they had contributed £10,000 to the cost of a banquet. The frantic Lord High Steward pushed them into places at a table reserved for Peers of the Realm, which created further angry disputes. There was no place for the Knights of the Bath and they were eventually seated in lonely isolation in the Court of Bequests. The Barons of the Cinque Ports, trailing their robes, scurried round the Hall, finding places anywhere they could squeeze themselves in.

But for the unfortunate Lord High Steward the crowning indignity was still to come. It was the custom for the Lord High Steward to ride on horseback into the Hall during the banquet. Lord Talbot had spent days patiently schooling his horse to withdraw backwards from the royal presence. On this occasion, the well-trained animal lost its sense of direction and despite the frantic efforts of the Lord High Steward to reverse its motion, the horse continued to progress backwards down the Hall to present its large backside to the royal gaze. The Hall hooted with laughter and derision. It was Wilkes's insulting reference to this humiliation which later provoked the notorious duel between him and Lord Talbot.

At last even the good nature of George III had reached its limit; he sent for the deputy Earl Marshal and complained sharply about the confusion of the day.

The reply was the ultimate blunder of the day. 'It is true, sir', he replied humbly, 'that there has been some confusion, but I have taken care that the *next* coronation shall be regulated in the best manner possible.'

There are many records of the event being marred by mistakes and confusion in the ordering of the ceremony. Even as late as the coronation of Queen Victoria, the ecclesiastical dignitaries had fumbled their way through the service. Queen Victoria confided her opinion to her diary. When at the Recess she retired to St Edward's Chapel she was astonished to find the altar 'was covered with sandwiches, bottles of wine, etc. etc.'. The Archbishop of Canterbury was 'confused, puzzled and knew nothing'. One of her two supporting bishops, the Bishop of Durham, 'was remarkably maladroit, and never could tell me what was to take place'. The Archbishop insisted on forcing the coronation ring on her wrong finger, causing her intense pain during the rest of the service.

In May 1952 we received a summons to a meeting in the Abbey with the Earl Marshal. Within a few moments of our meeting, I knew that this Earl Marshal would ensure that this Coronation would be 'regulated in the best manner possible'. There would be no confusion, no fumbling and no excuses on this occasion. Bernard Marmaduke Fitzalan-Howard, 16th Duke of Norfolk, Premier Duke and Earl, Hereditary Earl Marshal, knew precisely how a coronation should be arranged.

He had gained experience of his hereditary role at the coronation of George VI in 1937. At 29 he had been one of the youngest Earl Marshals to officiate at a coronation. His expert knowledge of heraldry and ceremonial matters had been widely acknowledged. He was now bringing this experience and his organising ability to this new occasion.

He went about the immense and complicated business with a quiet competence. Matters went as he directed, because he obviously knew better than most what had to be done. He had the air of authority, but none of the ostentation of rank. It was, however, perhaps the long hereditary standing of the Dukes of Norfolk which made him seem like a man who had his feet very firmly on solid ground. He could be friendly, relaxed and amusing. He was on occasions a generous and entertaining host to me and my colleagues. He could also puncture pomposity with a single verbal arrow. He had a devastating gift of fitting very apposite nicknames to people which fitted them as smartly as a boot.

He wore dark charcoal-grey suits, white stiff collars and pearl grey ties. He always wore his waistcoat with the bottom button undone. I noticed that all the Heralds and Pursuivants wore waistcoats with their suits. The Archbishop of Canterbury also had an expressed preference for conventional dress – when his Grace was around all the senior clergy invariably appeared in gaiters.

That morning the windows of the Abbey were luminescent with sunlight. We were standing in the great crossing in front of the High Altar in the place where the Coronation would take place. The Earl Marshal arrived, punctually almost to the second, followed by Dr Alan Don, the Dean of Westminster.

The Dean gave me the impression that reincarnation was a feasible hypothesis. I watched him walking through the choir to join us – black garbed like his Benedictine predecessors, with a monkish stoop and the hollow-cheeked features of those Abbots who must often have come that way during the long centuries of monastic rule.

In this place the Dean was also a man of authority. It was an authority which was confirmed, like the Earl Marshal's, by tradition and by Royal Charter. After the Reformation the power and privileges of the former Abbots had been perpetuated by the Charter of Queen Elizabeth I in 1560. The old Abbey of Westminster had enjoyed special privileges as custodians of the Regalia and keepers of the church of the coronation. The *Liber Regalis* gave the Abbots a place in the ecclesiastic ceremony next to that of the Archbishop of Canterbury himself. The Deans of Westminster had continued to exercise these ancient privileges within the Abbey.

Dr Don wore his authority with a certain austerity of manner. There were times during the following months, when the Abbey was filled with timber and scaffolding, when the patience of the Dean was sorely tried. Dr Don was, however, a man of impressive dignity, with a wide knowledge of Church matters, and a strong protective feeling for the great church in his care.

The main business of the meeting was swiftly settled. The Earl Marshal had been sent the architect's plans for the construction of the raised platform for the ceremony which would occupy the space before the High Altar and between the four great pillars down almost to the choir. This had been done from century to century, from one coronation to the next, as laid down in the *Liber Regalis*. The architect had shown me the construction drawing for the platform, and then laid alongside it the structural elevations of the platform used at the coronation of Queen Elizabeth I.

'The structural details are remarkably similar,' he had pointed out. 'The main beams cross the same areas, the working drawings for the supporting frames and the uprights are almost identical. We could almost have used the plans for the first Queen Elizabeth for the base of the Theatre for the second Queen Elizabeth nearly four hundred years later.'

Over the centuries the main variation had been in the height of the Throne above the platform. For the coronations of the two boy kings – Henry VI and Edward VI – the pedestals for their thrones had been raised to unusual heights so that these royal small boys should be clearly seen and recognised by the congregation. The Throne of Edward VI had been ascended by a flight of twenty-two steps.

This morning the Earl Marshal had not had to consider any such problems. The plans showed the steps up to the platform, bringing the Theatre level with the Sanctuary and five steps from this up to the Throne. This arrangement of the steps of the Theatre had been used at the coronation of King George VI and his consort Queen Elizabeth. The Queen Consort's throne had, however, been raised three steps instead of five. This time, however, there would be only one throne. The Duke of Edinburgh would be with the other two Royal Dukes in the South Transept in the front rank of the peers.

On one point the Earl Marshal wanted an assurance. He had heard that the timber stocks in the country were new and unseasoned. He wanted to be sure that there would not be any noise from the platform as the ritual movements of the ceremony went on. The Queen mounting her Throne to the sound of groaning timber might be regarded as bad an omen as the jewel which fell from the crown of George III at his coronation, which was later regarded as presaging the loss of the American colonies.

The Earl Marshal was assured that the timbers would be fully seasoned, treated and tested for their sound-proof qualities.

He nodded. 'Very well.'

He turned to look up into the South Transept where in due course the tiers of seats would rise almost to the level of the great window far above. In these seats the peers would sit in their traditional positions at the Coronation.

'I was speaking to your Minister about the possibility of getting more people into the Abbey. I will be under great pressure to provide more room. There will be more Commonwealth representatives and still more people will feel that they should be here on this occasion. I shall have to hold a ballot for places for the House of Lords and the Commons. I do not wish to restrict the number of seats for people with traditional claims, so every extra seat will be important.'

We had been anticipating this request and Eric Bedford had scrutinised the plans of every available inch of space in the Abbey. 'On this occasion we shall be using lighter steel framework to support the tiers of seats, instead of the heavy timber, in some places. This may give us some extra space, but I do not think it will amount to very much.'

'Do what you can,' said the Earl Marshal. 'I would like to see the seating plans as soon as they are ready.'

As we stood there that morning in 1952 it suddenly occurred to me that we were re-enacting a discussion which must have been held many times before. Down the centuries similar small gatherings of men had come together at intervals for the same purpose which had brought us there that very day – the preparations for the crowning of an English sovereign.

The Dukes of Norfolk had been doing the job for quite a long time. It was in 1483 that King Richard III appointed John Howard, Duke of Norfolk, as Earl Marshal and instructed him to prepare Westminster Abbey for his coronation. This Duke also became Commander of the English Army until he was assassinated in his tent on the night before the Battle of Bosworth in 1485.

A vestige of the former military role of the Dukes of Norfolk is that as Earl Marshals they are heads of the College of Arms. The hereditary post of Earl Marshal had, however, moved at times to collateral branches of the family, returning again to the Dukes of Norfolk in 1672.

The Dukes of Norfolk have not only been the great ceremonial officers of the Realm. They have played an illustrious, and sometimes fatal, part in the history of their times. It was the 4th Duke whose marriage to a Fitzalan heiress brought Arundel Castle into the family. He lost his head after he gained the Castle. Queen Elizabeth I regarded him as the friend, and possible lover, of Mary Queen of Scots and he was beheaded in the Tower.

His son nearly suffered the same fate. He was also imprisoned in the Tower. Queen Elizabeth offered him his freedom and the restoration of his estates if he would abandon the Roman Catholic faith. He refused and he died in prison. His descendants eventually won back their titles, their estates and their ancient hereditary position.

As Roman Catholics there were times when they could exercise their function as Earl Marshals only through the Protestant branches of the family. It required an Act of Parliament in 1824 to restore the Dukes of Norfolk fully to their ancient role at the coronation.

It is only in Britain that one could witness such a strange anomaly as a Roman Catholic duke exercising wide authority in one of the most famous Anglican churches in Christendom, preparing the ceremonial for a religious service which would be conducted by a staunchly Protestant Archbishop of Canterbury!

The Hereditary Earl Marshal was also one of the Great Officers of State whose position still keeps some of its ancient authority. He was not, like most of them, appointed 'only for the day'. His most important duty was the coronation but he was also in charge of ceremony on other state occasions.

The Earl Marshal's fee for his services at the coronation had once been that he should receive 'the horse and palfrey on which the king rode to his place of coronation, together with the bridles, saddles and caparisons; also the cloth spread at the table whereat the king dined; the cloth of estate which hung behind the king at dinner; the chines of all swans and cranes served up, and sundry other fees appertinent to the office of High Usher.'

But times have changed. The Earl Marshal now had to support the dignity of his office on a fee of £20 per annum, paid half yearly.

Certainly in modern times the appointment has been no sinecure. I doubt if the Earl Marshal had any leisure time during most of 1952 and 1953. He had to superintend all the arrangements for the Coronation ceremony in the Abbey, with the exception of the Church Liturgy. His other responsibilities included the sending out of the summonses to peers and the other invitations to attend; the compiling of the seating positions within the Abbey; issuing dress regulations; the organisation and timing of the Abbey processions; and the appointment of Gold Staff Officers.

As Chairman of the Coronation Joint Committee he was involved in many complex problems far beyond the realms of ceremony. Somewhat to his astonishment in 1953, he found himself undertaking some of the new duties of his office – appearing on television and holding press conferences.

As *ex officio* head of the College of Arms he was served by a capable and experienced group of officers from the College. The chief was the Garter Principal King of Arms, Sir George Bellew, once the Somerset Herald and then the youngest officer ever to hold the senior post at the College of Arms. In the months before the Coronation I met Garter frequently as we went about our tasks in the Abbey. His manner had none of the flavour of old parchment once popularly associated with the pursuit of heraldry. He was always informative about the historic background of the Coronation, and he could give the subject of royal ciphers and ancient crowns a genuine fascination.

The Kings of Arms, Heralds and Pursuivants in their brilliant tabards have moved down the centuries as the proclaimers of sovereignty, the precursors of peace or war, and the guiding masters of the great ceremonial occasions. They came to their full status

8   The Earl Marshal in Coronation Robes with his two pages, Duncan Davidson (right) and James Drummond.

in the Courts of Chivalry of the twelfth century. A knight in full armour was recognisable only by the individual charge – or symbol – on his shield. At a time when few could write, a personal armorial seal was indispensable for charters and other documents. The Heralds devised these symbols; in time the arms became hereditary, a protected privilege.

The registering of pedigrees and the devising of coats of arms still occupy most of the time of the officers of the College. From time to time, however, they are summoned from the rather drab building in Queen Victoria Street, and changed from sober-suited men into strange figures of impressive dignity, blazoned with the richness of the golds, reds and blues of their medieval tabards. They reach the summit of their responsibility and their splendour at a coronation.

The Ministry, after some search, set up operational headquarters for the Earl Marshal in October 1952 at 14, Belgrave Square. The thirteen officers of the College of Arms could not possibly handle the whole complex operation. Clerical and other staff were seconded from Government departments and specialised staff were recruited. The officers of the College became in effect the heads of the departments, each handling one aspect of organisation; with Garter, in the current phrase, acting as chief executive.

The ceremonial movements and positioning of each participant in the event were set down on scale plans. Everyone received the plans relating to his movements at each stage. Later all the movements were carefully rehearsed in the Abbey. Everyone was thoroughly familiar with his part, his place and his progression well before 2 June. I received the same meticulous attention on my appointment by the Earl Marshal as a Gold Staff Commander. I had twenty-eight pages, the complicated layout of the Abbey and other matters to master as well as taking part in the rehearsals in May 1953.

The movements of nearly 500 people were thus co-ordinated into the smoothly flowing progression of ceremony and timing which millions of people were able to watch on 2 June 1953. I am sure that none of the Earl Marshal's ancestors had ever done better.

7 The Archbishop of Canterbury

The Archbishop of Canterbury was seated on some planks of timber in Westminster Abbey, occupied with the *Times* crossword puzzle.

He looked up and said, 'This one is somewhat difficult. I usually do them in half an hour.'

I said, 'I don't want to interrupt your Grace. We are ready to test the lighting, but we can delay for a while.'

'No, no,' he replied, and folded the newspaper. 'The crossword is not important. The solution will probably come to me while I am occupied with something else.'

He brushed wood dust off his black coat before striding briskly towards the Sanctuary, where the lighting engineers were waiting.

The Most Reverend and Right Honourable Geoffrey Francis Fisher, MA, DD, the ninety-ninth Archbishop of Canterbury, was a very remarkable man. He carried his high dignity with a total lack of pomposity or affectation. His immediate predecessor, William Temple, had been an Archbishop in whom every inch was impressive with ecclesiastical dignity. His most simple words were a splendid oration.

Geoffrey Fisher was a complete contrast. He was unassuming, easy in manner, very approachable, and he had a real interest in all manner of men. He was the sincere and simple Peter following in the footsteps of the eloquent and masterful Paul.

On his frequent visits to the Abbey, he walked briskly around, asking questions of the workmen, taking a knowledgeable interest in every aspect of the preparations. One of the men working on the scaffolding said to me: 'Excuse me – is that nice parson really the Archbishop of Canterbury?'

I assured him that he was. He nodded and said, thoughtfully, 'It's a pity there aren't more parsons like him.'

Behind this simple directness, the ability to reach out to ordinary people, was a very able and informed mind. At Exeter College, Oxford, he had gained academic distinction. Throughout his life he went on adding to his knowledge of ecclesiastical history. He had a good teacher's ability to communicate. He had, in fact, been a schoolmaster. He was headmaster of Repton before he had been appointed Bishop of Chester in 1932. Like all his appointments it caused a lot of surprise.

'He has no parochial experience,' one clergyman complained in his parish magazine. 'I cannot see any reason why he should have been appointed. We prayed about the matter beforehand, and this is what we have got.'

Not the friendliest way to greet your bishop! The power of prayer, however, may have been greater than the doubting Thomas believed. Dr Fisher was an able and efficient administrator of his diocese. He moved easily into the affections of his clergy and his people. They were sometimes, however, disconcerted by his simple and direct approach to practical problems. When the local hospital was in need of money, the people saw their bishop, gaiters and all, grinding out tunes on a barrel organ at a fund-raising fête.

There was, however, nothing unorthodox about his approach to religious questions. His Christianity was simple, sincere, and without compromise on essential principles. He condemned both the increasing permissiveness of society and the immorality of some business practices.

His appointment as Bishop of London in 1939 came again as a surprise. He took up his residence at Fulham Palace shortly before the Blitz. When the bombs began to fall he opened part of the Palace as a shelter and hostel for the homeless. At the end of the Blitz Fulham Palace was virtually a bomb-shattered wreck, and the bishop and his wife were sleeping on camp beds in a corridor.

William Temple died in October 1944. Winston Churchill put forward Geoffrey Fisher's name as the successor to the See of St Augustine. It was another surprise appointment. Most churchmen regarded Dr George Bell, the Bishop of Chichester, as the obvious choice. The nomination also took Dr Fisher by surprise. He wryly commented that Churchill had asked him about his opinion of Renan's *Life of Christ*. He replied that he had not read it. Churchill drew on his cigar, for once nonplussed; it was incomprehensible that there should be a bishop anywhere who had not read Renan. This deplorable omission, however, did not prevent Churchill from making the nomination. The voice of protest was heard again.

'This appointment does not meet with Heaven's approval,' shouted a man at the ceremony of Geoffrey Fisher's translation to the See of Canterbury. Heaven, as usual, was silent. The Archbishop seemed to grow in stature with his office; he won respect and affection far beyond the Anglican community.

He stepped across the boundaries to take the hand of Pope John – the first Archbishop of Canterbury to visit a Pope since Archbishop Arundel in 1397. His gift to the Pope was, strangely, a beautifully bound copy of the Coronation Service!

The simplicity and informality fell from him each time he took up the duties of his office. He seemed to put on an immense authority with his vestments. All those who watched the Coronation Service on film or television will never forget the dignity, solemnity and the deep religious feeling with which the Archbishop imbued the whole ceremony.

I watched him strive to secure that dignity and solemnity in the ordering of the Service. The Archbishop and the Earl Marshal worked well and closely together. The parts of both the Church and the State had to be developed into one co-ordinated ceremony. The Archbishop made certain that the clergy were rehearsed in their roles to the same degree of perfection that the Earl Marshal was determined to secure from the officers of the state.

The Archbishop had gone carefully through the records of past coronations. He knew that Archbishops and clergy had sometimes fumbled their way through the service. At the end of the confused coronation of Queen Victoria, Archbishop Howley had sadly confessed, 'I think we should have had a rehearsal.' Geoffrey Fisher made sure that there were sufficient rehearsals in 1953.

King George VI had also recorded in his diary some of the unrehearsed moments at his coronation. He wrote:

> The supreme moment came when the Archbishop placed the St Edward's Crown on my head. I had taken every precaution as I thought, to see that the Crown was put on the right way round, but the Archbishop and the Dean had been juggling with it so much that I never did know whether it was right or not. The St Edward's Crown, the Crown of England, weighs seven pounds and it had to fit.

Archbishop Gordon Lang gave his own explanation of the incident: 'It had been arranged that a small thin red line of cotton should be inserted under one of the principal jewels in the front. It was there when I saw the Crown in the Annexe before the ceremony. But when the Dean brought the Crown to me on its cushion from the Altar, and I looked for my little red line, it was not there! Some officious person must have removed it.'

I mentioned this incident to the Archbishop. He smiled and told me, 'We will make very sure that it is right first time.' As indeed it was.

He had from the beginning very great doubts about the wisdom of televising the Coronation Service. He felt that the religious significance of the Service could not be captured on a medium for popular entertainment. He was anxious that the participants should not be distracted by the knowledge that every word and action was being instantly recorded by the TV cameras. At the best he felt that the religious significance of the Service would be an impression at second hand.

The Dean and the Canons of Westminster came to share the Archbishop's doubts about televising the Service. Their reservations were strengthened by some unfortunate incidents when the BBC arrived at the Abbey for the first lighting tests. Equipment was carelessly piled on a royal tomb and cables were draped where they should not have gone. One of the technicians gave a Canon the impression that the event was regarded 'as a change from the usual run of Saturday night show business'. Almost from the beginning the opposition to the televising of the religious service was hardening.

The decisive factor at that stage was the lighting required in the Abbey. I arranged for the Ministry engineers to instal lighting over the area of the Sanctuary to the standard given to me by the BBC.

Our engineers looked at the suggested lighting with astonishment. 'It is sufficient to raise the temperature inside the Abbey to intolerable levels,' Sir Charles Mole told me.

The Earl Marshal was informed of our reservations. He suggested that, none the less, we should go ahead with the installation so that everyone could be convinced, or otherwise, by an actual demonstration.

The Archbishop, the Earl Marshal and the Dean were among those who gathered to see the test. As soon as the system was switched on the Sanctuary was filled with a fierce blaze of light. It was immediately rejected as totally unacceptable by everyone present. Actors on a film set would only have to endure such lighting intensity for the few minutes of each 'take'. It was unthinkable that the Queen should be subjected to an ordeal by light during the long and complicated service. Elderly peers in their heavy robes could not have supported it, and there would have been casualties among the rest of the congregation in the Abbey.

At a meeting with BBC officials later that day I had to tell them that their lighting standards would have to be substantially reduced to allow the televising of the Service even to be considered. Within a remarkably short time they came back with substantially reduced lighting requirements.

It was after this that the calm and competent S. J. de Lotbiniere, chief of the television outside broadcasts, took over the technical arrangements. He was to control the biggest and most complex operation that the BBC had ever carried out. 'Lobby' smoothed away many difficulties but by then the first impressions were firmly entrenched in several important minds. The subsequent public controversy over the televising of the Coronation had its beginnings, I am convinced, in those crucial early days. It was after this that the Dean and Chapter of the Abbey decided to recommend that the use of television should be confined to the procession down the nave and that the whole of the ceremony should be excluded.

There were some early and public indications of the clerical opposition to television. The *Daily Telegraph* of 25 September 1952 reported that Dr Jocelyn Perkins, the Sacrist of Westminster Abbey, had told an Ilford meeting that he hoped that 'nothing so dreadful as televising the Coronation would be allowed'.

Even more significant was a statement by the Archbishop to *The Times* on his return from New York, also in September. He criticised television as a 'mass produced form of education which is potentially one of the great dangers of the world'. He did make the cautious reservation that TV might be useful at the Coronation because it would enable a lot of people to see it who otherwise wouldn't, but 'even if the Coronation were not televised it could be seen over the world a short time later'.

The Archbishop regarded the films, and particularly the colour films, as being more important than television. It should be recalled as some justification that TV was not the great mass medium that it has since become. In Britain out of nearly twelve million BBC licences only one and a half million were TV licences. Even in the USA television had not really begun its spectacular growth and there were only embryo TV services in a few other Western countries.

On the other hand, the films of the British newsreel companies were screened in every cinema in the country to audiences many times bigger than TV and they also claimed a world coverage of 350,000,000 people. In comparison at the time TV lacked stature and influence. The small screen provided a 'key hole' view of an entertaining world. It needed the Coronation to prove that television had grown up.

The film producers did not, however, leave their fortunes to chance. Castleton Knight, the producer for the Rank Technicolor film, handed me a beautiful leather-bound volume – 'A Queen is Crowned' – the proposed film treatment for a full-length colour film for world distribution.

It was a compelling exercise in diplomatic presentation. It had been prepared with the help of expert liturgical knowledge of the ceremony; the cameras discreetly turned away at the Anointing and the Communion. It was illustrated with little miniatures of camera angles like the drawings for a medieval missal. I looked at the production titles:

Produced by	Castleton Knight
Narration by	Laurence Olivier
Written by	Christopher Fry
Musical Adviser	Sir Malcolm Sargent
Special Music by	Guy Warrock
Played by	The London Symphony Orchestra

Castleton Knight had seen my reaction and he was beaming with satisfaction.

I said: 'My congratulations! I presume you are giving copies to the Earl Marshal and the Archbishop?'

'If you don't mind,' he said diplomatically. 'Do you think I might discreetly get a copy over to the Palace?'

'I have no doubt you might,' I told him, knowing that the book was possibly already there.

The opposition of the Archbishop and the clergy to television was not based on opposition to a record of the Coronation being made. That had been done for centuries in illustrated manuscripts, woodcuts, engravings and paintings. Sir Benjamin Stone had taken the first photographs of the actual ceremony at the coronation of George V in 1911. Copies of these photographs were in our files and they were of very good quality, taken with the available light in the Abbey! On that occasion, too, a film camera had also made a record of the Procession of the Regalia through the Cloisters.

In 1937 there was not any opposition to a film record and still photographs of the ceremony, but the request for a live sound broadcast aroused very strong opposition. Once again, like television, the 'immediacy' of the medium was the obstacle – the word and the deed were instantly gone beyond recall.

Archbishop Lang, on the other hand, was strongly in favour of the live broadcast while the ceremony was actually taking place. He argued that its 'immediacy' would have a great impact on the listening millions throughout the world. The opposition was not easily overcome until George VI himself came down decisively in favour of the broadcast – as I believe his daughter, Queen Elizabeth II, did in favour of television in 1953.

A few days after the TV lighting test the Archbishop and the Earl Marshal were present at the lighting tests for the colour film producers. The lighting was considerably below that first requested by the BBC but it was still too high to be acceptable. Sir Gordon Craig, the chairman of the producers association, was sure, however, that the problem could be overcome by increasing the film sensitivity and by improved techniques of laboratory processing.

During one of the tests I made a remark which may have had ecclesiastical consequences. The Archbishop had been standing beside me when the lighting had been reduced to more tolerable levels. He looked up at the lights far overhead and slowly passed his hand over the smooth pink dome of his head.

'You have plenty of hair,' he said to me, 'so you may not appreciate that a bald head can feel an uncomfortable impact from bright lights – especially over a long period.'

I looked at him in complete liturgical ignorance.

'But your Grace will be wearing your Mitre,' I replied spontaneously.

He looked at me for a thoughtful moment. 'It has not been the custom for a very long time for the Archbishops to wear their mitres at a coronation. I think the last occasion was before the Reformation.'

He smiled, passed his hand again over his head.

'It is something to consider,' he said.

For the first time – possibly since before the coronation of Henry VIII – the Archbishops of Canterbury and York wore their mitres for part of the time at the Coronation.

Early in 1953 we supplied the Earl Marshal with scale plans of the Theatre with the positions of the Chair of Estate, the Faldstool, King Edward's Chair and the Throne shown in their precise positions. The movements of the Queen during the progress of the ceremony were marked in continuous lines by officers of the College of Arms. These positions were then measured out on a floor at Buckingham Palace so that the Queen could become familiar with the movements and distances of the long complicated ceremony.

The Archbishop during several visits to the Palace explained the liturgy which accompanied the movements. The Earl Marshal had also to acquaint the Queen with the pattern of the secular part of the Service.

The Archbishop felt that there was another aspect of his responsibility – the duty of preparing the Queen for the act of religious dedication which the service involved.

Dr Fisher could preach a very fine sermon on the tenets of the Christian faith. He was not, however, one of those clerics who could easily discuss religion on a personal basis. He would never enquire, so it seemed to me, about the degree of your religious convictions. I think he also felt this personal reserve in relation to what he felt to be his pastoral duty to the Queen. I also believe, from my own observations, that he stood, in the old phrase, somewhat 'in awe of Majesty'.

At the end of March he went for a holiday in the Peak District. He settled down to prepare a book of devotion for the Queen, which she could read day by day in the month before the Coronation. There was a page for each day, which was related to some aspect of the Coronation liturgy, followed by a short prayer or meditation. It was printed and bound by the Cambridge University Press into a book the size of a church prayer book. He gave a copy to the Queen, and others to the Queen Mother and the Duke of Edinburgh. I heard that he was very content with what he had done.

He had a sense of humour which saved him from being too sensitive about his dignity. On one occasion he made an amused comment about the ancient customs of the Dean and Chapter of Westminster.

The Abbey in 1221 had been exempted from the authority of any bishop, including the Archbishop of Canterbury himself. After the Reformation the Charter granted by Queen Elizabeth I continued the privilege of making the Abbey a Royal Peculiar, with the Sovereign as the Royal Visitor.

It seemed that the Dean had reminded the Archbishop of this ancient privilege by reading to him the traditional statement which, while welcoming him to the Abbey, pointed out that he had no legal or episcopal rights there.

'I think they do make an exception for the Coronation,' Dr Fisher said with a smile.

There could be no doubt whatever about the Archbishop of Canterbury's traditional rights to be there for the Coronation. The *Liber Regalis* was very firm and precise on the matter:

> The right of anointing the Kings and Queens of England belongs above all by ancient custom, hitherto followed, to the Archbishop of Canterbury, if he be present, and be of sound health. And if it happen that on account of bodily weakness or infirmity he cannot in his own person duly perform the ceremony, or if he be hindered by any cause so that he cannot be present, another of the Bishops is to be found to perform the ceremony of unction and coronation, or one to whom the Metropolitan wishes to commit the said office.

The rights of the Archbishop were already of 'ancient custom' in the fourteenth century. There are numerous references to the predominant position of the Archbishops of Canterbury at the coronation of the Anglo-Saxon kings.

William the Conqueror was consecrated by Ealdred, the Archbishop of York. William may have decided to exclude the Archbishop of Canterbury, Stigand, because of doubts about the validity of his appointment.

The first Norman primate of Canterbury, Lanfranc, re-established the ancient rights of the See. He pointed out to William that if the authority was given to the Archbishop of York, far away in the north, he might be tempted to confer the sovereign grace on some rebel Saxon, marauding Dane, or even a Scottish princeling. The ancient rights of Canterbury were fully restored.

Secure in their See, established in their rights, the Archbishops of Canterbury were formidable and often fearless men. At the coronation ceremony itself the Archbishops have more than once risen like the prophets of the Old Testament to call kings to repentance and even at the very threshold of their reigns have publicly condemned the very means by which they had reached their thrones.

In the past 800 years only four sovereigns have not been crowned by the Archbishop of Canterbury.

At the accession of Edward II in 1307, the Archbishop Winchelsey was in Rome, too ill to travel. The status of Canterbury was preserved. The Archbishop entrusted his duty to a commission of three bishops, and Woodlock, Bishop of Winchester, conducted the service.

Queen Mary, the first Queen Regnant, in 1553 refused to receive the crown from the 'unworthy Cranmer', who with the Archbishop of York and the Bishop of London was imprisoned in the Tower. Gardiner, Bishop of Winchester, officiated and was later condemned by other bishops for acting 'without any express right or precedent'.

Elizabeth I was confronted with a hopeless problem for her coronation. The Archbishop of Canterbury had died a few days before. His proper deputy, the Bishop of London, was in the Tower. A score of dioceses were vacant through deaths from the plague. Other

9   The Archbishop of Canterbury, Dr Geoffrey Fisher, in his Coronation cope, with his chaplain, Dr Eric Jay.

bishops had been appointed by Queen Mary and they would not act. Eventually an obscure bishop, Oglethorpe of Carlisle, borrowed the robes of the imprisoned Bishop of London and performed the service. It is alleged that his death soon afterwards was hastened by remorse.

The last coronation at which the Primate did not officiate was that of William III and Mary II. In 1689 Archbishop Sancroft, who had strong Jacobite sympathies, shut himself in Lambeth Palace. His place was, however, with his reluctant consent taken by his proper deputy, Henry Compton, Bishop of London. Many of the other bishops stayed away.

Parliament, influenced by the refusal of Archbishop Sancroft, decided to terminate the traditional rights of the Archbishops of Canterbury by law. It was enacted by Parliament that 'the coronation may be performed by the Archbishop of Canterbury, or the Archbishop of York, or any other bishop whom the King's Majesty may appoint'.

The sovereign's powers of discretion have not been exercised since in favour of the northern Metropolitan. In 1953 the Archbishop of York took his place on the north side of the Sanctuary in front of the bench of bishops.

In 1953, Dr Fisher made a gesture which was in keeping with the traditions of many Archbishops before him and of his Christian faith. In 1948 at the Lambeth Conference, the Right Reverend M. H. Yasiro, Bishop of Kobe, had brought him a wonderful cope worked by the churchwomen of Japan. It was, said the little bishop, a peace offering, a gesture of Christian reconciliation after all that had happened during the war.

Feeling in this country was angry and bitter following the revelations of the torments and suffering of our prisoners of war on the notorious Burma railway and in the Japanese prison camps. The Archbishop wore the Japanese cope at the Coronation. There was no protest.

In 1961 Dr Geoffrey Fisher resigned from his high office to make way for a younger successor to the See of Canterbury. He filled in the gap in his life about which the clergyman in Chester had complained – his lack of parochial experience.

He became an assistant priest in a rural parish in Dorset. A leaflet in the Trent church near Sherborne had a bald little sentence. It read – 'The rector has the permanent help of a former Archbishop of Canterbury.'

8 The Splendour of the Past

For many centuries the kings of England on their accession hastened to the Tower of London to await their coronation. In perilous times it was no doubt a wise precaution for the new king to take up residence 'in the castle royall and cheefe house of safetye in this kingdom'. It could also have been at times a means of overawing the turbulent City of London, or of gaining the extravagant endorsement of its citizens when riding with great pageantry to the Palace of Westminster.

The chroniclers have left many vivid descriptions of the royal processions from the Tower. On St Swithin's day in 1377 the ten-year-old Richard II rode out from the Tower, bareheaded on a white horse. He looked a delicate child and the pallor of his features was accentuated by the whiteness of his attire. He wore a white tight-fitting jacket with trumpet-cuffed sleeves with the points trailing below his long white boots with their golden spurs. With him rode a splendid cavalcade of his nobles, as well as the Lord Mayor and leading citizens of London, in embroidered robes, on richly caparisoned steeds, bearing gold and silver cups in their hands. In front the royal trumpeters sounded the approach of the King.

The narrow streets of the City exploded into a tumultuous welcome for the young son of the Black Prince. The streets had been swept and sanded; the fronts of the houses were hung with carpets and rich damasks.

Holinshed in his chronicle relates that at the upper end of Chepe was a castle with four towers, spouting wine, and in each tower a beautiful virgin 'of stature and age like to the King' in white vestures 'the which blew in the King's face at his approaching neare to them, leaves of gold, and as he approached also they threw on him and his horse florins of gold counterfeet'. They filled goblets of wine for the King and a golden angel between the towers held a crown which 'when the King came he bowed down and offered him the crowne'.

The most sumptuous of all the processions from the Tower was undoubtedly that of Queen Elizabeth I. The Queen loved a pageant and the City of London gave her one of unparalleled splendour. The Tower could not have been an easy residence for the young Elizabeth, but past memories must have been swept away when she rode out to the most rapturous welcome ever given by the City to a sovereign of England.

Elizabeth was received with 'prayers, wishes, welcominges, cries and tender words' to which the quick-tongued young Queen was alert to reply with 'louing answers and gestures'. She halted her progress frequently to listen to some petition, to hear a child dressed as an angel read a poem of acclamation; she paused before every tableau, listened to 'musick', exclaimed at ingenious displays and was piously impressed by the Scriptural allegories.

The huge crowds watched the play of emotions in her face, saw her hands uplifted in delighted surprise, and rapidly repeated from mouth to mouth every one of her clearly heard responses, 'which indeed emplanted a wonderful hope in them touchyng her woorthy government in the reste of her reyne'.

She passed on through streets hung with banners and tapestries, between the houses with their gilded frames and crowded windows, past fountains running with sack and rhenish wine. The guns boomed; the joy bells rang; there was the 'heavenly melodie of boys and virgins' and the 'noise of music' and the great roaring tumult of the crowd which followed her in a flowing tide until she hushed it into silence with her gestures so that she might hear every word which characters like the Eight Beatitudes were addressing to her – 'the Queen's Majestie giving most attentive care'.

The figure of Time with the scythe emerged from a large tableau to greet the Queen in Latin and English as 'the daughter of Tyme'. The Queen replied thoughtfully, that, 'It was Tyme which has brought me here.' The wit and wisdom of her reign were there at the beginning.

'James I', writes Stowe, 'rode not through the City in royal manner as hath been accustomed', because of the plague, and the same dreadful affliction cancelled the progress of Charles I.

The last of the royal processions from the Tower was that of Charles II on 22 April 1661. The diligent pen of Samuel Pepys recorded the details of the event in his diary.

'There attended upon his Majesty at the Tower, all the nobility and principal gentry of the kingdom.' The king rode out with all his nobles, the heralds, the great officers of the household and the newly created Knights of the Bath – 'a brave sight in itself,' wrote Pepys.

'The streets were all gravelled,' confided Pepys, 'and the houses hung with carpets before them, made a brave show, and the ladies out of the windows. So glorious was the show with gold and silver, that we were not able to look at it; our eyes being at last so overcome.' With pride he wrote, 'Both the King and the Duke of York took notice of us, as they saw us at the window.'

It was already getting dark and the torches were being lit as the last royal progress from the Tower reached its final destination.

'James II', wrote Lord Macaulay, 'ordered an estimate to be made of the cost of such a procession and found it would amount to half as much as he proposed to spend in covering his wife with trinkets. He accordingly determined to be profuse where he ought to have been frugal and niggardly when he might pardonably have been profuse. More than a hundred thousand pounds was laid out in dressing the Queen, and the Procession from the Tower was omitted.'

Since 1661 no English sovereign has ridden in progress from the Tower. The custom of 'offering himself to be seen by the people' has now taken a new form. The great processions to and from the Abbey have moved the royal progress to the wide streets of central London; in 1953 the Queen drove out after the Coronation in a progress to each of the four quarters of London separately. The unique position of the City was not over-looked. On Friday 12 June, after her Coronation, the Queen drove in state to the Guildhall to be received with the ancient pomp and panoply with which the City has greeted so many kings and queens.

The progress from the Tower once brought the king to his Palace of Westminster on the eve of his coronation. There, on the morning of his inauguration, he summoned what seems to have been a Great Council of the Realm. This was the procedure from very early times. Henry I for his coronation in August 1100 called a meeting which has been described as being of 'the clergy of England and the whole people when divers laws were both made and declared'.

In 1308, the writ of summons for the coronation of Edward II required the attendance of the people by their knights, citizens and burgesses.

The *Liber Regalis* again gave very precise instructions:

On the day on which the new king is to be consecrated, early in the morning the
prelates and the nobles of the realm shall assemble in the Royal Palace of Westminster
to consider about the consecration and election of the new king, and also about
confirming and surely establishing the laws and customs of the realm.

When this has been done with the agreement of all, a lofty seat shall be prepared
in the royal hall [i.e. Westminster Hall] and suitably adorned with silken cloths
of gold on which the king that is to reign is to be raised with gentleness
and reverence. . . .

The proceedings in Westminster Hall were a great secular ceremony, an affair of state. What the king promised in the Hall was solemnly confirmed by the Coronation Oath he was called upon to take by the Archbishop in the solemn and sacred service in the Abbey.

The *Liber Regalis* went on:

When these things have been duly performed, a procession shall be arranged in the
church [i.e. the Abbey] by the Archbishops, Bishops and the Abbot and Convent
of Westminster in silken copes with Gospel-books and other things suitable for the
procession and so vested they shall go in procession to meet the king in the
Palace . . . and they go before him to the church singing and chanting those anthems
which are usually sung at the reception of kings.

This was the great Liturgical Procession which for centuries conducted the king from Westminster Hall to the Abbey. It proceeded along a raised platform from Westminster Hall to the Abbey Church. Altogether there were 1,000 magnificently or picturesquely attired personages in that procession.

It has gone from the coronation scene. George IV was the last sovereign to walk from the old Hall to the ancient Abbey, as so many English kings had done.

With the passing of the Liturgical Procession there also went the Coronation Banquet which was once held in Westminster Hall, which was newly finished when Henry I on 5 August 1100 held the first Coronation Banquet within its walls. His successor Stephen on St Stephen's Day in 1135 continued the practice with a lavish feast for his subjects.

It is not until we come to the Coronation of Henry III's Queen, Eleanor, in 1236 that we have a detailed eye witness account by Matthew Paris. 'At the nuptial feast', he tells us, 'were assembled a multitude of the nobility of both sexes, such numbers of the religious, such a vast body of people, and such a variety of players that the City of London could scarcely contain them in her capacious bosom.' Matthew Paris found the description of the actual feast beyond his powers of expression: 'How shall I describe the dainties of the table. . . . Whatever the world pours forth of pleasure and glory was there displayed.'

The splendour of this feast was surpassed by the one arranged for the coronation of Edward I in 1274. The country was ransacked for supplies. There were gathered in 440 oxen and cows, 430 sheep, 450 pigs, 16 fat boars, 278 flitches of bacon and 22,460 capons beside other poultry. The tables were laden with pies and sweetmeats.

The culinary arts also grew in extravagance. At the Coronation Banquet of Henry VI in 1429 almost everything edible which walked, ran, flew or swam was brought to the table. In addition to the traditional meats and fish there were served grouse, char, swan, heron, pike, crane, coney, partridge, peacock, bream, egrets, larks, carp, plovers, snipe and so on to an infinity of gluttony. There was also 'a red soup in which white lions were swimming, golden leopards immersed in custard, roast pigs gilded like gingerbread, and the head of a leopard crowned with ostrich feathers.'

It was at the coronation of Richard II in 1377 that a Dymoke appeared as the King's Champion. This office was held by Roger Marmion in the reign of Henry I by virtue of his tenure of the manors of Tamworth and Scrivelsby. The Dymokes obtained the manor of Scrivelsby in the fourteenth century by the marriage of Margaret, co-heir of the last Marmion, with Sir John Dymoke.

The Champion made his spectacular entry into Westminster Hall through the great north door to 'a long and cheerful flourish of trumpets'. In full armour, mounted on a milk-white steed, escorted by a brilliant retinue of esquires, heralds, mace-bearers, riding between the Earl Marshal and the Lord High Constable he advanced down the Hall. The Earl Marshal cleared the way to the King's table, the trumpets sounded three times, and the herald in a loud voice proclaimed the challenge: 'If any person, of whatever degree deny or gainsay that our Sovereign Lord, Richard, the heir to our Sovereign Lord Edward be the rightful heir to the Crown of this kingdom, or that he ought not to enjoy the same, here is his Champion who saith that he lieth, and is a false traitor; being ready in person to combat with him, and in this quarrel will adventure his life against him on what day soever he shall appoint.'

The Champion threw down his glove, which, when no one accepted the challenge, was returned to him by the herald. The challenge was twice more proclaimed. The Cupbearer presented a gold cup to the King from which he drank the Champion's health, and sent the cup to him. The Champion, cup in hand, bowed low and drank to the King. He retained the cup with its cover for his fee. With the same escort, the Champion and other riders backed their horses out of the Hall.

So it was at the coronation of Richard II. So it was done by the Dymokes for nearly 450 years. It was not surprising that in that armed citadel of the king the challenge was never taken up.

There are, however, romantic rumours that Prince Charles Stuart was present at the Coronation Banquet of George III. The Champion's gauntlet, it was reported, was picked up and returned by a woman who said, 'Young man, you should take more care of your property.'

In time long galleries were erected down both sides of the Hall to accommodate the privileged as distinct from the actual élite sitting at the Banquet down below. At the coronation of George III on 22 September 1761 the galleries were filled with crowds of hungry and impatient people sitting in the dark. The return procession had been delayed by the confused and chaotic proceedings in the Abbey.

When the lights were lit, the King seated at the royal table and the dignitaries began to carry in the profuse and luxurious dishes of the first course, the sights and smells proved too much for the hungry multitude. With urgent cries and gestures they sought to attract the attention of their friends and relatives among the noble lords below. They proved not unresponsive. The ladies in the galleries tied their scarves together and even stripped off their stockings to make ropes which dangled enticingly over the heads of the diners. Whole capons, savoury pies, daubed geese, hot joints and other viands from the first course of the banquet rose up to the eager hands and mouths in the galleries. Presently bottles of wine were also dangling their way upwards.

This unofficial refreshment of the galleries was only the *hors d'oeuvre* before the real feast. As soon as the King and the principal nobles had left the Hall, the people in the galleries rose to their feet in a wild stampede for the stairs leading to the Hall. Women struggled and fought to keep in front.

In a few moments every bottle on the tables was emptied. The elaborate confections were pillaged, sweetmeats vanished, the table ornaments were torn to pieces as the struggling press of people reached hands and thrust with bodies and elbows to seize every scrap and bottle left on the tables.

With the food disappeared the table ornaments – baskets, sauce boats, vases, figurines, cups, spoons, plates and dishes disappeared into pockets or were concealed under the capacious dresses of the women. Table ware with the royal arms were the most coveted and the first to disappear.

The scenes of looting, drunkenness and disorder after the Banquet seem to have been on an even more riotous scale at the coronation of George IV. When the Hall had been thoroughly looted many were too weary or too inebriated to get away from the Palace. A contemporary account describes the company throwing themselves down indiscriminately in the rooms of the Palace: 'peers and peeresses, judges and privy councillors, knights of all orders and commons of all degrees lay promiscuously, some on sofas, some on chairs and a still greater number on the matted floors of the rooms and corridors in which they happened to have sought refuge.'

The eccentric King William IV had been present at his brother's Coronation Banquet. As Duke of Clarence he had lived penurious years, and he was appalled by the vast expenditure incurred at his elder brother's inauguration. He would have none of it. In fact, there would not be any coronation at all!

When he went to dissolve Parliament he took up the Imperial Crown, placed it on his head, and turning to the Lord Chancellor said firmly, 'This, my lord, is my coronation day.'

It needed a great deal of pressure to get King William IV into King Edward's Chair. When private persuasion failed, the mighty Duke of Wellington rose in the House of Lords to ask the Prime Minister, Lord Grey, if he had received any instructions on the subject of his Majesty's coronation. The embarrassed Lord Grey replied that he had not.

'Why the delay?' demanded the Duke. 'Was it not necessary that His Majesty should take certain oaths connected with his coronation?'

The issue was clear. No coronation – no oath. No oath – no king! King William IV is possibly the only monarch in English history who dragged his feet all the way to the Throne. But not another jot of ceremony would he have beyond the confines of the Abbey walls. There would be no progress from the Tower; no ceremony in Westminster Hall; no Liturgical Procession to the Abbey doors, and, most definitely, no Coronation Banquet!

With a final emphatic smack of the royal hand on the royal desk the King also flattened the aspirations of scores of dignitaries, hereditary title holders and royal servitors, who had performed hitherto in Westminster Hall by virtue of their ancient tenures and traditions. They were suddenly cast into abeyance.

There was now the question of the one thousand or more very important personages who had walked in the procession. They could not be marshalled inside the Abbey. The King's solution was simple – fit them in – or leave them out! Many were left out including the Barons of the Cinque Ports with their tinkling 'canopy with little bells' whose misfortunes at other coronations were thus further compounded.

The King was eventually persuaded to accept the compromise of building an Annexe outside the West Door of the Abbey. Its hasty preparations had presented every sort of difficulty, including finance, to our predecessors. It was a cramped building, leaked in places, looked like an ugly fort for toy soldiers; it infuriated the clergy and the personages who had to use it and reduced the Earl Marshal to a state of impotent fury.

The Annexe to the Abbey has remained the compromise for assembling the grand procession on every occasion since William IV and his 'penny coronation'.

A large number of picturesque figures from the feudal and later pages of English history had departed from the coronation scene. They included the Royal Herbswoman who 'in a gown of scarlet cloth, with a badge and cipher on it' had walked before the procession to the Abbey, strewing flower petals and scented herbs, and the 'Six Clerks in Chancery in gowns of black flowered satin'. The Chief Cupbearer, the Serjeant of the Silver Scullary, the Dapifer, the Grand Carver and the Chief Larderer passed from sight. The Lord of the Isle of Man could no longer pay for his tenure by striding into Westminster Hall with two gaily caparisoned falcons perched on the jewelled guard on his wrist. For the first time possibly since William the Conqueror, the holder of the Manor of Addington in Surrey could no longer come forward to present the king with a mysterious 'mess of dilligrout'.

When all had been cut, pruned and cast out much was saved of the traditional order of things. The Great Lords and the Clergy were in their traditional places with other ancient officers of the Crown. The bishops were given privileged seats on the north side of the Sanctuary; the judges had a gallery to themselves and most of the peers who were not in the procession were given places in the south transept with the peeresses in their ranks opposite them. When all was done the procession which escorted King William IV to his place in the Theatre still retained in its traditional order all the main religious and historical elements of the previous centuries. And so it has remained.

The doors have not finally been closed on Westminster Hall. The proclamations at every coronation since dispensing with the services rendered there, expressly reserve to all concerned their rights at future coronations.

In past centuries the claims to perform special services had come before a court specially set up for the purpose. The Lord High Steward sat in the White Hall of the King's Palace at Westminster to decide between rival claims. The coronation of Richard II has provided us with the first detailed records of the Court of Claims, when John of Gaunt presided as the Lord High Steward of England.

The Court of Claims was still there in 1952 – possibly an example of the permanency which the monarchy gives to our institutions.

It had been set up by the Queen for the same purpose as the Court of John of Gaunt.

The Lord High Steward had, however, lost his place. The Lord Chancellor of England now presided over the Court of Claims.

9 The Court of Claims

The Court of Claims for the Coronation of Queen Elizabeth II was convened on 31 October 1952. It met in the oak-panelled room of the Judicial Committee of the Privy Council in Downing Street.

The Lord Chancellor of England, Lord Simonds, was presiding over a meeting of the highest judicial authorities of the United Kingdom. They included the Lord Chief Justice of England, the Lord Justice General of Scotland, the Lord Chief Justice of Northern Ireland, the Master of the Rolls, and a former Lord Chancellor and a Lord of Appeal. In addition there were present the Duke of Norfolk in his capacity of Earl Marshal and the Earl of Clarendon, the recently retired Lord Chamberlain.

It might seem to be a great weight to bear on some ancient formalities. In fact, the business before the Court could sometimes be very complex. The feudal system of land tenure had been, until a few decades previously, the basis of the English law of real property. Generations of lawyers had grown fat in law courts and in chambers unravelling the complexities of grand serjeanty, subinfeudation and common socage in the conveyancing of landed estates. The claims before the Court could involve the original ownership of a tenure in Norman times. It might have to follow the succession of ownership through the centuries. A complex jungle for even the keenest legal minds to explore.

The Court might also have to adjudicate on the validity of the hereditary claims to offices which had long ago been conferred by Plantagenet kings. The tangled patterns of inheritance are often a Minoan maze with only the faintest thread to follow.

Under the feudal system the king was the paramount lord of all land in the kingdom. Estates were held in fee from the king. The great nobles were the 'tenants in chief' holding their lands on the obligations of fealty and services to the king. The principal services were the providing of armed knights for the royal army and such money 'aids' as providing for his ransom, the marriage of his daughter and the knightly installation of his son. Under the system of tenure of grand and petty serjeanty the holding of the land was subject to the performance of a personal service to the king, the holder under grand serjeanty providing the greater or more intimate personal service.

The services were obviously not related to the value of the land. These services were often menial or very trivial – to provide a towel for the king, to serve him at table, to hold his cup or even to hold his head when he was seasick!

The humble nature of the services emphasised the great gulf between the exalted king and even his most powerful subjects. They were his servants. The small services rendered for great possessions showed that the king, like the overlord with his lesser tenants, valued fealty more than gain. Fealty – loyalty – was the social bond of feudal England.

As time went on the menial aspects were forgotten. Great lords contended for such honours as 'bringing the salt and the serving knives from the pantry to the king's table'.

These claims clustered most thickly around the king's coronation. Here the services were prominently and proudly performed. Clothed in splendid robes, the fortunate holders of their tenures moved to perform their 'services'. The envied cynosures of all their peers.

With the passing of time, too, the rewards for the services became substantial. The Chief Butler, for example, claimed for his fee 'the best gold cup and cover, all the vessels and wine remaining under the bar, all pots and cups, except those of gold and silver, which be in the wine cellar after the banquet'. The Grand Almoner got a silver dish and a tun of good wine. The Grand Pannetier collected the salt cellars, knives and spoons laid before the king at his coronation banquet. The Royal Napier took all the table linen for his fee. When all the fees were collected for all the services rendered, the hall, bedroom and kitchens of the king must have been remarkably bare!

In the course of centuries it often became difficult to ascertain who was entitled to perform the coronation services. Estates were forfeited, sold or broken up. The lines of succession became divided, extinct, or could be traced only on the distaff side. There were furious disputes between rival contenders. Who should be the Dapifer and arrange the dishes on the royal table? Out of these disputes in Plantagenet times there had come into existence the Court of Claims. It made its brief appearance at every coronation, and in 1952 was again called into session by Royal Proclamation.

The Law of Property Act 1922 finally swept away the old feudal systems of land tenures and simplified the law of real property. The Act carefully preserved the services, however, formerly rendered under the tenures of grand and petty serjeanty. The former feudal servitors were thus thrown their lifeline, and many ancient and picturesque services by manors and chartered towns to the sovereign, as well as to various other mesne lords, survived.

The Court of Claims, therefore, still had to consider the complexities of the past. In the words of the Proclamation, it had to consider the claims of those who 'by ancient customs and usages, as also in regard of divers tenures of sundry manors, lands and other hereditaments, do claim and are bound to do and perform divers several services at the time of our said coronation'.

Lord Simonds dealt with each case as it was read to him by the clerks to the Court. In those cases where no legal argument was necessary he announced the decision which the Court had reached since 1 October 1952 when all claims had to have been received.

The first claim before the Court was a venerable one. The Dean and Chapter of Westminster Abbey claimed the right to 'instruct the Queen in the rites and ceremonies, to assist the Archbishop of Canterbury, and to retain the robes and ornaments of the coronation in the vestry of the Collegiate Church of St Peter in Westminster, and to have certain allowances and fees'.

Their claim had solid foundations. The old Abbot Lytlington had again set it down for posterity in his *Liber Regalis*. Translated from the Latin it said:

The Abbot of Westminster for the time being, by the space of two or three days before the coronation of the king or queen shall instruct them what duties they are to perform in the celebration of their coronation, as also to prepare their consciences before receiving the sacred unction. And if the Abbot be dead, or absent in some remote country, or lawfully detained, then shall one of the monks of the said Abbey . . . supply the office of the said Abbot in this case.

It was a claim which over the centuries had never been contested. The right of even the Archbishop of Canterbury to conduct the coronation service has at times been vigorously contested, but the Abbots had gone unchallenged in their own place. The Dean and Chapter claimed as the rightful successors of the former Abbots and monks of Westminster.

The Court allowed the claim, and that the robes and ornaments should be kept in the vestry 'unless Her Majesty were pleased to order that they should be kept elsewhere'. With regard to the fees which were claimed, that was a matter for the pleasure of Her Majesty.

Another ecclesiastical claim before the Court in 1952 was the petition of the Bishop of Durham and the Bishop of Bath and Wells, 'as of old custom', to support the Queen throughout the coronation ceremony, the former walking on her right hand and the latter on her left.

This privilege had been claimed by these two prelates since the coronation of Richard I in 1189. The *Liber Regalis* gave its sanction to this claim: 'The king that is to be crowned shall be supported by the Bishop of Durham and the Bishop of Bath and Wells, if they be present.'

The two prelates were not always present. At the coronation of Henry VII their claims were denied because of their Yorkist sympathies. At the coronation of Elizabeth I not a single bishop was available for the Queen's 'support' and their places were taken by the secular earls of Shrewsbury and Pembroke. Once again, at the coronation of William and Mary, the two bishops were excluded from the Service, this time because of their Stuart sympathies.

The term 'support' was meant in both its physical and liturgical senses. There were times when they had to support the St Edward's Crown on the royal head, since it was then regarded as too sacred to be greatly altered. It was these two bishops whose arms held up the boy king Richard II through the long Service until at its end he was carried exhausted from the Abbey on the shoulders of his knights. The two bishops came again to the help of Queen Anne, crippled with gout and corpulency at the age of 37, when she had to be raised on to her swollen feet during the ceremony.

Unfortunately, their liturgical support was not always quite so competent. Greville recounts at the coronation of Queen Victoria how they created some confusion. 'They made her leave her chair and enter into St Edward's Chapel before the prayers were concluded much to the discomfiture of the Archbishop.' The Queen had to be brought back into the Theatre. 'Pray tell me what I am to do,' she said to the acting Dean, Lord John Thynne, 'for they do not know.'

Their undisputed claim was allowed again in 1952. At the Coronation in 1953, their physical support was certainly not required, although I saw them glance at the Queen from time to time during the long, exacting and complicated Service.

The Bishop of Durham on that occasion was the Rt Rev. Arthur Michael Ramsay, DD, who was to succeed Dr Fisher as Archbishop of Canterbury.

In 1952, the Barons of the Cinque Ports claimed to bear the canopy over the Queen. As there was doubt if a canopy would be used they put in a secondary claim – to be assigned stations in attendance on the Queen.

It was a very ancient claim by the ports of Hastings, Romney, Hythe, Dover and Sandwich. The privilege of carrying the canopy with silver bells over the king had been awarded to them by King John. They were also once entitled to sit on the king's right hand at the Coronation Banquet, and their fee was the canopy with its bells. As we have seen, the Barons had suffered many misfortunes at the Banquet. There was also an occasion when they had to fight the royal servants in the Hall to keep their canopy.

The Court decided that if a canopy should be carried in the procession it would be borne by the Barons of the Cinque Ports. The canopy was not so used and they were awarded the somewhat diminished privilege of standing by the Abbey Choir entrance to receive the standards from their bearers. Their Lord Warden of the Cinque Ports had, however, high office and a prominent seat within the Abbey. He was Sir Winston Churchill.

The Lord Mayor of London claimed the right of attendance at the Coronation and to bear the Crystal Mace of the City of London. There were historical precedents for this claim, which was granted.

Lord Hastings and Lord Churston both claimed the honour of bearing the Golden Spurs. Spurs were the badge of knighthood and the sovereign as head of the Orders of Chivalry has always been invested with them at the coronation since the time of Richard Coeur de Lion. When a Queen Regnant is crowned, however, the Spurs were not put to her heels; she touched them with her hands. The ancient claims of the two lords were granted, and each carried one of the Golden Spurs.

A claim now came before the Court which was presented by counsel, with a great weight of legal argument and the skilful presentation of references to former claims, precedents and privileges. The Duke of Newcastle was claiming through counsel that as Lord of the Manor of Worksop in Nottinghamshire he should present the embroidered Glove which the Queen would wear on her right hand while holding the Sceptre with the Cross.

This was another claim with the weight of centuries behind it. It was an already established claim at the coronation of Richard II in 1377. The service of the Glove was originally attached to the Manor of Farnham in Buckinghamshire. That manor was exchanged by the Earl of Shrewsbury with Henry VIII for the priory and Manor of Worksop. The tenure 'by glove service' was transferred by letters patent, and the claim had been allowed at each coronation.

However, there had now been a total change in the vesting of the tenure. The estate was now vested in a limited company, the London and Fort George Land Company. The company was of high reputation, but the claim, if allowed, opened up wide possibilities for the future. Holders of ancient estates were often compelled to sell them to pay death duties. There was, therefore, the chance that the ancient coronation services might in future be performed by a gathering of land speculators around the throne. There might also be the strange anachronism of a nationalised industry performing a humble service by acquiring an ancient tenure!

The Lord Chancellor asked to see the memorandum and articles of association of the company, and said that the Court would later give its reserved judgment. The claim was not allowed. The embroidered Glove was presented by Lord Woolton, the Chancellor of the Duchy of Lancaster.

Counsel also appeared before the Court to present the claim of the 17th Duke of Somerset to bear the Orb, or the Sceptre with the Cross, which he had borne at the coronation of George VI. The 15th Duke had also borne the Orb at the coronation of Edward VII and that of George V. The 1st Duke, Edward, had been the Lord Great Chamberlain at the coronation of Edward VI, and the Lord Protector during his reign. On the death of the young Edward, he had sprung the daring plot to exclude both Mary and Elizabeth from the throne in favour of his daughter-in-law, Lady Jane Grey. They both paid the forfeit of their lives.

On this occasion the Duke paid the forfeit of his claim. The Court decided that there was not sufficient evidence to justify a continuing and hereditary right to perform the service of the Orb, or the Sceptre. A rider added that the decision did not prejudice any hope the Duke might have of 'an act of grace from her Majesty'.

In the event, the Orb was borne by Earl Alexander of Tunis and the Sceptre with the Cross by Viscount Portal – two wartime leaders of the armed forces.

Three claims were excluded from consideration by the Court since they related to services once performed at the Coronation Banquet. Mrs Long, by virtue of the tenure of Heydon Hall, claimed to carry the Queen's towel, and the other two concerned the presentation of a cup to the Queen.

The claims of the old Kingdom of Scotland were next considered. For centuries before the Union with England, the Kings of Scotland had been crowned with their own ancient crown in the Abbey of Scone. It was there that Malcolm who vanquished Macbeth was crowned in 1057. After the Union of the two crowns the separate Scottish ceremony was not considered necessary. Charles I, however, in an effort to keep the loyalty of his northern subjects had himself crowned in the Kirk of Holyrood. Charles II also had two crownings. Two years after his father's death the fugitive young King received the ancient crown of Bruce from the hands of the Duke of Argyle in the parish church of Scone.

The Countess of Errol claimed to be permitted to take part by deputy as the Lord High Constable of Scotland, and to have a silver baton of twelve ounce weight, tipped with gold at each end, bearing the Royal Arms and her own arms. The Lord High Constable of Scotland is the chief subject of the realm in Scotland next to the blood royal. The Lord of Errol was a co-regent of Scotland in 1255. His grandson was created by Robert Bruce hereditary Great Constable of Scotland. The Court allowed the claim and the staff.

Since by the system of feudal tenure a female cannot render service, Lady Errol was represented by her deputy, Lord Kilmarnock, himself of a collateral branch of the House of Errol.

The next Scottish claim had some of the dramatic quality of a novel by Sir Walter Scott. The right to bear the Royal Standard of Scotland was claimed by the Viscount of Dudhope, as head of the Scrymgeour family. The right to bear this standard had been hereditary since the reign of William Wallace. A Scrymgeour had borne the standard at Bannockburn in 1314. The Earl had only recently succeeded in satisfying the Committee of Privileges as to his right to the earldom. The family papers had been stolen and it had been impossible to claim the title until recently. The claim was granted.

The Lord Lyon King of Arms and the Heralds and Pursuivants of Scotland claimed and were granted their traditional places in the Coronation ceremony.

Other representatives of the Ancient Kingdom of Scotland had their place in the ceremony without the necessity of appearing before the Court. Scotland as well as England had in former times her Great Steward, and like the English sovereigns the Scottish kings found it necessary to merge this powerful office in the Crown. At the time of the Coronation this office was held by the young Prince Charles, then Duke of Cornwall and Duke of Rothesay in the Kingdom of Scotland. By royal prerogative, therefore, the Earl of Crawford and Balcarres appeared as deputy for the Great Steward of Scotland.

A fascinating claim which went by default through lack of appearance was the claim by His Highness Prince O'Brien of Thomond to attend the ceremony and perform service. The ancient claims of the Irish prince remained obscure.

Before the Court sat there had been some lively speculation that the Queen's Champion might appear to press the family claim of the Dymokes to fling down the historic gauntlet yet once more. To the great disappointment, particularly of the American TV companies, it was explained that this service had been performed at the coronation banquet. It was, therefore, excluded from the consideration of the Court.

The Dymokes could no longer ride in shining armour, but they had their place in the Coronation of Elizabeth II. Captain John L. M. Dymoke carried the Union Standard in the great procession in Westminster Abbey. Kings and centuries pass, dynasties fall, customs change, but the Dymokes of Scrivelsby seem to have an enduring quality about them.

10 Lords of the Day

The Coronation was like a picture book of history. The pageantry from the past moved across its pages. Great lords who had strutted in Norman courts, or rode in the lists of chivalry, or who had stood by the thrones of the Yorkist kings, or sat in the Council of the first Elizabeth, had their counterparts in the age of the airliner and the atomic power plant.

These titles of state were once names of great power. The Lord High Steward of England, the Lord High Constable and the Lord Great Chamberlain were once the highest officers in the realm, and they still retained their ancient precedence at the Coronation. The Earl Marshal, the Lord Chancellor, the Lord President of the Council and the Lord Privy Seal also moved into their historic and ancient places at the Coronation. The history of their offices is part of the complicated pattern of English history.

The Lord High Steward is an office of descent from Saxon times. Originally, the Lord High Steward was the 'steadward' – the ward of the king's stead or place. The Lord High Stewards became the most powerful men in the kingdom; especially when the office was held by men of such ambition as Simon de Montfort and John of Gaunt. The Steward was the first subject of the realm next to the Blood Royal. He was viceroy of the realm during the minority or absence of the king. In time, kings grew wary of allowing so much power to one subject and the office of the Lord High Steward reverted to the Crown under Henry III in 1265.

Since the fifteenth century the office of the Lord High Steward has been revived only for special occasions, such as the trial of a peer, or for a coronation. It is a temporary office of state. The Lord High Steward at the coronation of Elizabeth I held the office 'from the rising of the sun on the same day to the setting thereof'. In 1953 he was still 'the lord of a single day' and by the warrant of his commission his white staff should be formally broken at sunset.

At the coronation ceremony the Lord High Steward walks in front of the Sovereign in the Abbey procession carrying St Edward's Crown, the most treasured privilege of all the coronation honours.

At the Coronation of Queen Elizabeth II the Lord High Steward was Admiral of the Fleet, the Viscount Cunningham of Hyndhope, the famous wartime commander of the Mediterranean Fleet at the battle of Matapan.

Another ancient office at the Coronation was that of the Lord Great Chamberlain – who should be distinguished from the Lord Chamberlain of the Household. The office of Lord Great Chamberlain originated with the duties of the 'bower thegns' of the Saxon kings.

On the night before the coronation he had personally to mount guard on the king's chamber. On the morning of the coronation he brought the royal clothing and assisted in dressing the king. In return for these services of the royal bedchamber he received as his fee 40 yards of crimson velvet for his own robe, the king's bed and bedclothing, all the furniture in the room and the king's nightgown and other clothes.

When James I arrived for his coronation he refused to comply with this eccentric custom. He was not going to be parted from his shirt, drawers and stockings. After much discussion the service was compounded for a fee of £200.

Even greater was the royal embarrassment when the Great Chamberlain offered to perform the ancient services for the good Queen Anne. She paid £300 to keep her under-clothes and bedding. George I paid £350 – a large sum at that time – to keep his shirt. It was not until the coronation of King Edward VII that the Lord Chamberlain lost even his remuneration of the 40 yards of crimson velvet.

The office of the Lord Great Chamberlain had been granted as an hereditary tenure by Henry I in 1133 to the de Veres, Earls of Oxford. The line expired in the male succession in 1702, and the daughters of the last earl claimed the right to appoint their husbands as deputies. These claims led to disputes at the beginning of each reign. The office is now shared in succeeding reigns between the Earl of Ancaster, Lord Carrington and the Marquess of Cholmondely whose turn it was in 1952.

The Lord Great Chamberlain has other duties than those at the coronation. He is respon-sible for the arrangements when the sovereign opens Parliament and officiates at the introduction of a new peer.

In the Coronation Theatre he carried out the traditional offices of the wardrobe – he assisted the Mistress of the Robes in divesting the Queen of the Crimson Robe, presented the Golden Spurs, and fastened the clasp on the Robe Royal of the Cloth of Gold.

Another Great Officer of State called into being by the Coronation was the Lord High Constable, once the 'staller' of the Anglo-Saxon kings.

William the Conqueror gave Ralph de Mortimer his staff of office as the Constable of England. It was a position of very great power and became a hereditary office held by the Earls of Hereford. Through the female line it passed to the houses of Lancaster and Stafford. The last Lord High Constable of England was Edward Stafford, Duke of Buck-ingham. When he was executed by Henry VIII, this office was also merged in the Crown.

It had become too powerful to be held by one subject under the autocratic Tudor king since it combined in one person the duties of commanding the royal armies, Master of the Horse, joint president with the Earl Marshal of the Court of Chivalry, and the adminis-trator of martial law throughout the realm. The office was revived only for a great state pageant or a coronation.

In keeping with the old military tradition, the office is usually held by a famous soldier. The Duke of Wellington held the title at the coronations of George IV, William IV and Queen Victoria. In 1953 the Lord High Constable was Field Marshal, the Viscount Alan-brooke, Commander-in-Chief of the Home Forces in 1940–1, and later Chief of the Imperial General Staff. He also held the position of Constable of the Tower of London, and was commander of all the troops on parade for the Coronation.

In the Abbey Procession the Constable walked beside the Sword of State, borne by the Marquess of Salisbury, in step with his martial and hereditary colleague of times long past, the Earl Marshal.

The duties of the Master of the Horse are all that the title implies. He is officially responsible for the royal horses, hounds, stables, studs and the Royal Mews. In 1953 the appointment was held appropriately by the Duke of Beaufort, the Master of the famous Beaufort Hounds. Fourteen generations before his ancestors had also been Master of the Horse to Queen Elizabeth I and his grandfather held the same position to Queen Victoria.

As Master of the Horse the Duke was responsible for the safety of the Queen when she rode on horseback or in a carriage. He rode immediately behind the Queen on horseback when she drove to her first State Opening of Parliament and also in the same close proximity to her when the State Coach carried her to the Abbey for her Coronation. In the Abbey he walked wearing his blue Garter mantle between the Vice-Admiral of the United Kingdom and the Gold-Stick-in-Waiting.

The Lord Chamberlain is also another title of long descent and great authority in times past. He has wide and more permanent responsibilities, too many to enumerate here. They range from his responsibilities for matters 'above stairs' in the Royal Household to Court Ceremonial, Court Mourning, the care of the Chapels Royal and the royal swans. He officiates at Courts and Garden Parties, State Visits and Banquets. He has nominal charge of the Ecclesiastical Household, the Medical Household, the Gentlemen at Arms, the Yeomen of the Guard, the Gentlemen Ushers, the Serjeants at Arms, the Royal Bargemaster and Watermen. He is also the official custodian of the Regalia and the Crown Jewels – a duty which he delegates to the Keeper of the Jewel House at the Tower of London.

The Lord Chamberlain in Coronation year was the 11th Earl of Scarbrough. He belonged to one of the oldest families in England. His ancestor was created Baron Lumley by Richard II in 1380. Another ancestor lost his head and his title in Robert Aske's rebellion against Henry VIII in 1537, when he attempted to take Scarborough Castle. The title is taken from the castle lost in that abortive attempt, but a clerk in the Crown Office in 1620 omitted the 'o' from the warrant; so Scarbrough it remains.

We have still not completed the account of the 'Great' Lords of State who were, by custom, summoned to the Coronation. They held, however, more familiar titles and have permanent places in the administration of the realm.

Edward the Confessor, who had admired the highly organised court of the Dukes of Normandy, introduced the office of Chancellor into England. It was an office which, unlike some others, did not diminish with time. The Lord High Chancellor has become the highest judicial officer in England, the Speaker of the House of Lords and the guardian of the Great Seal.

At the Coronation of Queen Elizabeth II, the holder of this high office, Lord Simonds, a stately figure in full-bottomed wig and damask robe trimmed with gold, walked in the procession immediately behind the Archbishop of York. He was attended by his Official Pursebearer, bearing the gold embroidered purse with three splendid tassels which, nominally, held the matrices of obverse and reverse of the Great Seal of England.

The Lord President of the Council, the 5th Marquess of Salisbury, who like his ancestors of the house of Cecil had held many offices of State, did not on this occasion walk in the now traditional place of the Lord President behind the Prime Ministers of the Commonwealth. He had been appointed by the Queen to carry the Great Sword of State and he walked with the Lords bearing the Regalia.

The Lord Privy Seal is another ancient office of State which has its place in the coronation. As early as the fourteenth century Parliament wished to impose a check on the issue of public money, and to prevent the use of the Great Seal by the sovereign by connivance with the Lord Chancellor. The Privy Seal was, therefore, introduced as the authority needed for the issue of money for the Exchequer. The office has been shorn of much of its former authority but has been retained as a convenient method of appointing a minister to undertake special responsibilities. At the Coronation of the Queen this ancient office was held by the Rt Hon. Harry F. C. Crookshank.

On the morning of 2 June 1953, the holders of many ancient offices of State were standing in their positions in the Annexe to the Abbey to await the arrival of the Queen. There were the Great Lords of England, and the hereditary title holders from the old kingdoms of Scotland and Ireland. There were the standard bearers of the quarterings of the Royal Arms – the leopards of England, the lion of Scotland and the golden harp of Ireland. There was the 4th Baron Harlech, former constable of Edward I's castles of Harlech and Caernarvon, holding the standard of the Principality of Wales. The emblem on the standard of Wales was not the red dragon of Cadwaller, but the four lions which formed the Arms of Llywellyn ap Gruffydd who in 1282 was the last ruling Prince of Wales.

Standing in splendid isolation was Viscount Montgomery of Alamein, holding the Royal Standard, the personal banner of the Sovereign, which united in its gold, red and blue quarterings the ancient realms of the British Isles.

There were also the High Commissioners of the new countries of the Commonwealth, bearing the colourful standards of the nations which acknowledged the Queen as their liege lady and Head of the Commonwealth. There was the white crescent and star of Pakistan; the tricolour with the Union Jack of South Africa; the maple leaf of Canada; the splendid standard of Australia with its stars of the Southern Cross and the black swan; the standard of New Zealand with its three ships, the golden fleece and the Southern Cross; and the banner of Ceylon with the lion of the ancient Sinhalese kings.

Around them during these waiting moments were clustered many of the other ancient offices and pageantry of the British Isles. The glittering Kings of Arms with their ceremonial batons in their hands; the Gentlemen Ushers of the Orders of Chivalry, with the colour of their rods taken from the colour of the mantle of their order of Knighthood; the Gentlemen at Arms with their bright gilt helmets with swan plumes; the Chaplains of Westminster in scarlet cassocks and their Dean in the beautiful cope of red velvet worn at the coronation of Charles II, and everywhere in the Annexe were the peers in their rich scarlet Robes of State with the ermine capes covering their shoulders.

Other ancient officers came to take their place in that gathering – the Rear Admiral of the United Kingdom, the Keeper of the Jewel House, the Serjeants at Arms with their maces, the Mistress of the Robes and the train bearers, the Groom of the Robes, the Gold-Stick-in-Waiting, the Silver-Stick-in-Waiting, the Captain of the Queen's bodyguard of Yeomen of the Guard, and the holders of other offices in the long history of the British Crown.

All the bright and splendid colours of chivalry blossomed within the old Abbey for those few hours.

Coronation Appointments

THE GRAND PROCESSION
To Carry the Standards

The Union Standard	Captain J. L. M. Dymoke
The Standard of the Principality of Wales	The Lord Harlech, KG
The Standards of the Quarterings of the Royal Arms	
Ireland	The Lord de L'Isle and Dudley, VC
Scotland	The Viscount of Dudhope
England	The Earl of Derby, MC
The Royal Standard	The Viscount Montgomery of Alamein, KG, GCB, DSO

Four Knights of the Garter to hold the Canopy for the Anointing

The Viscount Allendale, KG, CB, CBE, MC	The Earl Fortescue, KG, CB, OBE, MC
The Duke of Wellington, KG	The Duke of Portland, KG

Bearers of the Regalia

St Edward's Staff	The Earl of Ancaster, TD
The Sceptre with the Cross	The Viscount Portal of Hungerford, KG, GCB, OM, DSO, MC
The Spurs	The Lord Hastings and the Lord Churston
The Pointed Sword of Temporal Justice, or Third Sword	The Duke of Buccleuch and Queensberry, KT, GCVO
The Pointed Sword of Spiritual Justice, or Second Sword	The Earl of Home
Curtana, Sword of Mercy	The Duke of Northumberland
The Great Steward of Scotland, as Deputy to the Duke of Rothesay	The Earl of Crawford and Balcarres, GBE, LLD
The Lord High Constable of England	The Viscount Alanbrooke, KG, GCB, OM, DSO
The Sword of State	The Marquess of Salisbury, KG
The Rod with the Dove	The Duke of Richmond and Gordon
The Orb	The Earl Alexander of Tunis, KG, GCB, GCMG, CSI, DSO, MC
The Lord High Steward to carry St Edward's Crown	The Viscount Cunningham of Hyndhope, KT, GCB, OM, DSO

11 The Royal Regalia

In January 1953 the Lord Chamberlain requested the Keeper of the Jewel House to have the Imperial State Crown removed from the Tower of London. The priceless and beautiful crown was taken to the workshops of the Crown Jewellers to be altered to fit the Queen. While it was there the settings of all the jewels were tested and the platinum framework and arches were carefully polished. This delicate work was supervised by the Crown Jeweller, Cecil Mann, CVO. St Edward's Crown, the one with which the Queen would be actually crowned, was not taken from the Tower until the end of April.

Crowns have seldom been easy to wear. Charles I complained of the weight of his crown during the ceremony. Princess Anne, later herself to succeed to the Throne, had commiserated with Queen Mary II after she was invested with the crown.

'Madam, I pity your fatigue.'

'A crown, sister,' sharply replied the newly crowned Queen, 'is not so heavy as it seems.'

Due to its awkward weight St Edward's Crown had not been used at the coronations of sovereigns from George IV to Edward VII. The existing Imperial State Crown had been used, or a new one made with the jewels reset in the new frame and arches. Queen Elizabeth II, like her father and grandfather, decided to use the traditional St Edward's Crown for her Coronation.

The Crown Jewels in the Tower of London are the most tempting prize ever put on display. Nowhere else in the world has such a priceless collection of jewels been laid out to the public gaze. The incredible radiance of the Koh-i-noor is at eye level; the immense Cullinan Diamond is an arm's length away.

'How are the Crown Jewels?' I used to ask Colonel E. H. Carkeet James, the Resident Governor of the Tower and acting Keeper of the Jewel House.

'They are still here! Come and see for yourself,' was his smiling invitation for another visit to the Jewel House.

One gang did succeed in lifting the Crown Jewels from the Tower of London. They got as far as Tower Wharf. This was the attempt to steal the Crown Jewels by the notorious Colonel Blood.

He was an Irishman who had risen to his rank in Cromwell's army. For some reason his hatred of the Duke of Ormonde, Lord Lieutenant of Ireland, was so intense, that in 1663 he tried to seize Dublin Castle to capture the Duke. The attempt was foiled and Blood escaped. Seven years later, with armed associates, he again tried to seize the Duke in St James's Street, London, with the stated intention of hanging him publicly at the 'hangman's corner' of Tyburn. The Duke was injured but escaped. A thousand-pound reward was offered for Blood's arrest. It was never claimed.

Blood was not intimidated. A few months later in May 1671 he reached the summit of his audacity with the attempt on the Crown Jewels. The plot was carefully laid. The Regalia in the Tower were in the care of an aged custodian, Talbot Edwards, who was allowed to show them to the public for a 'modest fee'.

Disguised as a clergyman, Blood cultivated the friendship of his aged victim. The path of cordiality was garnished with presents and flattery. When they dined, Blood, 'taking it upon himself to say Grace performed it with great seeming devotion, and, casting up his eyes, concluded it with a prayer for the king, the queen and the royal family.' The Crown Jewels, he obviously felt, were by then past praying for!

On the chosen day, Blood returned with three companions. He told Talbot Edwards that his friends would like to see the Jewels. Once in the Jewel House all pretence was abandoned. Edwards was seized, gagged and stabbed in the stomach. The jewelled swords and sceptres were attacked with files to reduce their length. Blood began to flatten the Imperial Crown with a mallet to make it more portable.

Blood was near success when his plans were shattered. Edwards's son returned un-expectedly to see his parents. When his entrance to his father's residence in the Martin Tower was prevented by a stranger, he raised the alarm. Blood thrust the battered crown under his cloak and fled with his companions. They rushed across the drawbridge to their waiting horses, but young Edwards and a few of the guards were upon them.

Blood struggled to keep his booty until it was wrested from him. Arrogantly he declared, 'It was for a crown!'

The outcome of his crimes and audacity was astonishing. After a brief sojourn in prison, he was released, given a pension of £500 a year for life – a large sum in those days – and 'received into the intimacy of the court'.

We shall never know the reasons for the King's clemency and his astonishing generosity. A dark suspicion at the time was that the impecunious Charles II was in the plot to steal his own Crown Jewels!

What was the reward of Talbot Edwards and his son for saving the priceless gems in the Tower? After long and desperate pleading he was awarded £200. He had to wait so long for the money that the sick old man had to pledge the future payment for half the amount.

The raffish Earl of Rochester wrote this sardonic comment:

Blood that wears treason in his face,
Villain complete in parson's gown,
How much he is at Court in grace,
For stealing Ormonde and the crown.
Since loyalty does no man good
Let's steal the King, and outdo Blood.

The Crown Jewels which Blood had tried to steal had been newly made for the coronation of Charles II. The ancient and historic crowns of England had been destroyed twenty-five years previously – by Act of Parliament.

The destruction of the ancient Regalia was the work of Cromwell's followers. The ancient crowns and sceptres were regarded as symbols of the 'detestable rule of kings'. On 3 June 1643 Parliament resolved 'that the locks on the doors where the Regalia are kept, in Westminster Abbey, shall be opened . . . and a search made there, and Inventory taken of what things are there'.

The order was enforced by Henry Martin, a future regicide, and George Withers, a Puritan poet. We have a contemporary account of the macabre scene which followed their entry. They forced open the great oak chests and piled on a table the crowns and sceptres 'belonging anciently to King Edward the Confessor, and used by all our Kings at their Inauguration'.

They had great fun with the ancient crowns and the coronation robes of long dead kings and queens. Martin dressed Withers in the royal robes and St Edward's Crown, 'Who thus crowned and Royally arranged, marched about the room with a stately garb, and afterwards with a Thousand Apish and Ridiculous actions exposed these sacred ornaments to contempt and laughter.'

St Edward's Crown, which so many English kings had worn at their coronation, was among the ancient treasures in the Abbey. The relics of St Edward there also included his staff, his ring and the vestments taken from his body when it was moved to its new shrine by Henry III.

The old chests in the Abbey may also have held the regal ornaments of some of our Saxon kings. The coronation robe of Wiglaf, King of Mercia in the ninth century, for example, had come into the keeping of the Abbey. It is possible that the greatest of all the royal treasures had been kept in the Abbey – the crown of the greatest Saxon King, King Alfred the Great.

It was so named in the inventory made for Parliament – 'King Alfred's crown of gold wyerworke, set with slight stones and two little bells'. Robert of Gloucester in 1250, describing the meeting between Alfred and Pope Leo IV, wrote: 'The Pope blessed him, and the king's crown of this lande, which is in this lande yet.'

Much later the crown was still in this land, in an old box in the Abbey with the inscription, 'This is the principal crown with which were crowned Alfred, Edward, etc.'

Was this really the crown of the Great Alfred? We shall never know. The ruthless decision was taken. All the Regalia were 'broken and defaced'. The jewels were sold or plundered, the gold melted down. So vanished for ever the royal treasures of the centuries, possibly King Alfred's crown but certainly the Crown of St Edward as well as the crowns, sceptres, and other regalia of many English kings and queens. This priceless Regalia, including the jewels, were valued at the absurd price of £2,647 18s 4d! Some of the jewels from the ancient Regalia appeared after the restoration of Charles II. They had been bought by Stuart sympathisers. They included the famous ruby of the Black Prince, which had been worn in the helmet of Henry V at Agincourt; and the four pear-shaped pearls, once the ear-rings of the first Queen Elizabeth. They were set again in the new Imperial State Crown.

I   The Royal Regalia. St Edward's Crown, the Ampulla and Spoon, the Sceptre with the Cross, the Rod of Equity and Mercy, the new Bracelets or Armills, the Coronation Ring.

II   The Imperial State Crown – worn by the Queen after her Coronation and henceforth on State Occasions like the opening of Parliament. A Crown of priceless splendour.

III   The Orb, the Spurs and the Coronation Ring.

IV   The Abbey and the Annexe immediately before the Coronation.

In 1660, therefore, Charles II was restored to a kingdom which was, literally, without a crown. His coronation was delayed while the new Regalia were designed and made by the goldsmith, Sir Robert Vyner, at a cost of £32,000.

There is space for only a brief description of these priceless regal ornaments.

St Edward's Crown

The arches are depressed at the centre to indicate that it is the crown of a kingdom, and not a 'crown imperial'. The framework is of gold set with about 440 precious and semi-precious stones. It is worn only once in each sovereign's lifetime, at the coronation. When the sovereign retires into St Edward's chapel at the end of the coronation service, it is replaced by the Imperial State Crown.

The Imperial State Crown

The most beautiful and most priceless crown ever made for any sovereign in Christendom. Its delicate platinum framework and arches seem to shimmer with the white splendour of 2,700 diamonds and hundreds of other precious stones. Most conspicuous among the other gems are the great ruby of the Black Prince; the sapphire of Edward the Confessor, and the four long pearl drops known as Queen Elizabeth's ear-rings. The second 'Star of Africa', cut from the fabulous Cullinan Diamond, shines with incomparable splendour in the front of the crown. The Cullinan Diamond, the largest ever discovered, was found in 1905 at the De Beers mine in South Africa. It was presented by General Smuts to Edward VII – a generous gesture from a Boer leader.

The arches of the crown are not depressed in the centre, indicating that it is an imperial crown. It is the crown the Sovereign wears on all state occasions.

The Sceptre with the Cross

This Sceptre was delivered into the Sovereign's right hand at the Coronation, as the 'Ensign of Kingly Power and Justice'.

It is of gold, about three feet long, the upper part wreathed with collars of gems and enamels. In the head is set the first 'Star of Africa'. This huge diamond of 530 carats can be detached and worn as a pendant. The Cross is a cross-patée, heavily encrusted with diamonds and with a large amethyst.

The Sceptre with the Dove

This Sceptre was placed in the Queen's left hand. It has customarily been called the Virge or Rod. It is first mentioned at the coronation of Richard I in 1189. The Dove is the symbol of the Holy Ghost, and this sceptre symbolises the royal duty to be the wise guardian and guide of the people.

The Dove on top is of white enamel with outstretched wings, its eyes, back and feet are of gold. Four jewelled bands encircle this sceptre.

The Orb

The Orb is delivered only to a Sovereign Regnant, as was Queen Elizabeth II. The Roman emperors used the globe, or orb, as a symbol of their universal dominion, adding the cross after their conversion to Christianity.

The Orb is of gold, six and a half inches in diameter and weighs nearly three pounds. It has a band of rubies, sapphires and emeralds between two rows of pearls.

The Swords

Five swords made their appearance at the Coronation, all of them of ancient use and symbolism.

The Jewelled State Sword is the most beautiful and valuable sword in the world. It was made for the coronation of George IV. Even a brief description of its magnificence would fill several pages. The blade is of damascus steel; the diamonds, sapphires and emeralds on the scabbard form the emblems of the Tudor rose, the thistle and the shamrock.

It is the symbol of honour and a king is girded with it. As Queen Regnant, the Archbishop placed it in the Queen's hand. The Queen carried the Jewelled Sword back to the Altar, symbolising that the Sovereign placed the sword at the service of the Church. As the *Liber Regalis* directed, it was then redeemed for one hundred shillings.

The Sword of State is the symbol of majesty and authority. It is a large two-handed sword, and its crimson scabbard carries the arms of William and Mary, and the emblems of the rose, thistle, harp and fleur-de-lis.

It is a heavy sword of eight pounds, and is very difficult to carry upright for a long period in a two-handed grip. I heard Lord Salisbury, who carried it, give a faint sigh of relief when he surrendered it to the Lord Chamberlain after the Queen's anointing. He received in exchange the Jewelled Sword of the Offering.

This Sword of State is carried before the Sovereign on other state occasions.

The Sword of Mercy or Curtana has a blunt end to represent justice tempered by mercy. Its name is said to have been derived from the fabled sword of Ogier the Dane, who was one of the peers of Charlemagne. With his sword uplifted to strike, he was commanded by a voice from heaven to show mercy. Tradition also says that this sword passed into the keeping of Edward the Confessor. It could have been among the Regalia broken and defaced by the Puritans.

The Sword of Justice to the Spirituality. The traditional name of this sword has given rise to disputes on whether it implies any spiritual authority by the sovereign over the clergy. It has a scabbard of crimson velvet ornamented with gold.

The Sword of Justice to the Temporality symbolises the royal authority to administer justice to lords and people. It is similar to the previous sword with a scabbard of scarlet and gold.

The Spurs

The golden spurs are the symbols of honour and chivalry. They were once fastened over the buskins, later they were simply touched to the heels of a king or offered to the hand touch of a Queen Regnant. They were first mentioned at the coronation of Richard I.

The Ring

It was made for William IV and used at the coronation by every sovereign, except Victoria. It consists of a sapphire background with a St George Cross of rubies.

A ring has been used at every coronation since that of Edgar in 973. It has been called the wedding ring of England, the bond which unites sovereign and people.

The Bracelets

The bracelets for the Queen's Coronation were presented by the nations of the Commonwealth. In some reigns there has been some confusion between the bracelets and a stole, part of the coronation vestments. The ancient name for the bracelets was 'armills' from the Latin *armillae*. Through a faulty translation the term came to be applied to a long piece of silk worn stole-wise round the neck and tied to the arms. In 1953 the confusion was resolved. The 'armills' were 'bracelets' again and the silk was named the 'Royal Stole'.

The Regalia which were brought to the Abbey in June 1953 were laden with the symbolism and significance of many centuries, even from times long before the old Abbey itself was raised on the marshes of the Isle of Thorns.

12   The Abbey and the Annexe

The Great West Entrance to the Abbey was closed to the public. The Earl Marshal had issued his warrant to the Ministry and the preparations for the Coronation could begin. The Dean and Chapter announced that the nave of the Abbey would be closed from 1 December 1952, but the Transepts and the Sanctuary would still be open for services. On 1 January 1953 the whole of the Abbey would come into the possession of the Ministry.

In the grey light of a December morning the prefabricated boarding was placed around the Broad Sanctuary in front of the Abbey, where more than four centuries ago William Caxton had set up his first printing press. By mid-morning the heavy lorries were lumbering into this enclave loaded with timber. It was being stacked under awnings to keep it dry.

When I came into the nave the usual noise of shuffling tourists was replaced by more purposeful sounds. Chairs, carpets and the other removable ecclesiastical fittings were being taken out. Electricians had begun to fit temporary lighting. Huge rolls of felting and bags of clean sand were being carried in. The sand was used to fill any uneven spaces in the floor before the heavy felting was laid. On top of the felt the pre-cut lengths of timber flooring would be laid.

We disturbed the ancient dust of the Abbey as we were guided by Mr W. Bishop, the Clerk of Works, up the narrow winding stairways to the Triforium.

In this high place the passing of the centuries seemed to have drained away every particle of colour – the grey light came through grey glass windows, falling on grey stone and the grey dust of the high arched passageway.

Mr Bishop pointed to a faint glitter of glass on the dust-shrouded floor.

'A reminder of the war damage,' he said.

'Was there much damage?' I asked.

He smiled. 'I think St Edward in his shrine below us must have worked some of his greatest miracles to save his Abbey. During the early Blitz we had several near misses. The great west window was damaged, the Choir School hit, and the east window in the Henry VII Chapel was blown in. The night of 10 May 1941 was the worst. Showers of fire bombs fell on the South West Tower, the Nave, the Triforium. The Chapter Library roof was soon well alight. The Fire Brigade couldn't get through the blocked streets, the water supply failed. I don't know how we coped, but in the morning the Abbey was still there.'

We looked down at the Sanctuary and the long cavern of the Nave far below us, where the tiny figures of the workmen were moving around. In seven months' time that space would be filled with crowded splendour.

The Abbey of Westminster has been the coronation church of the English kings and queens for nine hundred years. Only two English sovereigns have not been crowned in the Abbey. Edward V was born in the Abbey but not allowed to return for his coronation. He was one of the two young princes murdered in the Tower. The other non-crowned king was Edward VIII who had abdicated in 1936 before his coronation.

King Edward the Confessor had begun building the Abbey in 1055 and lay dying while his great new church was being consecrated.

One by one, the Norman kings had come to the Abbey for their crowning, but they conferred few other favours on the Abbey, apart from the dubious bounty of King Stephen who appointed one of his illegitimate sons, Gervase of Blois, to be Abbot. He lived richly on the Abbey revenues.

For over 100 years the Abbey had a precarious existence. There was often trouble between the Norman Abbots and the Saxon monks. The community had also to provide for the upkeep of twenty-five knights from its tenures scattered from Sunbury to Islip in Oxfordshire with which Edward had endowed it.

These tenures were coveted by their secular neighbours. The Abbey, therefore, strengthened its defences by a little judicious forgery of its charters and other evidences of title. At the same period other great ecclesiastical establishments throughout England – monasteries, churches, abbeys and minsters – were also in many instances fortifying their unchartered titles by the careful arts of penmanship. Monks from Paris were the great masters of the craft. It has been called the 'golden age of forgery'.

Henry III, proud of his descent from Alfred the Great, was captured by the popular devotion to St Edward. He set about proving his own devotion by pulling down St Edward's church to make way for his own much more splendid building. There was pride in his devotion. He wanted his church to outshine the high and lovely cathedrals of France.

Set amid the soaring columns, below the intricate vaulting, surrounded by every ecclesiastical splendour, was the chapel and shrine of St Edward, raised above the Sanctuary, 'like a candlestick to enlighten the church'. Soil was brought from the Holy Land to raise the floor of the chapel six feet above the ambulatory. St Edward's body was transferred to the most splendid gold and jewelled shrine in Christendom. It remained such until it was stripped of all its splendour by Henry VIII.

The gold has been taken from St Edward's shrine but his name has run like a golden and recurrent thread through English history. Eight kings of England have borne his name. For centuries the English kings came to the Abbey, until the time of James II, to swear before crowning to keep 'the laws of King Edward'. At each coronation the crown has been called 'St Edward's Crown'. The jewel at the top of the Imperial Crown is 'St Edward's Sapphire'. 'St Edward's Staff' has been carried in the coronation processions and for centuries the 'St Edward's vestments' may have been those actually worn by the king.

Henry III sleeps beside the king he chose to venerate. He built a shrine for a saintly king, but it was also his intention that the Abbey should be the royal resting-place for himself and his successors, as well as the coronation church of the English royal line. The Abbey was built like no other church in England. The two wide Transepts were brought forward beyond the Choir to form a wide open space before the Sanctuary. This was the 'Place of the Crowning', later called the 'Theatre', where the kings of England could be recognised, acclaimed, consecrated and crowned in the 'gaze of their peers and of their people'.

The Abbey was a place we had to approach with reverence and care. There had been damage to the monuments and structures of the Abbey at some previous coronations. Even Queen Victoria's coronation had taken its toll. At her coronation and at the Golden Jubilee in 1887 an enormous spectators' gallery had been erected at the east end of the Abbey, rising above the High Altar with towering tiers of seats. This structure enclosed the whole of St Edward's Chapel below it. The heavy timber supports had damaged some of the royal tombs, including the shrine of St Edward. The preparation of the Abbey from that time onwards was approached with much more care.

The Abbey in 1953 was made to accommodate 7,700 people. As on previous occasions the people in the Nave were able to witness only the processions and could see little of the ceremony beyond the Choir Screen. In 1937 they could listen to the Service on the public address system. The peers and peeresses beyond the first ten or twelve rows in the Transepts also had their view completely cut off. Henry's splendid Theatre had been designed when there were only a few hundred noblemen and important clerics in the land. The viewers on TV had a far better view of the proceedings than the great majority of the congregation in the Abbey.

The usual careful survey of almost every inch of the Abbey's stonework was undertaken. The building was full of the wear and stress of time, and there was the risk that some worn finial, or a loose piece of old stone might suddenly descend on some distinguished head far below.

The great galleries which filled the public space in the Abbey would reach high up the ancient walls. Behind these galleries an immense access and supporting system had to be built. To every level stairways had to be constructed, lavatories, control rooms and a telephone exchange provided. Miles of conduits stretched round inside the Abbey for the cables for lighting, telephones and TV and broadcasting lines. A powerful system of air conditioning had to be provided. There had to be a control room for the lighting and public address systems. A committee of doctors under Sir Horace Evans asked us to provide five medical centres for the Abbey.

Space had to be found for the Army signal units, the emergency radio links, overnight sleeping quarters for Yeomen, police, troops and security staff. The BBC and foreign broadcasting systems would need control rooms for their massive equipment. We would have to build commentary boxes and hidden camera positions.

St Edward's Chapel, behind the High Altar, had also to be prepared. Here the 'Traverse' would be built. This was the traditional curtained enclosure in which the Queen would

10   The Abbey is prepared. With meticulous care the carpenters erect the framework for the Throne.

be disrobed of her coronation vestments and attired in the Robe of Purple Velvet for her return journey to the Palace. The 'Traverse' has been built at least since the coronation of Richard II in 1377. The secular orders for his coronation said, 'And also it is to wite that a certain place nere the shrine must be prepared with travers and curteyns', where the King could retire to break his fast after the communion 'yf hym wyste'. The 'closed place with curtains' was also required by the *Liber Regalis.*

All this had to be fitted into an ancient building originally designed for the royal tombs, the devotions of a few score monks, and once every reign to provide a place for a few hundred dignitaries to assemble for a coronation.

When the timber and scaffolding was cleared from the Broad Sanctuary to the inside of the Abbey, the erection of the steel framework for the Annexe could begin. In addition to the marshalling hall for the processions, it would have to contain retiring rooms for the Queen, the Duke of Edinburgh and other members of the Royal Family.

Finally there was the structure that nobody seemed to see! During the night before the Coronation a bridge was raised across St Margaret's Street linking the Abbey to the Palace of Westminster. It would provide a convenient entrance for the peers and commons and avoid a great deal of congestion around the entrance to the Abbey. It was not a new idea. The Bayeux Tapestry shows a similar link between the Abbey and the Palace in 1066.

Within a few days the floors were laid in the nave, and the workmen were laying the 'railway line' which would run during the construction period from Broad Sanctuary through the West Door, down the Nave and along the Choir to the Sanctuary. This system of transporting material was first used in 1937. It had speeded up the handling of heavy materials, ensured an even stress on the floors and lessened the risk of accidental damage. It was not so incongruous as it seemed. The medieval master masons had hauled their heavy stone burdens into that place on sledges running over heavy baulks of timber.

The number of workers employed in the Abbey began to rise from about 30 in December to just over 200 at the peak in February and March. Sharp eyes watched in Parliament. Eccles had to explain that the number of workers in and around the Abbey who might have been engaged on housing work was 95 but that none of them had actually been taken off housing. In reply to another question he stated that 85 per cent of the timber used in the Abbey would be later used in housing.

At the coronation of Richard II in 1377 there had also been a similar shortage of labour and building materials. The solution was then regarded as perfectly straightforward. It was dealt with by a Royal Proclamation.

Know ye that we have appointed our beloved William Hanaway, clerk, to take and provide by himself and by his deputies stone, mortar and other necessaries for our works which we have ordained to be executed in our Palace of Westminster for the Solemnity of our Coronation. And to take carpenters, and all other workmen necessary for the works aforesaid in our City of London and Counties of Middlesex and Surrey, and to put them on the works aforesaid, to remain in the same at our command as shall be necessary.

And all those whom he shall find perverse or disobedient in this matter, to arrest take and commit them to our prisons, there to remain until by deliberation we shall be induced otherwise to ordain.

By the end of February 1953 the galleries in the Nave had been completed and the tiers in both Transepts had risen far up the walls. It was shortly after this stage that the Queen and the Duke of Edinburgh came to see the progress of the work. The Earl Marshal with the Minister received them on arrival, but after the formal reception they walked around the Abbey by themselves. The Queen was very interested in the changes which were taking place in the Abbey.

She had been eleven years old at the coronation of her father. She had walked in the great procession with her young sister Princess Margaret. She had seen the splendour of the Abbey on a coronation day but she had not before seen the timber and scaffolding behind the setting. While the royal couple walked around the Abbey the workmen went quietly on with their work.

The Queen stopped to ask questions and the Duke was amused by the 'railway' when a laden trolley moved down the Nave.

The Queen and the Duke paid several other visits to the Abbey during the preparations. The journalists and photographers used to arrive with remarkable promptness on these and other important occasions. These visits were supposed to be private arrangements and I used to speculate on how the Press got the 'tip-off'. When the Coronation was over a journalist revealed the secret.

'We gave a few quid to an old chap who made the tea and handled the post in an office opposite the Abbey. We gave him reference pictures and he was soon able to recognise almost everyone going into the Abbey. The arrival of your Minister – dragged away from Parliament – was the tip that something important was due to happen.'

Outside the Abbey the light tubular steel frame of the Annexe was rapidly assembled before the West Front of the Abbey. Since the first Annexe was built for the coronation of William IV, the architects had striven to harmonise the design with the Abbey buildings. They had been structures in the Gothic style with battlements, turrets and high windows. Their interiors were as heavily conventional as their Gothic exteriors. The interior design of the Annexe for George V, for instance, had been 'pillared and cross beamed with oak within, and hung with stamped leather and tapestries, halberds, pikes, swords and armour'.

The Annexe in 1953 was certainly unlike anything which had gone before. It paid no tribute to any Gothic antecedents yet it seemed to harmonise with the twin towers of the Abbey. It may have owed a little of its inspiration to the pavilions of the Festival of Britain in 1951, but there was a feeling of dignity about it which had not been necessary in the airy castles of the South Bank. The large mullioned window at its west end, decorated with the engraved emblems of Britain and the Commonwealth, seemed to claim its own contemporary affinity with ecclesiastical architecture.

The entrance to the Annexe was the focal point of the plan. The water-lily shape of the top canopy, supported by delicate white columns, sheltered the huge Royal Coat of Arms

11 Interior of the Annexe, or Vestibule, where the processions were assembled. The Regalia Table is on the left and the beautiful engraved window beyond.

which, with its bright colours, made a brilliant contrast to the flat north screen wall.

At that time it was a very revolutionary building to set in front of the venerable Abbey. The new cathedrals and churches had not yet appeared to accept and sanctify contemporary design.

The main work of Mowlems inside the Abbey and on the Annexe was completed by the end of April. Some features were left to the last moment like the hide-covered main entrance doors to the Annexe, the Royal Coat of Arms above them, and the glazing of the great west window. The Queen's Beasts did not make their appearance in front of the Annexe until two days before Coronation Day. We shall meet these strange heraldic creatures later in this book.

When the workmen had gone and the 'railway' had been taken away an unusual tranquillity settled on the Abbey. The galleries in the Nave and Transepts, awaiting their seating, were showing their long expanses of new boards; the raised platform of the Theatre was wide and bare. The treatment of the wood had turned it a faint yellow colour. Looking from the Choir towards the Sanctuary the honey shades of the side galleries merged into the daffodil yellow of the Theatre's floor. As the bright April daylight outside changed with a passing cloud the quality of the light inside the Abbey was also altered. The colours ran before the light, from a deep bronze through a changing chiaroscuro of yellows. There were times when the whole Abbey was filled with a rich translucent light, a honeycomb of radiance. It was a halcyon place, a Royal House of Gold. The Abbey was beautiful before it was adorned.

12   The Abbey in its Coronation setting. On the left the Chair of Estate; centre, King Edward's Chair and the Throne; right, the three rows of seats for the Bishops.

13 The Queen's Beasts

None of the adornments of the Abbey aroused so much interest as the ten great heraldic statues which stood guard outside the Annexe. Millions came to stare up at them with curiosity; the cameras clicked away during every daylight hour.

The Minister, David Eccles, first introduced these strange beasts to the world under the blazing lights of a press conference at Church House, Westminster on 17 February 1953. He was very proud of those beasts.

'Here', he said pointing to a large model of the Abbey, 'the Queen will alight from her Golden Coach. She will see a line of sculptured animals sitting upright, with expressions of ferocious loyalty on their aristocratic faces.'

Several hundred journalists made a careful note of Eccles's picturesque description. The 'ferocious loyalty on their aristocratic faces' was the caption to every picture which appeared all round the world.

He went on. 'You will not meet these animals anywhere on the level of humdrum reality. But then on that plane there is no place for the Queen's Golden Coach. These are dream creatures, aristocrats of an heroic species, real and formidable in the world of the imagination.'

These royal creatures were ranged like sentinels along the western side of the Annexe. They were known as the 'Queen's Beasts'. They had a long heraldic ancestry. They were derived from the badges of the Queen's ancestors.

The appearance of the Queen's Beasts in 1953 was the result of a shared inspiration. Eccles had felt that the design of the Annexe would not be complete until the space below the great west window was filled in some appropriate way. A procession of ideas passed over the drawing boards into the waste paper bins.

Eccles woke up in the middle of the night inspired by his sudden recollections of Henry VIII's beasts at Hampton Court Palace. Twenty miles away the Chief Architect was sitting up in bed drawing strange monsters on scraps of paper. The 'beasts' were born.

They had to be born anew. The beasts at Hampton Court were typical of their century and the emblems on their shields were personal to Henry VIII and Jane Seymour. The houses of Stuart and Hanover had since brought their own heraldic emblems to share

13   The Queen's Beasts. The Minister, David Eccles, with the Chief Architect, Eric Bedford, at the studio of the sculptor, James Woodford.

14 The Queen's Beasts in position before the Annexe. The sculptor gives the final touches.

the royal bestiary. Some thirty heraldic creatures had been inherited by the Queen.

Ten of the royal beasts more closely related to the Queen's ancestry than those at Hampton Court were selected by Mr H. Stanford London, a Fellow of the Society of Antiquaries and an expert in the field of medieval heraldry. He guided the sculptor on heraldic principles, including the bearings on the shields which the beasts would present to the world.

The chosen sculptor was James Woodford, RA, who had worked on the heraldic designs for the Whitehall façade of the Ministry of Agriculture and the heraldic beasts for the Imperial War Graves Commission.

The heraldic antecedents and most interesting artistic forms were agreed between medieval scholar and modern sculptor. In the autumn of 1952 James Woodford came to the Ministry to present his designs. He showed us the fabulous monsters in miniatures – ten little figures, nine inches high, modelled in Plasticine and executed in perfect detail. After the first examination the figures were placed in position on the scale model of the Annexe, and everyone knew that the design of the Annexe was satisfyingly complete.

I spent a morning watching the progress of the work in the sculptor's studio at St Peter's Square, Hammersmith. Mounds of clay lay under damp sheets of sacking. The sculptor himself was perched high on a scaffolding putting the finishing touches to the crown on the Lion of England's head.

From the huge clay figures the plaster casts were taken in sections for ease of transport. They were given a protective coating against the weather for their vigil. The Beasts were not painted in their heraldic colours since it was felt that their neutral shades blended better with the architectural setting. The shields which they held were emblazoned, however, with all the vivid hues of chivalry.

They were placed in their positions below the great west window two days before the Coronation. Above the tall window were the vivid colours of the Coats of Arms and insignia of the nations of the British Commonwealth.

I asked Woodford which of the beasts had been the most difficult to design. He replied that it had been the Falcon of the Plantagenets because 'it had not been easy to depict gracefully a bird sitting down and supporting a shield'.

The place of honour next to the Royal Entrance was given to the Lion of England, the oldest beast in the royal pedigree and the only animal to wear a crown. Along the western façade of the Annexe beyond the Lion were placed the other beasts – the White Greyhound of Richmond, the Yale of Beaufort, the Red Dragon of Wales, the White Horse of Hanover, the White Lion of Mortimer, the Unicorn of Scotland, the Griffin of Edward III, the Black Bull of Clarence, and the Falcon of the Plantagenets.

Most of them had appeared in various heraldic renderings on the coronation scene many times before. They had been seen on silken banners, had been embroidered on cloths of gold and appeared as the ornaments on royal liveries. They had been carved for the adornment of many royal palaces. In 1953, they seemed to have come again to their proper places.

14 The Textures of Tradition

The Queen's Beasts outside the Abbey derived their strange shapes from ancient royal insignia. Within, the Abbey had to be prepared in accordance with other ancient traditions.

Abbot Lytlington still pointed to the way the Abbey should be prepared for the Coronation of Queen Elizabeth in 1953: 'The King . . . shall follow the procession into the Church at Westminster and he shall go on a blue cloth spread upon the ground . . . to the stage erected in the aforesaid church.' Like many other rubrics of the *Liber Regalis* this was the perpetuation of a practice at even earlier coronations.

On a bright morning in June 1952, when it was hoped that the light inside the Abbey would be comparable with that a year hence, we held the 'trial of carpets' in Westminster Abbey. The Earl Marshal, the Lord Chamberlain, the Minister and the Dean solemnly surveyed the long stretches of carpets of many shades of blue which were stretched down the aisle. There were pieces of the carpets which had been used from the coronation of Queen Victoria to the coronation of the Queen's father in 1937.

There are many shades of blue and there were several divergent opinions on what the appropriate shade should be! Many rolls of blue carpet were laid down and rolled up again before the final decision was taken – the carpeting of the processional ways in the Abbey would consist of two shades of blue. The 17-foot width would comprise 10 feet of light blue carpeting in the centre with contrasting darker blue borders both $3\frac{1}{2}$ feet wide. The contrasting colours would enhance the decorative effect and also serve as a guide for the processions, with the outflankers and escorts, such as the Gentlemen at Arms and the Yeomen, keeping to the dark blue borders.

The longest carpet of continuous weave, 188 feet long by 17 feet wide, was for the Nave from the Annexe to the Choir Screen; from there a further length of 56 feet of carpet would reach to the Coronation Theatre.

For the Coronation Theatre, the Sanctuary, and the Traverse in St Edward's Chapel, the uniform carpeting like the drapings were to be of a golden colour. There would be twelve separate carpets in this group, the largest single woven carpet on the grand scale of 86 feet by 32 feet.

Within the Annexe the carpeting would be in contrasting shades of blue and gold. Altogether in the Abbey there would be laid 508 square yards of blue carpet and 971 square yards of gold, while the Annexe would have 1,298 yards of blue and 187 yards of gold.

The manufacture of the Abbey carpets was entrusted to James Templeton & Co. of

Glasgow, who had also provided the carpets for the coronations in 1911 and 1937. They were at that time the only firm in the world with a power loom sufficiently wide to weave in one piece the great carpet for the Theatre.

The carpets were of Chenille Axminster, woven seamless – a process which had been invented by James Templeton in 1839. They were of exceptional fineness, having 288 tufts of 6 ply worsted yarn to the square inch. The pile was short in order not to impede the passage of the robes and trains of the peers, peeresses and other robed or mantled participants in the procession. The weight of the pile was $3\frac{1}{4}$ lb per square yard compared to the household grade of $1\frac{1}{4}$ to $1\frac{1}{2}$ lb.

The final consignment of carpeting for the Abbey weighed 13,709 lb and the cost was £18,000. The cost was fully recovered since most of the Abbey carpeting was later cut into suitable lengths and sold for the sanctuaries of churches in the United Kingdom and throughout the Commonwealth. The feet of many a clergyman should be able to walk on those carpets for many centuries to come.

The Ministry was offered large sums of money for one of the Coronation carpets. A Hollywood film studio offered 'ten times its cost' for the carpet in the Theatre, and a big New York department store also made a princely bid.

It is only once in each reign that such skill and richness has been brought to the design and the spinning and weaving of such superb and beautiful fibres and fabrics. For generations of designers a coronation has been the supreme challenge to their artistry and skill.

In 1952 the Ministry, as I have mentioned, invited Professor Robert Gooden, RDI, FSIA, to create the designs for the silk warp tissues for the frontals of the rising tiers of seating in the Abbey. These silk frontals would be the largest display areas in the Abbey and their design was of very great importance.

Since Tudor times the crown has been associated with the Tudor rose in coronation drapings. Robert Gooden based his design on these symbols. On the blue silk ground the centre of the design was worked in gold enriched with metallic thread. The Tudor roses, like other national emblems, were delicately stylised. The design of the crown itself was the summit of Robert Gooden's inspiration. Above the Tudor rose, the thistle, the shamrock and the leek, the outlines of the crown were composed of the fleur-de-lis, ivy leaves, pinks and other flowers – a unique floral bouquet for a Queen!

We saw how right the designs were on Coronation morning. When the Abbey was filled with the waiting guests in the Nave, the blue frontals – appropriately called 'Queensway' – lifted into prominence the long lines of uniforms, mantles, robes and the dresses of the women. The metallic sparkle of the thread was picked out by the flood of light from high overhead.

The floral crown and the national emblems of the 'Queensway' design were also used for the gold tissue frontals of the Theatre – as old Abbot Lytlington had directed 'silken cloths of gold are to be hung around the theatre'. Over this golden tissue below the Royal Gallery was laid a magnificent silk embroidery of the Royal Arms. The same beautiful golden tissue was also used to cover the Regalia Table in the Annexe.

The blue and gold tissue had been woven by Warner & Sons, Ltd at their New Mills in Braintree, Essex. I went with David Eccles to see the weaving of the silk tissues.

When we arrived we seemed to have entered an Aladdin's workshop of the most splendid fabrics in the world.

We saw wide swathes of cream silk lute, or lustring, which would be embroidered with the Royal Coat of Arms and lengths of rich crimson satin which would cover the chairs of the three Royal Dukes. This rich satin would also be used inside the State Coach. A rich crimson damask with 28,000 silk threads in its warp of 63 inches was being woven for covering the Throne Chair; it would also be used for the cushions on the Coronation Chair and on the Chair of Estate.

The looms were also laden with the rich silk tissue for the copes of the canons of Westminster – a traditional offering from the new sovereign. The gold figures in its beautiful blue ground were derived from a fifteenth-century Italian design known as 'Milan'.

There was the superb red silk damask in the design called 'Canterbury Rose' for the Faldstool on which the Queen would kneel during various parts of the ceremony.

Finally, there was the purple velvet for the Royal Robe of State with which the Queen would be invested in St Edward's Chapel at the end of the ceremony and before she left the Abbey.

By long tradition an uncrowned monarch does not wear the royal purple; it is assumed only after the coronation rite and before each of the newly crowned sovereigns showed themselves to their people. The Royal Robe of State is, therefore, more traditionally known as the Robe of Purple Velvet. An uncrowned monarch wears a robe of crimson velvet – this was the colour of the robe the Queen wore for the opening of Parliament before her Coronation and it was also the colour of the robe in which she drove to the Abbey.

The silk for the purple velvet had been spun by a special strain of silkworms at Lady Hart Dyke's 'farm', where the silk for the Queen's wedding dress had also been spun. The silk mills at Glemsford, near Long Melford, 'threw' the silken threads together. The yarn was then passed to Joshua Wardle of Leebrook, Staffordshire, for dyeing before it arrived at the Braintree Mills of Warners, to be woven in the lengths of purple velvet 20 yards long by 21 inches wide on a handloom identical with those used 100 years ago.

The royal fabric was then sent to the unpretentious shop of Ede & Ravenscroft in Chancery Lane, London, where gowns had been made for lawyers, clergymen and scholars for nearly 300 years. It was here that the coronation robes of the Queen's parents had been made in 1937. The fabric was cut to shape before it was passed to the Royal School of Needlework for the elaborate gold embroidery on both edges of the long train. This embroidery depicted olive leaves and ripening corn – to symbolise peace and prosperity for the new reign. Incorporated in the train was a gold embroidered crown and the Royal Cipher EIIR. An edging of white ermine and gold lace completed this most magnificent of all robes of state.

At other coronations the robe had been lined with ermine, but because there could have been a heatwave in June, the Queen had broken with tradition and chosen an oyster silk lining which was woven at the mill of Stephen Walters & Son at Sudbury in Suffolk.

While coronation fabrics were being woven, other experts were looking at the most ancient of all the surviving coronation relics – the Coronation Chair. This venerable seat

15   The Coronation Chair in which most English sovereigns have been crowned.

had shared the glories and vicissitudes of the Abbey itself for over six and a half centuries. Nearly all the sovereigns of England since Edward I had been crowned in that Chair.

The Chair had been made by royal command. In his invasions of Scotland about 1296 Edward I had captured the legendary Coronation Stone of the Scottish kings – the Lia Fáil, or 'Stone of Destiny'. He sent the stone to London with instructions to his Serjeant Painter, Walter of Durham, to make a chair which would hold the stone beneath its seat, so that the future kings of England should assert their claim to the Scottish throne by being crowned seated above the 'Stone of Destiny'.

Walter of Durham was a superb craftsman. His Chair was a masterpiece which had endured the wear and stress of centuries. He received 100 shillings for his work.

The Chair had survived the abuses of time. For the coronation of Richard III it was covered with baudikin; at Elizabeth I's coronation it was covered in 'cloth of silver incarnate' and at later coronations it seems to have been covered with cloth of gold. These coverings were nailed to the Chair and by custom as soon as the procession left the Abbey, the waiting spectators swarmed up the Nave to strip pieces of the covering off the Chair for souvenirs.

During Hanoverian times the Chair suffered the ignominy of neglect. Visitors carved their names on it, and Westminster schoolboys practised mock coronations in it. For the coronation of George IV the carved pinnacles on the arms were cut off and in 1887, for the Golden Jubilee of Queen Victoria, the Chair was covered in a coat of thick brown varnish – possibly to hide the graffiti!

Early in 1953 the Ministry suggested an examination of the Chair by the new scientific techniques. The Dean consented on the condition that the Chair should not be taken from the Abbey. In all the centuries the Chair had been removed from the Abbey on very rare occasions – once when Cromwell ordered the Chair to be placed in Westminster Hall for his own almost regal installation as Lord Protector, and after the bombing began in the Second World War when it was sent for safe keeping to Gloucester Cathedral. The 'Stone of Destiny' was buried within the Abbey precincts.

The expert examination was an astonishing demonstration of the ability of modern scientific techniques to recover the past. Stage by stage, with the careful use of X-rays, infra-red photography, the chemical analysis of microscopic fragments and other means, not only was the original form of the Chair revealed but also the successive changes in its shape and its decoration.

When the report was passed to me before publication, my first reaction was one of incredulity. How could that old, worn Chair, covered with the grimy patina of centuries, be made to reveal so much? There was a reconstruction of the Chair as it had been made by the skilful hands of Walter of Durham over six centuries ago – decorated in white and gold with its four carved corner posts with inscriptions painted in vermilion overlaid with letters of gold. The exterior of the Chair had also been enriched by twenty-one painted shields. It had indeed been a seat for the crowning of a king.

Many decades later another craftsman had completely altered the appearance of the Chair by decorating inside it with the painting of an enthroned king with his feet resting on a lion. He had added some beautiful designs of birds perched among oak leaves and vines, as well as grotesque animals like a strutting bird wearing a headcloth. This unknown craftsman had also sumptuously gilded the Chair and set it with mosaics of deeply coloured lustres.

Centuries later the Chair was altered again by raising its base on the supports of the golden lions and by other structural changes. By modern skills the old Plantagenet oak of the royal Chair had been made to tell its story.

The Coronation Chair was not covered for the Coronation of Queen Elizabeth II. It was simply decided to remove the clumsily attached velvet arm coverings and to place a cushion of crimson damask on the seat.

It was only after the Chair had been placed in the Coronation Theatre that the 'Stone of Destiny' was replaced in its base. It was a necessary precaution.

For many centuries the Stone had been the object of the dreams, demands, conspiracies and aspirations of many Scots. Many attempts had been made to get it back. An article in the Treaty of Northampton in 1328 which ended the long war between the two countries required the restoration of the Stone to Scotland. The king sent his royal writ to the Abbot of Westminster and the Sheriffs of London requiring them to return the Stone. They remained strangely deaf to the royal command. In spite of other treaties and entreaties it remained in the Abbey until Christmas Day 1950 when after six centuries it began a secret and tortuous journey back to Scotland. A few young Scots had spirited it away.

The incident had all the elements of daring, comedy, mischance and luck. There was a chance meeting with an unsuspecting Archdeacon in the Abbey, a young man without shoes found hiding in Poets' Corner, and a young girl sitting in a 'broken down' car outside the Abbey as the midnight notes of Big Ben were sounding the advent of Christmas Day.

The young people were soon known. Wheels moved within wheels. On 11 April 1951 three men deposited the Stone at Arbroath Abbey and it was returned to the Abbey of Westminster on 13 April 1951 with a very strong police escort. This episode in the history of the ancient Stone is one of those occasions when those who know the most can say the least about it!

When the Stone was put in its historic place beneath the ancient Chair it was the final act in the preparation of the Abbey for the Coronation.

The fabric fitters had worn canvas felt-soled shoes and white gloves as they had carefully fixed the blue silk tissues along the front of the tiers of seats down the long line of the Nave. Once again the quality of the light in the Abbey began to change as the bright yellow of the wood was covered by the blue draping. The light in the Nave held a clear coldness until it was filled with all the resplendent colour of Coronation Day. By comparison, the Theatre was a place of warm and shining gold.

The Abbey was ready for its carpets. They arrived on the last day of April, their journey supervised by the police from Glasgow to London.

The carpets were laid exactly over the guidelines marked on the floors. It was a job for strong and expert carpet layers. Foot by foot the heavy blue carpet moved forward along the Nave, and as it unrolled it was immediately protected with a covering.

16 Laying the carpets in the Abbey.

The laying of the great gold carpet in the Theatre was a much easier task. The carpeting of the Annexe was not done until the great engraved glass window had been fitted.

The Ministry had placed contracts for 2,000 chairs and 5,700 stools for the seating of the congregation in the Abbey. The chairs were for the peers and peeresses and other guests 'beyond the screen'. They were upholstered in blue velour with gold braiding and the chairs had the Royal Cipher on their backs. They were of English hardwood – oak and beech – from the woods of Berkshire and Buckinghamshire. The costs were recovered by the sale of the chairs and stools to those who would use them on Coronation Day. Finally the Throne Chair, the Chair of Estate, and the Faldstool were placed in their positions.

When this part of the Ministry's work was completed the Earl Marshal walked slowly through the Abbey to the Theatre. He looked carefully around and slowly nodded his approval. As the Ministry's work in the Abbey was finishing his was about to commence. The long and complicated series of the rehearsals for the Coronation could now begin.

15 The Robes of Byzantium

'Early on the morning of the coronation,' states the ancient rubric, 'care is to be taken that the Ampulla be filled with oil for the anointing, and, together with the Spoon, be laid ready on the Altar of the Abbey Church.'

When the Dean and Prebendaries with the choir of Westminster moved down the church carrying the Regalia to the West Door, they had left behind two small articles which were insignificant compared to the gleaming magnificence of the Abbey plate on the Altar behind them. Few people could see them. In a short time they would be lost among the glittering splendours of the Regalia which would be laid alongside them.

The Ampulla and the Spoon were the vessels of the royal consecration. They had made their appearance for the 'hallowing' of many English kings and queens, and they were the oldest objects in the Regalia. They had survived the looting of the Abbey treasures by Henry VIII, and the destructive hands of Cromwell's fanatics.

The Ampulla, or Golden Eagle, is 8 inches high with a wing spread of the same width. Its body has been hollowed out to hold the sacred oil, which is introduced by unscrewing the head and pouring in the oil. The oil is slowly dripped from its beak on to the Spoon at the anointing.

The gold work on its wings and base was applied by Sir Robert Vyner in 1661, but the screw by which the neck is attached to the body was already ancient in the days of Charles II. The Ampulla was possibly the 'egle' used at the coronation of Henry IV in 1399.

Some would give the Ampulla an even earlier date. Sir George Younghusband, for many years the Keeper of the Jewel House, considered that the Ampulla bore 'distinct traces of Byzantine origin and thus may be fourteen hundred years old'. It was not the only link between the Coronation and the 'sunbright glory of Byzantium'.

The Ampulla was once regarded as a celestial gift. The legend relates that when Thomas à Becket was living in exile at Sens, the Blessed Virgin appeared to him in a vision holding an eagle of gold and a phial of oil for the anointing of the kings of England. Henry II, said the Virgin, was totally unworthy.

Thomas à Becket hid the precious gifts in the Abbey of Poitiers. In due time a holy man gave the eagle and the oil to the Duke of Lancaster and from him it passed to the Black Prince. There is, in fact, the record of sacred oil being deposited in the Tower, possibly by the Black Prince, in 1345.

After Henry IV seized the crown he fortified his claim by being anointed at his coronation with the potent oil in the little eagle. The sacred unguent was used until the coronation

The Queen's Beasts.

V   The Lion of England wears a royal crown and bears on its shield the Royal Arms of the United Kingdom.

below

VI *left*   The Unicorn of Scotland wears about its neck a royal coronet and supports a shield with the Arms of former Scottish kings.

VII *centre*   The Falcon of the Plantagenets holds a shield with the livery colours of the House of York whereon is the falcon with a golden fetterlock partly open.

VIII *right*   The Yale of Beaufort descends to the Queen from Henry VII. Its shield is divided, white and blue, and on it is a crowned portcullis.

IX   The Abbey, all preparations done, is ready for the Coronation.

of James I when it was exhausted. It seems to have become somewhat pungent. Elizabeth I, in her customary forthright manner, complained that the 'grease smelt ill'. Charles I had a new unguent prepared which had forty ingredients; and there was no complaint about the unction compounded for James II. He was so pleased with its fragrance that he rewarded the apothecary with the enormous fee of £200.

The companion of the Ampulla, the Spoon, was also of ancient origin. Some experts give its date as the twelfth century. Sir George Younghusband considered that the long handle with the four pearls was also possibly of Byzantine origin. The link with Byzantium was again suggested.

The bowl of the Spoon is divided by a ridge. After the oil is poured from the Ampulla, the Archbishop dips his first two fingers into the separate hollows in the Spoon. It is the prelude to the anointing.

The anointing of kings in Western Europe was obviously a rite derived from the Old Testament. When Saul was made King over Israel, the aged Samuel 'took a vial of oil and poured it upon his head'. David, and later Solomon, were thus also anointed to be kings in Israel. The anointing of the king thus became for the Church the sacred purpose and the climax of the coronation service.

At the anointing in 1953 the familiar attributes of royalty began to recede: they were, so to speak, withdrawn from the Queen. The jewelled diadem was taken from her and with her Collar of the Garter was carried away by the Groom of the Robes into St Edward's Chapel. The Mistress of the Robes and the Lord Chamberlain of the Household divested the Queen of the Royal Robe of Crimson Velvet. The Queen, white garbed, bareheaded, moved forward to her anointing in King Edward's Chair. The Knights of the Garter held the concealing canopy of cloth of gold while the Archbishop anointed her.

The canopy was taken away and the slow and formal vesting was begun. The robes were of ancient usage. Robes decorated like those were worn at their inaugurations by Saxon kings. They were found enfolding the body of Edward the Confessor in his tomb in 1163. Down to the Restoration 'St Edward's vestments' were used, so it has been claimed, by each sovereign in succession. It is not surprising that Archbishop Laud had complained that one of them was nearly torn when assumed by Charles I. The robes being placed upon the Queen were not the familiar robes of royal estate. For centuries only a few hundred people close to the scene had ever seen these garments. They were worn only for a few hours in each sovereign's lifetime. In 1953, when for the first time in history millions saw the Queen wearing these regal robes on colour film and TV, there was a universal feeling of perplexity and surprise. She had become remote from the traditional figures of royalty. The splendid garments which they were putting upon the Queen belonged to a very different tradition of regal splendour. They were the robes of the Emperors of Byzantium.

The first of these royal vestures was the Colobium Sindonis – a 'muslin undergarment'. It was made of white linen cambric, sleeveless and opened at the side so that it passed easily over the Queen's beautiful Hartnell gown. The ancient world once knew this garment – it was the *tunica* – or *talaris* – worn by all classes of society, by both men and women. The Emperors of Byzantium wore it at their coronation.

The Queen stood again to be invested with the Supertunica. It was a garment of great splendour – a long coat of cloth of gold with wide sleeves, and it was lined with rose-coloured silk. This gorgeous tunic was derived from the ceremonial dress of the Roman Consuls – the *tunica palmata* – which later became the imperial *sakkos* of the Byzantine Emperors. It was gathered at the waist by a girdle of cloth of gold, designed like a traditional sword belt with a sword frog, although the Queen as a Queen Regnant would not be girded with a sword. The girdle had been presented by the Girdlers' Company, a City Livery Company since 1327. Their tiny sign of the girdle iron was on the inside of the belt.

After the Queen had received the Spurs and made the offering of the Sword, she rose again from King Edward's Chair to be invested with the Stole Royal. This was a long richly embroidered and jewelled scarf, which included in its beautiful design the emblems of the four Evangelists and of St Peter on a background of the floral emblems of Britain and the Commonwealth. This was passed around the Queen's neck. The Stole was also worn as part of the imperial costume by the Byzantine emperors as the *loros*.

Finally, the Dean received from the Groom of the Robes, the Pallium, or Robe Royal of Cloth of Gold. It was a garment of great beauty. Its cloth of gold was worked with designs of silver coronets, fleurs-de-lis, thistles, shamrocks and the other emblems of the Commonwealth. Very prominent in the design were the shapes of the imperial eagles. It swathed the Queen in splendour as the Lord Great Chamberlain fastened the clasp of the robe.

The *Liber Regalis* described this garment as 'square and worked all over with golden eagles. Its four corners signify that the four corners of the world are subject to the power of God, and that no man can reign on earth who has not received his authority from Him.'

Similar robes had appeared on 'the day of joy and glory' when the Eastern Emperors came in their magnificence to the Church of St Sophia to be invested with the Imperial Mantle. This was the Chlamys, blessed by the Patriarch, and put on the Emperor by the Imperial chamberlain. The grey stone Abbey where Abbot Lytlington wrote down the *Liber Regalis* in the fourteenth century was a long way from the gorgeous mosaics of St Sophia in Byzantium.

The eagles woven in the fabric have appeared on this imperial mantle since Saxon times. They signified that Britain was an independent empire. In 925 Athelstan, the grandson of Alfred the Great, had been styled 'Emperor of the Kings and Peoples' of Britain. Edgar, in 973, took the Roman title of 'Imperator Augustus of all Albion' as well as the Greek imperial title of 'Basileus'.

How it came about that Queen Elizabeth II, like the numerous line of her royal predecessors, was garbed in the dazzling splendours of Byzantium, we do not know. A modern historian of the coronation rites, Edward Ratcliff, Ely Professor of Divinity at Cambridge, has written:

By the tenth century we find in England a Coronation Order that exhibits parallels with the Byzantine tradition of such a kind that it is difficult not to think them the result of imitation. Respect for the institutions of the Empire was universal, and their influence far reaching: and the Byzantine imperial title, as we have seen, was known and used in England.

The similarity between the coronation robes of the king and the vestments of a bishop gave rise to the theory that the anointing conferred a quasi-ecclesiastical status on the king. It was sometimes used as an argument to give the king a claim to spiritual authority over the Church. The Church like the state had come to use the ceremonial dress of the imperial courts. The parallel does not stretch to any close identity between the Robe Royal and the bishop's cope. The cope has the more humble origin – it was the raincoat of antiquity! The Robe was the imperial cloak of the Emperor.

16   The Royal Route

The first roll of drums startled the ducks by the lake in St James's Park. Their angry protests showed that they were not used to such a loud and ceremonial sound at a frosty hour before daybreak in November.

At 7.30 a.m. the Guards' drummers moved smartly off, keeping the unceasing roll of their drums along the route. Behind them marched detachments of Scots and Grenadier Guards, and a State Landau drawn by eight Windsor greys with a troop of the Household Cavalry closing up behind it. The Earl Marshal, stop-watch in hand, was holding a rehearsal of the Royal Route. With him were the Crown Equerry, officers of the War Office and the Ministry and the surveyors of Westminster City Council. We marched every yard of the 5 miles 250 yards of the processional route.

It was as well we did. The route had to be surveyed for the widths required for mounted and marching troops and also for the passage of the Coronation Coach, on this occasion represented by the State Landau. A surprising number of traffic islands had moved into the centre of the roads since 1937 which would have divided the procession and brought the huge coach to a halt. These islands were noted and they were all temporarily removed on the evening of 1 June.

The Queen would ride along the route in the Royal State Coach – the golden centre-piece of the coronation processions. No other equipage in the world can compare with it in splendour. It does, however, need very expert coachmanship. Its great weight has always restricted the progress of the coronation procession to three miles an hour, since even the eight Windsor greys can only safely draw its $4\frac{1}{2}$ tons at a walking pace. The rear pair of horses are trained to hold back its weight while the other six do the pulling.

In addition to the four riding postilions, there are eight walking grooms beside the horses. They carry a stick with a curved handle to hold up the traces as the Coach turns.

The State Coach had been designed by one of our predecessors at the Ministry, Sir William Chalmers, for George III. The accounts have been preserved – £2,500 to Joseph Walton for the ornamental carvings; £1,673 to Butler the coachbuilder; Pujolas the gilder got £933 and Cipriani, the painter of the beautiful side panels, among them that of Britannia holding the staff of liberty, attended by religion, justice, wisdom, valour and victory, received a mere £315 for his work. A more prosaic item was '£6 10s to Mr Haynes for the charcoal under the floor in his patent foot-warmers'.

What did George III receive for the money? He got a beautiful extravaganza, gilded in 18 carat gold, 24 feet long, 13 feet high which weighed over 4 tons. Four huge golden tritons supported the body of the Coach. The two in front proclaimed the approach of the Monarch of the Oceans while the two behind carried the imperial fasces, with tridents instead of axes. The framework was fashioned into eight golden palm trees, branching out to support the roof where three golden boys held aloft the Imperial Crown.

In October 1795 the London mob looked with disfavour on the coach's owner. They besieged it in Pall Mall and smashed the glass panels in George III's face.

The Coach has survived critics and assault to carry every sovereign from William IV to their coronation. The famous cream horses were used until the coronation of George V, when the last team were sold during the First World War. They were replaced by the Windsor greys for the coronations of King George VI and Queen Elizabeth II.

As for every coronation in this century, the State Coach was driven out of the Royal Mews to the Chelsea works of Messrs Hooper & Co. for a complete overhaul. It came back under tied covers, a strange sight to encounter in the grey light of dawn, lumbering along behind the eight greys who were also being rehearsed for their unfamiliar task.

The Superintendent of the Royal Mews, Major George Hopkins, had to cope with many problems. The Mews were short of both horses and carriages. The carriage horses needed would have to be already harness trained and geldings, because mares are liable to kick over the traces.

Carriages in the Mews had also been disposed of during the war. Some of the visiting royal guests for the Coronation might have to endure the indignity of riding to the Abbey in a mere Rolls-Royce!

Word of the predicament got around. A number of private owners came forward with offers of carriages. There was still a deficiency when help came from an unexpected quarter. Sir Alexander Korda, the film magnate, had carriages used on film sets. He was able to provide five two-pair broughams and two landaus. Without this generous help we would not have seen one of the memorable sights of Coronation Day – the huge smiling Queen Salote riding in her open carriage, undaunted by the rain.

The final problem was the shortage of trained coachmen. They were enlisted from members of the Coaching Club, who had to sacrifice some of the finest moustaches in the country before they could don the royal livery – the royal coachmen are traditionally clean-shaven.

The Ministry also had the Speaker's Coach overhauled and partly regilded, including new braces for its support. We know very little of its history since the Speaker's records were lost in the fire in 1834 which destroyed the old Houses of Parliament. Our experts thought it might have been one of William III's coaches which George III had transferred to the Speaker when he acquired the new State Coach in 1762.

The Speaker's Coach weighs over 4 tons, could only proceed at a walking pace and could not be taken up or down the slightest gradient. Fortunately the Coach had only to travel the flat 200 yards from New Palace Yard to the Abbey. Since the time of Speaker Shaw-Lefevre, who was in the chair from 1839 to 1857 and a director of the company, Whitbread's Brewery have supplied the two heavy and magnificent horses for the Speaker's Coach, as they did again in 1953.

Officially, we had to await the Coronation Commission's formal decision on the route. Unofficially the Ministry got on with the job of planning the public stands and viewing positions in the large area of central London along which the processions would certainly pass – the Mall, Trafalgar Square, Parliament Square, Whitehall and other important spectator positions like the East Carriage Drive in Hyde Park and the Green Park side of Piccadilly. We also acted on the assumption that, as in 1937, the seats in Ministry stands would be allocated to national organisations in Britain, with a substantial allocation for Commonwealth visitors.

The applications for seats in those stands began to pour in from the very day that the Queen was proclaimed. The first flood came from organisations and people who had seats in 1937, and from their adult children who remembered their parents' description of the spectacle. Later the requests poured in from people in every part of the Commonwealth and from the USA. Many of the applicants were native-born people who had served in many capacities. There was, for example, a beautifully illuminated scroll from an Indian which listed in support of his request the names of the regiments and of their commanding officers whose washing he had laundered for nearly a quarter of a century.

The ticket agencies and property owners were not waiting for the Coronation Commission. They knew which way the processions would have to go. There was brisk bidding for sites. Prices began to soar. We saw reports of £85 to £100 for a single place.

By the late summer the position about the Government seats had become confusing for the public. The situation could no longer wait for the formal decision. The Minister got the agreement of certain members of the Coronation Joint Committee to make an interim statement.

On 1 August 1952 several hundred journalists from many countries gathered at Church House, Westminster to hear David Eccles unfold the Ministry's plans. He began by stating the position on the public seats. He told them that 'while the Coronation Joint Committee was still considering how the seats would be allocated, I can tell you the principle on which they are working. The Committee will not allocate seats to individuals, but only to national organisations – local authorities, institutions representing science, learning, the arts and letters, women's organisations, trade unions, industrial and commercial organisations and so on. These organisations will select those of their members who are to occupy those seats. Only in this way can we be sure that the widest possible spectrum of our national life will be represented on this occasion.'

He went on to say that the Government stands would provide about 100,000 seats and one third of these would be reserved for Commonwealth visitors. The High Commissioners in London would make the allocations to people representing or coming from their countries. The Colonial office would make the allocation for all other territories of the Crown.

After the costings had been done we were able to announce that the price of the seats in the Government stands would be £4 in the open stands and £6 in the covered stands.

There was also another large group for which the Ministry had to provide. The peerage had greatly increased since Henry III built his 'viewing theatre' for a few hundred peers, abbots and bishops. In December the Earl Marshal held a ballot for those peers and peeresses not in certain degrees such as Privy Councillors, Knights of the Garter, the Thistle and St Patrick, Members of the Order of Merit and the Knights and Dames Grand

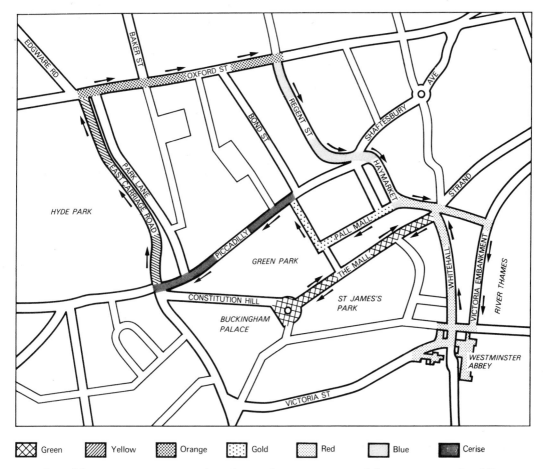

Green	Yellow	Orange	Gold	Red	Blue	Cerise

17 Plan of the Coronation Route. The colour references were used for transport and public access to stands.

Cross of the Orders of Knighthood. A ballot was also held for the House of Commons. Those of both Houses who were not successful in the ballot for the Abbey were allocated four seats in the covered stands in Parliament Square.

After the Minister's statement it was possible to get on with designing the stands with their 27 miles of seating. In 1937 the height of the stands in the Mall had been restricted by the need to avoid lopping the trees. A stand was, therefore, rapidly put up in the Mall to test possible viewing angles. The natural growth of the trees had solved the viewing problems.

A few weeks later there was a thunderous clatter from the Mall. It was a company of Grenadier Guards in their heavy boots jumping up and down on the stand to test its stability. It survived the test.

The work of stand building began in January 1953. The long period of building work attracted understandable criticism – notably from 'Peterborough' in the *Daily Telegraph*. The Royal Parks were not in their usual green and flowering state while the work went on. It had not been possible to gamble on the weather, especially after a year which had produced the Lynmouth and Lynton disasters and the serious flooding of the east coast. A shorter period of stand construction would also have required a much larger work force, some of which might have been diverted from housing. As it was, the Ministry was able to use the existing specialised labour of contractors like Mowlems.

Building the stands was an easy task compared to the complicated problems of filling them. It was easy to identify local authorities, trade unions, employers' organisations and other established strata of British life. They were allocated seats in proportion to their membership. Beyond them were cohorts, all claiming national status and seats for their members. The tendency to collective cohesion is one of the notable aspects of the British people. Let two or three men discover a common interest in old waggon wheels and the National Society of Waggoners is well on the way to being born.

By the end of January the allocations were completed and the notifications went out. We got few complaints; most organisations allocated their seats by ballot. We took precautions, but got no evidence of any black market in tickets. Those who got them guarded them like gold.

In the meantime, our architects had been getting on with the 'gay and colourful job' of designing the decorations. The local authorities were also working on the public transformation of their thoroughfares. Westminster had appointed Sir Hugh Casson to design its decorations, the City of London appointed Sir Giles Scott. There was close co-operation with our architects. Beyond London there could not have been a city, town or village without its own Coronation Committee, busy planning decorations and festivities.

It is seldom given to Ministers of the Crown, who usually have to crumble the dry bread of facts, to provide a vivid feast for the imagination. Eccles did that at his press conference. He presented the picture of a London which would be transformed. A rich profusion of gay colours would spread along the streets, delicate arches would hold aloft golden crowns, the plumes of chivalry would fly from tall standards, and the bright symbols and emblems of many lands would be blazoned above the heads of the vast rejoicing crowds.

The Minister took his listeners along the route as the Queen would see it on the day of her Coronation. As the Golden Coach left Buckingham Palace by the South Gate the first of her subjects to greet the Queen would be the holders of the Victoria Cross and the disabled ex-service men. The stands around the Queen Victoria monument would have long beds of thousands of Gustav Emich geraniums spread in front of them.

The coach would enter the 1,000 yards of London's royal highway – the Mall – with the triple avenues of plane trees in the full leaf of June. Rising high above the trees down

18   The Arches are erected in the Mall. The Lion and the Unicorn begin their 'fantasy dance' above the golden Princess Coronets.

the Mall would be four graceful arches, their delicate golden structures supporting two lions and two unicorns, 'poised in the manner of old-time dancers'. These tall rampant creatures would be profiled in steel filled with fine wire mesh, gold for the lions and white for the unicorns. A huge princess's coronet was to be suspended from each arch with wires threaded with aluminium spheres which 'if you are feeling fairly romantic you can compare with drops of dew on threads of gossamer'.

Eccles followed the processional route – the Admiralty Arch with its serried ranks of White Ensigns flying, and the giant coils of rope of the foul anchors. Parliament Square was to be an immense enclave of the peoples of the Commonwealth, so that the Queen on her way to her Coronation would figuratively 'drive through the lands of her subjects'. These stands would be emblazoned with their heraldic arms and emblems.

The stand outside St Margaret's would have the colourful badges of the county towns of the United Kingdom.

So to the royal entrance to the Annexe, with the huge plaque of the Royal Arms above the delicate transparent canopy with the Queen's Beasts, badges of her royal ancestors, waiting in strange and rigid attention to greet their Sovereign.

On the return journey the procession would pass down Whitehall with its flying plumes on tall standards, the red dragon of Wales on the Welsh section of the Home Office, the golden guineas scattered lavishly across the front of the Treasury, the scarlet and gold of the Horse Guards, the greenery of Agriculture and the red and blue rondels of the Air Ministry.

Everywhere there would be flowers, before the stands, in window boxes, around the Cenotaph; wherever a place could be found for them. There would be masses of red rhododendrons, verbena, salvia and azaleas. There would be the bright yellow of chrysanthemums, the blue of larkspur and delphiniums. The greenhouses of the Royal Parks were bulging with tens of thousands of flowers, all being carefully nurtured to bloom to perfection on Coronation Day.

Beyond the centre of London the decorations would spread for mile on mile, each street decorated to the extent of its own purse and its own taste, from the golden trumpets of Bond Street to the gay bunting spread across the small streets in Whitechapel, Hoxton and Tottenham where the children would gather for their Coronation parties. London would become a floral dance of colours on Coronation Day.

It was the only occasion I have ever heard journalists applaud a Minister at a press conference. The evening and morning papers reflected the journalists' enthusiasm. 'London the Enchanted City', 'Road to Royal Splendour', 'Blend of Majesty and Gaiety'.

It seemed that the bells for the Coronation were already starting to ring.

17 'No Foot Shall Slide'

'That', said Randolph Churchill, 'is the most distinguished and also the most shambling *corps de ballet* on the face of the earth.'

The Prime Minister's son was one of the Gold Staff Officers who had been watching the Great Officers of State rehearsing their movements when the Queen, after her crowning, would rise from King Edward's Chair and move across the Theatre to the Throne Chair for the Homage. It was not a moment for distraction. She had to move with great dignity wearing the heavy St Edward's Crown and holding upright the Sceptre in her right hand and the Rod in her left.

The noble lords had not performed very well. It was not easy for elderly gentlemen to follow a complicated pattern of movement, wearing an unfamiliar coronet, with a long robe sweeping their heels and holding a sword upright beneath their chins. Garter and the Heralds had tried gently to guide them. The Earl Marshal, standing by the north pillar, had pursed his lips into the shape of a small wrinkled prune.

Randolph's comment had echoed down the choir. A pursuivant left the side of the Earl Marshal.

'I have a message from the Earl Marshal,' he told Randolph. 'He has asked me to remind you that there is plenty of room in the Tower!'

Randolph glared at him, for once speechless – the pursuivant departed, treading with delicate precision back to his position.

Randolph found his tongue. 'There speaks Norfolk's ancestors. Where does he keep his bloody axe!'

The ancestral axe, if one existed, was hanging on a wall in Arundel Castle. The Earl Marshal was in sufficient command without it. He left his position by the pillar to take personal charge of the rehearsal.

He had cause for concern. In 1937 this stage of the ceremony had nearly led to a disastrous incident. King George VI had told the young Earl Marshal about it in plain words. As the King began to move towards the Throne balancing Crown, Sceptre and Rod, one of the attendant bishops had put a heavy and unwary foot on his robe. The King that evening wrote in his diary: 'I was brought up all standing. I had to tell him to get off it pretty sharply as I nearly fell down.'

The King also recorded other incidents. 'The Dean of Westminster insisted that I should put on the Colobium Sindonis inside out, had not my Groom of the Robes come to the rescue.'

'The Lord Great Chamberlain was supposed to dress me [in the robes] but his hands fumbled and shook so I had to fix the belt myself. As it was he nearly put the hilt of the sword under my chin!'

There had been other mishaps. The Marquess of Salisbury with St Edward's Crown had got the lace of the cushion entangled in the St George's pendant of his Garter Collar and had a struggle to tear it free. The Duke of Portland had the same mishap with the Queen Consort's Crown and was caught fast until Garter hurried to the rescue.

The incidents had been recorded in the capacious memory of the Earl Marshal. As the rehearsal began again I could hear Big Ben across the square sounding its strangely appropriate Handelian quatrain

> Lord through this hour
> Be thou our guide
> That by Thy pow'r
> No foot shall slide.

Everyone arrived for the rehearsals with the individual plans prepared for them by the Garter King of Arms. This preparatory work had been done for many coronations. The Egerton MSS in the British Museum, for example, has beautiful little sketches in pen and ink of the positions to be taken up in the Abbey at the coronation of the first Elizabeth.

There is, however, a great gap between plans on paper and people in action. The ceremony was rehearsed in its separate parts, not necessarily in the order in which they would come. There were moments when I felt that chaos would reign when the attempt was made to bring all the parts together.

What was happening within the Abbey had also to be co-ordinated with what was coming from without. Before the arrival of the Queen seven processions had to reach the Abbey and pass up the Nave to their positions. There would be only a ten-minute interval between the arrival of the 'Procession of the Members of the Royal Family', for example, at 8.50 a.m., and the long procession of the 'Royal and other Representatives of Foreign States' arriving in 80 cars from Buckingham Palace.

On their entry into the Vestibule these processions would have to be marshalled and escorted by the Heralds and Pursuivants, through the five long lines of those already waiting in their places to join the Queen's Procession. There could have been a tangle of confusion at this place if, for any reason, one of the processions had been delayed.

One procession had to be timed to move in the opposite direction. At 9.57 the Dean and Prebendaries of Westminster Abbey would move down the church to the West Door bearing the Regalia from the High Altar to the Regalia Table in the Vestibule. There was a possibility that they might, by a slight mistiming, meet the procession of the Princes and Princesses of the Blood Royal coming the other way.

The Dean and Prebendaries of Westminster were obviously well versed in their parts when the rehearsals began in May. The difficulties began when the bishops assistant joined them. Each bishop had his own idea of a liturgical pace. After several rehearsals the Earl Marshal's voice came loud and clear.

'If those bishops do not learn to walk in step we'll be here all night.' They got the message.

Another bishop felt his firm hand. He went off for a short holiday before a rehearsal. The Earl Marshal sent a police car to bring him back.

He came into the Abbey pink with indignation, followed by his chaplain carrying his hand luggage.

'Most humiliating,' he was protesting. 'Escorted from my hotel by the police. What on earth will people think? I consider it disgraceful.' His words faltered as he saw the gaitered figure of the Archbishop looking intently at him.

There were problems with a few of the peers, whose attendance at rehearsal was also obligatory.

'If you are not at rehearsals you will not be here on the day,' the Earl Marshal told a peer who was protesting that he knew it all.

There was not the slightest doubt that he meant what he said. No one would risk losing his place on that historic day.

The pages who carried the coronets of the peers in the Theatre had to wait in the Transepts until just before the crowning. They arrived for rehearsal full of eager excitement at this great opportunity. When the signal was given for the entry they rushed into the Theatre like a swarm of bees. It proved difficult to teach young boys to walk sedately.

By the middle of May the first confused and self-conscious actions of different persons had become the co-ordinated movements of a ceremony. The Queen was present at some of the later rehearsals. The Earl Marshal, the Archbishop and Garter had gone over every detail of the ceremony and service with her, but very understandably the Queen wished to make sure that her own part would be perfectly performed. She watched some of the main rehearsals and herself practised the difficult descent from the Throne Chair.

On 27 May the Queen Mother and Princess Margaret came to rehearse their parts in the procession which immediately preceded the arrival of the Queen. The four young men bearing the Queen Mother's train nearly lifted it from her shoulders at the start. She stopped, said some words of encouragement before they moved up the nave. At the bottom of the winding stair to the Royal Gallery, she expertly gathered the train over her arm and went on to her place.

Garter looked at the watch in his hand. 'Right first time,' he said. Princess Margaret, preceding her mother, found the rehearsal somewhat more difficult. She had had much less practice, like her train bearer, Miss Iris Peake, in handling the heavy robe falling from her shoulders.

On Sunday 24 May the choir and the orchestra with the trumpeters and organists took over the Abbey for the whole day.

Finally, on Friday 29 May, all the component parts of the ceremony were brought together for the Final Rehearsal. State dress, Court Dress or full dress uniforms were worn. The escorts were mounted in procession order; the Great Officers of State carried replicas of the Regalia.

All the seats in the Abbey were filled by invitation – peers and MPs who had been unsuccessful in the ballot, distinguished Commonwealth visitors, staff of the Royal Household, craftsmen and other workers who had helped to prepare the Abbey were there. The TV commentators and cameramen and the radio broadcasters were present to rehearse their own parts and the press photographers, film cameramen and journalists were given an 'off the record' opportunity to prepare for the day. The occasion also provided the Ministry with a final opportunity for testing all the complicated channels of lighting, sound, air conditioning and all the other services in the Abbey as well as communications with the waiting world outside.

The Duchess of Norfolk took the place of the Queen with great dignity and grace and with a well-rehearsed knowledge of all that was required of her – for which her husband no doubt deserved some credit! She had one awkward moment when the six Maids of Honour seemed to get into difficulties in their handling of the long train as she passed up the steps to the Theatre.

The rest of the rehearsal seemed to go with the smooth precision the Earl Marshal required. There were, however, many problems behind the scenes.

The police cadets who were my messengers got themselves lost in the network of passages. My control telephones went dead for nearly an hour. They began to operate again to warn me that one of the great lights over the Theatre was overheating and would have to be turned off. The light fell by a few degrees and the BBC and other cameramen turned urgently to me for information – one stop more and there would not be any colour films.

For a few minutes the public address system faltered. The ancient dust of the Abbey stirred by the warmth and breath of the great congregation was rising to lay its ghostly and insidious fingers on the modern electronic systems.

There were mishaps elsewhere. To test the Medical Centres they were sent a few simulated patients. Unhappily a few genuine unfortunates got mixed up with the 'deceivers' and were not immediately recognised.

While the rehearsal was going on one of the Queen's personal staff was investigating the amenities of the Queen's Robing Room. She found it very adequately furnished but lacking the one essential item which any woman would require on one of the great days in her life – a mirror!

Finally there was one moment in the rehearsal which opened up the risk that millions of people might be deprived of the sight they were all waiting to see – the placing of the Crown on the Queen's head. We were all watching intently as the Archbishop raised the Crown, then as his arms came down his cope fell forward cutting off the placing of the Crown. Within seconds my phones were ringing with expressions of dismay and despair.

I asked the *Times* photographer to send me a photograph he had taken at the crucial moment. Later that evening I was able to show the Archbishop how the fall of his magnificent cope had concealed the Crown and even part of the Coronation Chair itself.

He looked carefully at the photograph and said, 'I think this can be avoided. If I lift my arms higher when I raise the Crown the cope will fall much wider open. I will see it stays that way.'

I remarked, 'You will have much to remember.'

He smiled in reassurance. 'Do not be concerned. I will remember.'

The superb TV pictures, films and photographs of that moment are their own tribute to the Archbishop's attention to every detail on that day.

The BBC recordings of the rehearsal were later seen by the Earl Marshal and the Archbishop at Broadcasting House and given approval as the pattern to be followed on 2 June.

The Earl Marshal and Garter King of Arms considered that the rehearsal had gone well.

'The best Final Rehearsal I have seen,' was the opinion of the Lancaster Herald, A. G. B. Russell. 'But there is always the unwary step, the fumbling fingers, the forgotten detail. It has always been so. What is that verse of Big Ben you quoted to the Earl Marshal – "That by Thy pow'r no foot shall slide". That's what we must pray for.'

When the last rehearsal was over there remained for the Ministry the job of tidying up and getting the dust and other 'gremlins' out of the system.

The Abbey was then left for a few days in the tight guard of our security officers, with the waiting silence occasionally broken by the practising feet and fingers of the Coronation organists.

18 'The Exquisite Sound'

The Final Rehearsal had been the first opportunity to hear the full range of the music for the Coronation. The great choir of over 400 voices included the choirs of Westminster Abbey, the Chapel Royal, St Paul's Cathedral, St George's Chapel, Windsor, as well as members of other choirs throughout the country.

There had been, of course, intensive rehearsals by all the choirs before they came together in the Abbey with the orchestra, brass and organ in a great collective rehearsal on Sunday 24 May.

The Abbey had, however, often resounded with music before that date. As soon as the fall of the hammers had ceased in the Abbey, the great organ installed for the coronation of King George VI occasionally started into life as its pipes and keyboard were tried by one of the three organists who were to share the organ playing on 2 June – Dr O. H. Peasgood, Dr H. G. Ley and W. H. Gabb.

The sound of music has always been heard at the coronation. Thomas de Eltham, the biographer of Henry V, refers to the 'resounding notes of the trumpets' at the king's coronation and he also writes of the 'exquisite sound of instruments'.

Until the coronation of Charles II there is very little information about the musical scores and the composers of coronation music. We know more about the instruments and the performers. At Henry VIII's coronation the instruments were the 'shalmes, still shalmes and fifteen trumpets'. His son, Edward VI, had a grander assembly of instruments including flutes, viols, harps and a bagpipe. Among the choir of 'twenty gentlemen of the Chapel and fourteen other singers' on that occasion was Tallis, whose five-part setting of the Litany was still sung at the beginning of the Service in 1953.

The 'shalmes' and 'still shalmes' at the coronation of Henry VIII had passed from the ceremony, as have the 'regals, courtals and luteş' which were heard at the coronation of William and Mary in 1689. Through all the centuries only the lordly trumpet has held its own undisputed and compelling sway. In 1953 the trumpeters of the Royal Military School of Music from Kneller Hall from their high places on the choir screen filled the Abbey with the same fierce and resplendent sound which had pealed against its walls through the centuries.

The music for the coronation, unlike the other parts of the ceremony, can be chosen afresh on each occasion, but there are pieces which have their immemorial places; they may, however, be given a new setting. 'Zadok the Priest' was heard at the anointing of King Edgar in 973, as was also the anthem 'Be Strong and of Good Courage' which Queen Elizabeth II was to hear, like her predecessors, after she had been crowned.

In more recent times two composers have kept their places in the service. Handel's setting of 'Zadok the Priest', specially composed for the coronation of George II, has been used ever since, and Parry's 'I was glad', which greeted the Queen as she entered the Abbey, had been used at four successive coronations, with its very effective incorporation of the 'vivats' of the Westminster schoolboys.

In 1953 some of the traditional anthems were set to new music including the 'Introit' by Herbert Howells, the 'Gradual' by William Harris and the anthem 'Be Strong' at the crowning by Sir George Dyson.

In addition a new march by Sir William Walton and a processional by Sir Arthur Bliss were played before the Service began. Gordon Jacob had prepared a new setting of the National Anthem and Sir Arnold Bax had composed a Coronation March to be played at the end of the service.

The five anthems chosen to be sung during the Homage represented English church music from the time of Queen Elizabeth I to Queen Elizabeth II. 'Rejoice in the Lord Always', for example, was attributed to John Redford who was organist of St Paul's at the time of Henry VIII. The new anthem in 1953, 'O Lord our Governour', had been composed for the occasion by the contemporary Canadian musician, Healy Willan.

The 'Te Deum' composed by Sir William Walton gathered into a splendid climax of harmony from the choirs, orchestra, organ and trumpets as the crowned and consecrated young Queen withdrew from the Altar.

A complete musical innovation in the Coronation Service was Vaughan Williams's arrangement of the 'Old Hundredth', 'All People that on Earth do Dwell', to be sung by the whole congregation in the Abbey with the choir. This was the first occasion on which the congregation were able to join their voices to the choir during the course of the ceremony.

The new setting of the National Anthem caused a slight hesitation at the end as the Queen left the Theatre. There was a moment of brief uncertainty when people accustomed to the slow style of the familiar anthem paused before joining in the lighter and more majestic rendering in four-square harmony by Dr Gordon Jacob. The fifth verse, sung 'with all available trumpets', did, however, fill the Abbey with a surging wave of triumphant sound.

The orchestra of 60 included musicians from the 18 principal orchestras in the country under the leadership of Paul Beard. When the choir, the orchestra, organists and trumpeters were assembled they comprised nearly 500 people. The synchronisation of this musical multitude, many of whom could not see the conductor, had always been a major problem at each coronation.

At the coronation of James II in 1685 the choirs were accommodated in three widely separated parts of the Abbey. Matters were slightly better arranged for the coronation of Queen Victoria where the large choir was placed in the tiers above the choirstalls. On that occasion the bishops had returned to the practice of singing the Litany and a Mr Givelt stood beside them with a flag to signal the responses from the choir!

The conductors still had problems in 1953, since some of the choristers were again behind the organ above the nave. Sir Adrian Boult conducted the music but when

Dr William McKie in his turn took up his baton for the choral works his beat had to be passed on by two sub-conductors.

The results seemed to be beyond criticism. In June 1953 as in April 1413, the Abbey was filled with 'exquisite sound'.

19   The Coronation Service

Queen Elizabeth II was anointed and crowned with the solemn rites and ceremonies which represented more than one thousand years of the history, traditions and customs of her people in the British Isles.

Almost as soon as they arrived in Britain the missionaries of the Christian faith reached out their hands in the benediction of a newly appointed king. As long ago as 574 St Columba sailed across the sea to Iona and there ordained Aidan as King – 'laying his hand on his head he consecrated and blessed him'. Aidan was King of Dalriada, the modern county of Argyll.

The *Anglo-Saxon Chronicle*, that fount of English history, tells us that in 787 Ecgfrith of Mercia was hallowed as King and that Eardwulf was consecrated King of Northumbria in 795.

By the ninth century the form of the coronation had been set down in the book of the religious services performed by a bishop, called a Pontifical. The main features were the anointing, the investing with the royal Regalia, the king's promise of his duty to the Church and his people. This was the basic form of the service which was to endure over the centuries, including as well the Gospel reading and the anthem 'Zadok the Priest'.

The next order of the coronation service is attributed to Dunstan, the most formidable Archbishop of Canterbury of the Anglo-Saxon church. It was this scholar and statesman with a wide knowledge of the traditions of his own country and of Western Europe who, it is claimed, set down the order for the coronation of King Edgar at Bath in 973. In this coronation service we can see not only the unfolding of a splendid ceremonial for the hallowing of a king, but also a religious service in which the traditions, laws and customs of the people are embraced within the solemnity.

The King was brought to the church with great ceremony, escorted by nobles and clergy to the singing of anthems. Two bishops on each side led him by the hand. He put aside his 'diadem' and lay before the Altar while the 'Te Deum' was sung. He was then presented by the Archbishop for 'election' by bishops, the nobles and the people. Then, standing before the Altar he made his Promise – as all his successors were to do – saying:

Three things I promise in Christ's name to the Christian People Subject to me: First, the Church of God and the whole Christian People shall have true peace at all time by our judgment, Second, that I will forbid extortion and all kinds of wrong doing to all orders of men; Third, that I will enjoin equity and mercy in all judgments, that God who is kind and merciful, may vouchsafe His mercy to me and to you.

The King was anointed on his head with holy oil to the singing of 'Zadok the Priest'. He was invested with the Ring, the Sword, the Crown, the Sceptre and the Rod. Each item of the Regalia was given with a prayer which expressed the religious or royal symbolism of the object. There followed the solemn benediction of the King and the anthem 'Stand fast'.

The fabric of the coronation service which was to endure for a thousand years was thus established in the Church of St Peter at Bath on the feast of Pentecost in 973. It would be added to, it would be damaged and it would be restored and it would be enlarged and adapted in conformity with the needs of different times; but the central acts and some of the prayers and the anthems would hold their places in the service as the kings, queens and the centuries passed away.

The twelfth century saw a further development of the service for the coronation of Richard I. The anointing of the king became more elaborate and now included his head, his hands, breasts, shoulders and elbows. The Bracelets were added to the Regalia and the royal vestments were introduced.

I have already had much to say of the next great revision of the coronation service – the *Liber Regalis*, or Royal Book – which was probably prepared by Nicholas Lytlington, the Abbot of Westminster from 1362 to 1388. Like that of St Dunstan, the order was a work of immense scholarship. Like Dunstan, too, the Abbot had set out to preserve and build upon what had gone before. He set down also the arrangements for the procession from the Tower of London through the City to the Royal Palace of Westminster on the day before the ceremony and for the banquet which followed. He even, as I have described, prescribed the way the Coronation Theatre should be arranged in the form which we followed in 1953.

It was all patiently and beautifully inscribed on thirty-eight pages of vellum, illustrated by four superb illuminations and has been carefully preserved in the library of Westminster Abbey. It is said that the marks on its cover are those of the kings who held it during their coronations.

Queen Elizabeth I was the last English sovereign to hear the Service in its original Latin. For James I an English version was made. 'It was done in haste,' wrote the contemporary historian Heylin, 'and wanted many things which might have been considered in a time of leisure.' The defects were remedied by Laud for the coronation of Charles I. 'I had a perfect book of the ceremonies of the Coronation made ready, agreeing in all things with *Liber Regalis*,' he wrote in his diary.

The Reformation had made little difference to the service. The Communion Service was substituted for the Mass and the Dean and Prebendaries, stood in place of the Abbot and the monks.

Another reign brought alteration and shortening of the Service. As a Roman Catholic James II felt unable to take part in an Anglican Communion Service. Archbishop Sancroft was instructed to leave out the Communion Service and to abridge the rite as much as possible. He was, however, directed not to destroy the essentials. Some of the old prayers were omitted, the wording of others were changed and there were alterations in the order in which the Regalia were given. These changes caused great anguish to liturgical scholars, but the ancient pattern of the rite was certainly not destroyed.

The 'Glorious Revolution' which brought William and Mary to the Throne as co-sovereigns brought complex problems for the ceremonial officers of the College of Arms and for the Order of Service. Parliament itself determined the form of the Coronation Oath and Henry Compton, Bishop of London, was given four weeks to make the revisions. The task was not well done.

Other reigns brought other changes, but none of them were fundamental to the character of the coronation rite. The first Elizabeth, lying in her tomb but a few paces from where the second Elizabeth came to her crowning, would still have recognised the form and progression of the ceremony. The pattern of *Liber Regalis* was again enacted in the Abbey.

We may now consider, very briefly, the form of the Coronation Service for Queen Elizabeth as the centuries had brought it down to her.

The *Entrance* must always have been the moment when the Abbey began to fill with the splendour of copes and vestments, robes, mantles, tabards and uniforms as the great procession from the West Door of the Abbey conducted the Sovereign to the Theatre. The general composition and order of this procession has remained unchanged since the coronation of Richard I in 1189.

Since the coronation of James II in 1685 the triumphant shouts of the Westminster schoolboys have greeted each new sovereign on passing through the choir screen.

At the *Recognition* the Archbishop presents the Sovereign for the consent and acclamation of the people. It is a custom of immemorial antiquity. The Emperors of both East and West were raised high on their soldiers' shields. The Teutonic tribes in the forests of Northern Europe after electing their chieftains raised them high for popular assent and acclaim. They brought this custom when they came to Britain; after many Saxon kings were elected by the Witan they were raised on a shield and placed on a royal stone for popular recognition. The old stone still stands outside the Guildhall at Kingston-on-Thames.

The *Liber Regalis* perpetuated the form of Recognition as we were to see it again in 1953. 'The Metropolitan, or Bishop, that is to consecrate the King, shall address the people at the four sides of the Theatre, inquiring their will and consent about the consecration of the said King.' Only when 'the people give their assent, as is customary with loud and unanimous shouts' would the Bishop vest himself to begin the service.

In 1953 Dr Fisher, the Archbishop of Canterbury, was equally definite on the importance of this part of the ceremony. On 17 March 1953 he told a conference, 'In the Recognition, the People accept the Queen as their Sovereign and acclaim her as such.' He added the significant words: 'The willing consent of the People is necessary.'

The *Oath* has remained the solemn compact between the new Sovereign and the people at the beginning of each new reign from Saxon times. The changes in the form of the Coronation Oath bring into focus the constitutional, religious and social pressures at each period in England's history. The dispute between the barons and the king about the use of the royal power at the beginning of the reign of Edward I, for example, was reflected in the Oath which the King had to accept as the condition of his coronation in 1274.

'The barons', says the contemporary record, 'treated with the king on the oath before they would proceed with his election.'

Other centuries also brought their changes. The Abbot Lytlington recognised the need for change in the Oath when he wrote in the *Liber Regalis* that 'there shall be added to the aforesaid questions what is right'.

Henry VIII before his own coronation tried, unsuccessfully, to write his own version of the Oath: Charles I put his own fatal interpretation on it. Finally, after the abdication of James II, Parliament itself wrote the terms of the Oath by the Coronation Oath Act of 1689 and it has been revised, when considered necessary, by further Acts of Parliament.

The *Presentation of the Bible* was introduced at the coronation of William and Mary in 1689 and was put immediately after the crowning until 1937. In 1953 it was placed after the Oath. At this stage the Communion Service of the Church of England had not yet begun and it was possible to introduce an important innovation – the participation for the first time of the Moderator of the General Assembly of the Church of Scotland in the presentation.

Throughout all the centuries the *Anointing* has been regarded by the Church as the central act and purpose of the ceremony. It is only in recent centuries that the popular attention has been focused on the glittering spectacle of the splendid crown raised high in the Archbishop's hands. The word 'coronation' is now firmly embedded in the language as the name of the ceremony. In earlier times the ceremony was described as the 'hallowing', 'sacring' or 'consecration' of the king.

This view of the ceremony was expressed again by one of the most eminent authorities on the coronation, L. G. Wickham Legg. He wrote: 'Nothing which goes before and nothing which follows can approach the anointing in significance. Without it the king cannot receive the royal ornaments, without it, in a word, he is not king.'

This opinion was once held so strongly that in Plantagenet times, for example, the years of a king's reign were counted from the date of his consecration and until it was done it was customary to describe him as 'The Duke of Normandy'.

The anointing has been regarded as such a sacred and personal moment that for centuries it has been screened from curious eyes by a canopy. At the coronation of Richard II in 1377 this canopy was held by the Barons of the Cinque Ports. By the time of Henry IV in 1399, the Barons were dispossessed by four dukes; finally the canopy passed into the hands of the Knights of the Garter who have firmly held it since.

At the *Investiture* the Sovereign, having been consecrated, is invested with the regal vestments and those symbols of temporal power, the Regalia. An account of these robes and the royal ornaments has already been given.

The service now moves on to the climax of the *Crowning*. As the Archbishop places the crown on the Sovereign's head, the peers and peeresses put on their coronets, the Kings of Arms their crowns and the Abbey resounds with the fanfares of trumpets, the beating of drums and the loud shouts of acclaim. It must always have been a great triumphant moment.

Immediately afterwards the Sovereign, wearing the traditional St Edward's Crown, vested in golden garments and carrying the two Sceptres, moves from King Edward's

Coronation Dates

William I	25 December 1066		Edward VI	20 February 1547
William II	26 September 1087		Mary I	1 October 1553
Henry I	5 August 1100		Elizabeth I	15 January 1559
Stephen	26 December 1135		James I	25 July 1603
Henry II	19 December 1154		Charles I	2 February 1626
Richard I	3 September 1189		Charles II	23 April 1661
(and again at Winchester 17 April 1194)			James II	23 April 1685
John	27 May 1199		William III and Mary II	11 April 1689
Henry III	28 October 1216			
Edward I	19 August 1274		Anne	23 April 1702
Edward II	25 February 1308		George I	20 October 1714
Edward III	1 February 1327		George II	11 October 1727
Richard II	16 July 1377		George III	22 September 1761
Henry IV	13 October 1399		George IV	19 July 1821
Henry V	9 April 1413		William IV	8 September 1831
Henry VI	6 November 1429		Victoria	28 June 1838
Edward IV	28 June 1461		Edward VII	9 August 1902
Edward V (1483, never crowned)			George V	22 June 1911
Richard III	6 July 1483		Edward VIII (1936, never crowned)	
Henry VII	30 October 1485		George VI	12 May 1937
Henry VIII	24 June 1509		Elizabeth II	2 June 1953

Chair to the raised Throne Chair at the front of the Theatre. The peers and bishops gather around the steps of the Throne so that they can 'raise' the Sovereign into possession of the Kingdom.

The *Homage* is the next stage of the ceremony. The custom was based on the formal acknowledgment of the tenancy of land at each level of feudal society. The word embraced two acts, the homage in which the lesser tenant declared he was 'the man' or vassal, of the superior lord, and fealty, the oath to be faithful and true to his lord and to perform the 'services' of his tenancy. *'Jeo deveigne vostre home'*, 'I become your man', said the vassal to his lord and eventually the great tenant-in-chief repeated in his turn the words to his king, as the supreme lord of all land in his kingdom.

Until 1902 all the peers of Parliament present in the Abbey were entitled to perform individual acts of homage. At the coronation of Queen Victoria the Homage lasted nearly an hour. After the postponed coronation of Edward VII, his illness provided the opportunity to make a necessary change. Since then only the senior peer in each order ascended the steps to the Throne to do homage while 'the other peers in his degree, having put off their coronets, shall kneel in their places and say with him the words of the homage'.

At the end of the Homage the Sovereign descends from the Throne, takes off the Crown, and makes the traditional offerings including a 'wedge of gold' before the Communion Service is resumed. At the end of this Service the Sovereign, crowned and carrying the Sceptre and the Rod, returns again for a brief time to the Throne.

After the 'Te Deum' the Sovereign leaves the Theatre and withdraws in state into St Edward's Chapel behind the High Altar. In the curtained Traverse the golden vestments are removed. The Sovereign is robed for the first time in the Robe of Purple, and wearing the Imperial Crown and carrying the Orb and Sceptre, in the words of the *Liber Regalis* 'shall return with great splendour through the midst of the choir by the same way as they came into the Church'.

20 'The Eyes of the World'

King Edward IV, writing to the Pope after his coronation in 1461 referred to Westminster Abbey 'as placed before the eyes of the world of Englishmen'. Five hundred years later it had become true to say that the Abbey was placed before the eyes of the world as well as of Englishmen. At our press conferences the foreign and overseas journalists had begun to exceed the British press by two to one.

The College of Arms was besieged by journalists. The Heralds were not enjoying their customary immunity – they were vigorously assailed. The Ministry tried to help but even its historical resources could not answer questions about why Heralds wore tabards and Kings of Arms their crowns. In October 1952 an experienced Information Officer, R. G. S. Hoare, was appointed to the staff of the Earl Marshal and the harassed officers of the College were able to return to their traditional duties.

The pressures of the day often continued into the night. The ringing of my home telephone became too familiar. There was the occasion when I was awakened at 3 a.m., dazed with sleep, to hear a brisk transatlantic voice saying, 'You're on the air in California. Say, can you tell our listeners what Queen Elizabeth had for breakfast?' At the Palace, the Queen's Press Secretary, Commander Richard Colville, was also fielding just such questions.

Since the last coronation in 1937 there had been a world growth of newspapers, magazines and radio. News agencies spanned the world; thousands of cinemas in nearly every country, from the tin shack cinemas of Asia to the luxurious Plazas of the capital cities, had a generous supplementary diet of newsreels and documentaries. The British Newsreel companies – Movietone, Pathe, Gaumont British and Paramount – claimed a joint world viewership of 350 million cinemagoers. The American film companies estimated they had an almost equal share of the world's population. In the planning of the media coverage of the Coronation these film companies could claim our very serious attention.

Television in Britain was still the growing infant of the media. Closed down during the war, it had $1\frac{1}{2}$ million licences in 1952, compared with over 11 million for sound radio. Important parts of the country were without TV. Its coverage was small, therefore, compared with the vast world-wide audiences of film and radio.

This comparison influenced a lot of attitudes. Why bother about television with its small audience and big cameras and lighting requirements when the radio could project the service round the world, and the cinema screens could show the ceremony in all its rich colours to millions of people in every continent?

It was an attitude which gathered strength as time went on. It became known that the Dean and other Clergy were opposed to the televising of the ceremony; the Archbishop was hardening his opinion against it. It was difficult for politicians and others to oppose the ecclesiastical authorities responsible for the religious service itself.

There were members of the Coronation Joint Committee who were genuinely concerned about the burden which live television might impose on the Queen during the long service. There were also participants in the ceremony who feared that their slightest slip would be instantly transmitted to the watching millions. Finally, there were a few who were horrified by the idea that 'chaps in pubs would watch the Coronation over their third pint'. It all built up into strong opposition to the televising of the service.

Like other adolescents the BBC TV service did not help its cause by the manner of its approach. Many important people believed that television would mean one long unblinking stare at the Queen and other persons in the Theatre. The BBC did not offer to demonstrate how telephoto lenses could draw back from a scene, how the programme could be edited by switching from one camera to another and the ability of the TV producer to select his material during a live transmission.

When the decision came to restrict the televising of the Coronation, a lot of people were strongly criticised for what the *Daily Express* called 'a bad and reactionary decision'. The BBC should have shared some of the criticism.

On the other hand as I have already mentioned, the film companies had handled their own approach with great success. I was requested to intensify the efforts to solve the lighting problems for the colour films in the Abbey. A few days later the Duke of Edinburgh came to inspect the lighting arrangements. After brief introductions, he said: 'Let us see what it is like when the lights are on.'

At the signal the space around the Sanctuary was suddenly flooded with light. The Duke stood for a few moments while his eyes adjusted. Then he began to walk slowly around the space of the eventual Theatre.

He said to the Earl Marshal at one place, 'I think King Edward's Chair will be about here.'

He looked up thoughtfully at the lights far overhead and came back to us.

'There is some glare,' he said.

'Yes, sir, but that will be overcome, possibly by the use of diffusers, so long as we are able to match the colour of the light to the properties of the emulsions for the colour films.'

He was not deterred by the technicalities. He probed into the problems. At the end of our discussion he walked slowly into the centre of the lighted space.

He said, 'I am sure you will remember that everyone here will be under the lights for some hours.'

We understood perfectly what he meant.

He turned to leave, saying, 'Keep at it. I'm sure you will come up with the answers.'

I had another meeting with Sir Gordon Craig, Chairman of the British Newsreel Association, and the film companies. In the next few weeks film technicians arrived from the big film laboratories in America; other experts were called in. I was invited to see coils of film being lifted from strong smelling liquids. There was also a strong smell of triumph in the air.

The lighting requirements were finally met by a precisely controlled system of projectors mounted 60 feet up, augmented by lighting units at lower levels by adapting the existing Abbey chandeliers to use gold-coloured prismatic glass reflectors.

We were now ready to test the lights and the films.

Norman Hartnell, who was creating the beautiful Coronation dress for the Queen, loaned me the robes to dress a procession. My PA, Miss Sheila Bell, was arrayed as a marchioness, other officers donned robes of state.

The new lights were turned on; the cameras stared wide-eyed; Miss Bell, supported by the bogus barons, began to move in dignified processional order. The scene was impressed on film.

A few mornings later Castleton Knight appeared in my office. I looked at him and said, 'You look as though you have found a crock of gold.'

'True gold', he said, 'and full of every colour of the rainbow.' The colour tests had been successful.

The Coronation Joint Committee met to decide their attitude to the televising of the ceremony. I was sure that too many expectations had been aroused for an adverse decision to be quietly accepted. Three-quarters of a million people had rushed to buy or hire television sets. Even the most superb films would not compensate for the loss of the immediacy of live television. For the first time in history the Sovereign and the people could be linked in ways which were both unique and personal. The Queen could literally be crowned 'in the sight of all her people'.

I did what a civil servant could do to point out the implications. I was sure that the Press would explode, MPs react and eventually the decision would be reversed.

On the evening of 20 October 1952, the Earl Marshal's office made the announcement. It was carefully worded to indicate the shared responsibility of everyone concerned with the decision. It stated:

> The Earl Marshal announces that the Coronation Joint Executive Committee, with
> the consent of the Coronation Commission, and after receiving the advice of the
> Cabinet, has decided that still photography, black and white films and colour films
> will be allowed within Westminster Abbey during the ceremony. A sound broadcast
> of the ceremony will also take place. Live television will be restricted to the
> procession west of the choir screen, but a film of the ceremony will be available
> for subsequent showing in the television service.

Journalists seldom react with strong feelings to the news they are handling, but that evening when they telephoned me, they were angry men. The next morning's newspapers showed how deeply the editorial emotions had been stirred. The restriction on television was front page news in every paper. The Fleet Street drums had begun beating out the thunders of a national campaign.

The *Daily Express* called the ban illogical. 'The nation's desire to see the Queen crowned is a natural reflection of the esteem in which she is held. If her advisors cannot understand such communion between ruler and people, which television can invoke, it can only remain for the Queen to intercede and have a foolish deed undone.'

The London *Evening Standard* demanded that the ban should be 'reconsidered and revised'. The *News Chronicle* was angry and the *Daily Mirror* called it 'a truly astonishing decision. The people will be denied the climax of a wonderful and magnificent occasion in British history.'

Several newspapers asserted that the decision had been made in ignorance of television techniques. Had the BBC explained their techniques to the authorities? asked the *Star*. *The Times* complained that the pros and cons of television should have been explained from the beginning. If this had been done those responsible for the decision 'might have saved themselves embarrassment and kept an issue directly affecting Royalty out of discussion in Parliament'.

There were attempts to run before the storm. Some members of the Coronation Committee explained that they were away, or even, were not consulted about the ban. The Commission secretary, Sir Ronald Knox, replied tartly and publicly that 'the agenda papers containing all items under discussion had been circulated before each meeting'.

A Question to the Prime Minister quickly appeared in the Order Paper of the House of Commons, asking what advice the Cabinet gave to the Earl Marshal before the ban was imposed on direct television of the Coronation ceremony. I was in the Civil Service box at the back of the Chamber to hear the answer. The House was crowded for Winston Churchill's reply. He merely said that the arrangements for televising the Coronation were not a matter on which the Government, or indeed, Ministers of the Crown, alone advised the Crown. He fended off further questions by pointing out that several more questions were down for answer the next week and he wished to reserve any statement until then. The House saw he was playing for time, interpreted the familiar growl in his voice and guessed the likely outcome.

The newspapers guessed too. The drum beats slackened. Sir Ronald Knox confirmed that the 'Earl Marshal had been in touch with the BBC'.

The BBC stated that it was 'preparing a detailed memorandum designed to show that TV apparatus will be inconspicuous, that no extra lighting will be required and that the solemnity of the occasion will not be marred'. A belated shooting script was being prepared.

A few days later we began 'experimental tests' in the Abbey. The BBC set up its cameras and monitors to demonstrate the techniques and to discuss how far 'close-ups' might be used and other matters. The atmosphere was a little restrained.

There could not be an immediate *volte face*. On 28 October the Prime Minister satisfied the House, the Press and the public with a statement that the restriction on televising the ceremony might be modified. 'I believe it would be for the public advantage if the Coronation Commission were to consider any new report which later knowledge and study permit the Earl Marshal's Committee to make to them.'

Papers went from Committee to Committee, from Cabinet to Commission, until on 8 December 1952 the Earl Marshal was able to announce that with the approval of the Queen 'parts of the service east of the screen will be televised'.

From then the BBC television service went on to the crowning triumph of 2 June. It was the day when television came of age. It was, however, the technical skills of its

19   The Eyes of the World. The Queen Victoria Monument on Coronation Day – a focal point
of the world-wide circle of communications.

engineers, the careful planning of de Lotbiniere and Peter Dimmock and the outstanding quality of the commentaries by Richard Dimbleby in the Abbey and Chester Wilmot, Michael Henderson, Bernard Braden, Mary Hill and others along the processional route which placed the 'crown' on the Corporation's head.

By January 1953 the main technical problems of the colour films and television had been overcome, but the tests and experiments went on until the Earl Marshal and the Archbishop were satisfied.

In the meantime the reserves of press seats for 2 June had been vanishing. We combed the roofs of Whitehall for places, juggled with seats in the Mall, crammed more in the press stand at Trafalgar Square. By the evening of 2 June the eyes and ears of the world could see and hear. There were over 2,000 journalists on the route and 500 photographers from 92 nations.

We had worked closely with the Post Office to meet the unprecedented and complicated needs of the BBC for TV and radio. It was the largest operation the Corporation had ever attempted. Every line and panel in the control points was duplicated, every commentator had a spare microphone, there were storage batteries if the power failed and a radio link between the roof of the Abbey and Broadcasting House.

In every continent the national radio stations made arrangements to transmit commentaries along land lines from London or to pick up the BBC overseas short wave transmissions. The TV programme was relayed, with separate language commentaries, to France, Holland and West Germany, involving complicated equipment for the converting of the signal to different line standards.

In those days, before the communication satellites had taken to the skies, the US networks arrived to discuss the transmission of the Coronation direct from London. They arrived separately and in very competitive moods. I explained that there was not a single nook or ancient cranny in the Abbey where another camera could possibly be fitted in.

'Say, why can't you knock a little hole in the Abbey wall so that we can poke a lens through. We'll pay all the costs of repairs!'

I thought of the reactions of the Dean of the Abbey to that idea. I suggested they should discuss their proposals with the Earl Marshal and made appointments for them. The Earl Marshal had a great gift for polite and convincing statement. The Americans were back, still separately, in my office the next day to discuss other ways of getting their own exclusive pictures from London.

Our American cousins are not easily defeated. They agreed to make arrangements with the BBC to telerecord the scenes from the Abbey, but asked for their own camera positions facing the Palace and along the route. I offered all they required.

Then they set about finding the quickest way to get their own pictures across the Atlantic. They thought about bouncing the signal from one aircraft to another in a series of relays to New York. This scheme was given up before the prospect of one plane falling out of the series and plunging the millions of dollars invested into the cold waters of the ocean.

One of the networks spoke of building a tall tower at Land's End until the Post Office demonstrated the height required. They then turned to the idea of calling in the ships of the US navy to act as relay stations from ship to ship. I am sure that the US navy would willingly have patrolled the heaving waters of the Atlantic on Coronation Day if the proposal had been feasible. But it was not.

The RAF provided the solution. The Canadian Broadcasting Corporation had been offered three of the record-breaking Canberra PR 3s, fitted out as film processing and editing laboratories as they raced across the Atlantic. The Americans took to the air also, but it was still going to be a race to see which network first got on to the screens of the USA.

The RAF Canberras did the job for the networks, flying the films and telerecordings in three relays to Goose Bay, Labrador, where US Mustang P 51s were waiting to rush the recording to Boston and Canadian CF 100s were also ready to speed the recording to Quebec for Canadian viewers.

The NBC sprung a sudden surprise by announcing, after the planes had taken off, that it had secretly arranged for another Canberra to fly its own recordings direct to Boston, refuelling at Gander. To the great delight of Columbia Broadcasting the plane was obliged to turn back with a defective fuel tank two hours over the Atlantic. The NBC was still not defeated. They made impromptu arrangements with the Canadians and got a picture on their network screens about ten minutes ahead of Columbia.

These arrangements involved the solution of great technical problems. The BBC signal from Alexandra Palace was picked up both on microwave and regular broadcast in a control room at Heathrow. A new 'hot' processing technique developed the BBC recordings in seconds. Films from the camera positions on the route were rushed in by motor cycle messengers. In the afternoon the aircraft took off with a complete record of the Coronation from which Edward P. Murrow and other CBS newsmen prepared a one-and-a-half-hour programme for that evening.

Eighty-five million American viewers gathered round their TV sets to witness the crowning of a British monarch.

When the vice-president of Columbia came to express his thanks for all the facilities, he said that the technical developments had meant that 'TV had jumped ten years in ten hours'.

Another new development was forced along by the Coronation. Colour television made its first appearance. I arranged for Pye of Cambridge to have three camera positions for their new colour system on the roof of the Foreign Office. The pictures were relayed to the delighted children in Great Ormond Street Hospital.

The links to the outside world were the most comprehensive and complex ever undertaken. The Cable and Wireless Co. had finished laying the new transatlantic cable; direct phototelegraph services were also extended to places as far away as Hong Kong, Tokyo and Sydney. By a combination of wire, radio and facsimile techniques photographs of the Queen leaving Buckingham Palace were in Sydney newspaper offices before she had arrived at the Abbey.

Photographs transmitted at two-minute intervals were on the television screens of America within seven minutes, together with a sound commentary from London! 'Rush

editions' of newspapers throughout the USA with pictures were on the news-stands before the Abbey ceremony began.

The British provincial newspapers were served with equal speed by portable transmitters of the Muirhead-Belin type which were able to transmit photographs 5 inches by 8 inches in even less than seven minutes for reproduction in the big provincial newspapers.

For the journalists and commentators in the Ministry stands direct lines were provided. Altogether 3,280 special telephone circuits were provided on the processional route and from the Abbey.

Finally, arrangements had to be made to get additional photographs, films and colour photographs from the closed route. With the help of London District Command and Scotland Yard I made arrangements for police cadets to cross the troop and police lines to collect the material at regular intervals. Motor cyclists were waiting at collecting points.

As this world-wide system of communication was built up, rolling its problems before it one by one, it seemed that it could not possibly function without some hitch or breakdown on the day. Miraculously it worked. Almost at the same moment, all round the globe, newspaper presses were beginning to print that first picture – the Queen leaving the Palace for her Coronation.

'Every other coronation in history compared to this was a local, near private affair', later recorded the Britannica Book of the Year.

The *Times* correspondent, Derek Hudson, an author of a standard book on the press, also wrote later: 'It was generally acknowledged that never before had such satisfactory co-operation for a State occasion been achieved.'

It was also for those at the centre of the organisation, including the Post Office engineers, something close at times to being a waking nightmare.

The final problem was fitting in the artists. Their arrival was one of David Eccles's inspirations. He had set up in April 1952 a fund fed by private subscriptions to buy works of art for public buildings. Early in 1953 he invited artists to depict the scenes on Coronation Day. Over forty artists accepted the invitation, among them L. S. Lowry, Edmund Seago, Dame Laura Knight, Osbert Lancaster, Feliks Topolski, as well as artists from Australia, France, India and Roumania.

Newspaper and magazine sales in Britain and in many other countries had a boom period. Those with Coronation supplements like the *Illustrated London News*, the *Tatler*, *Picture Post* and *Illustrated* had record export sales. On Coronation Day the *Daily Mirror* achieved a sale of 7,000,000 copies.

After the Coronation the press cuttings from all round the world flowed in, thick heavy bundles of them.

It seemed that for one day in our troubled century the front pages of newspapers nearly everywhere were filled with pictures of happy, rejoicing people and of a young woman who had come to Westminster to be crowned before the eyes of the world.

20   A few of the many magazine and newspaper Coronation editions published in many countries.

21 Coronation City

The arches went up in the Mall, the sun shone and the crowds came out. The arches were lifted into place by giant mobile cranes on 13 May. The lions and unicorns were placed on top to begin their fantasy dance against the sky. Then the huge crowns were suspended from the arches and the twin lines of sixty tall crowned standards were set in position on each side of the Mall. The newspaper photographs and comments brought Londoners in their thousands to view the new vista of the Mall. The first tingles of anticipation and excitement were in the air.

The rising of the arches was the signal for the rest of London's decorations to come out. The pink Alexandra roses blossomed on the façades of Regent Street, lit at night by softly glowing lights. The gold and scarlet banners were draped across Victoria Street, and workmen began preparing a gilded cage for Eros in Piccadilly. In the East Carriage Drive the tall staffs bearing shields with the crests of the Commonwealth countries confronted the fluttering banners in Park Lane. A huge equestrian statue of the Queen appeared on the front of Selfridges store in Oxford Street. An archway of pennants spanned the approach to the Royal Borough of Kensington, and long golden trumpets were raised in silent salutes in Old Bond Street. The nightingales began to sing in Berkeley Square – their disembodied voices provided by tape recorders concealed among the trees.

There was new paint everywhere; the fronts of the buildings had been cleaned to reveal unexpected shapes and mouldings of brick and stone, and the familiar outlines of buildings themselves were given a fresh emphasis by flags, buntings, crowns and the new EIIR ciphers. London was putting on its Coronation dress.

From the middle of May every part of Britain was bursting out in its Coronation colours and hastening the preparations for every form of festivity. The Ministry of Food had even granted eighty-two applications to roast oxen where it could be proved that by tradition an ox had been roasted at previous coronations – an envied concession in a country where the meat ration was still only two shillingsworth a week!

On 23 May, Whitsun Saturday, I came back from a brief visit to the preparations for the Queen's visit to Caernarvon Castle on 10 July through towns and villages gay with decorations into a London which had almost been brought to a standstill by the huge influx of suburban Londoners and holidaymakers from every part of the country. The holiday lure of Whitsun at the seaside was forgotten. The coastal resorts from Southend to Brighton reported the sparsest attendance since the war. Over 2,000 coaches poured their passengers into central London; almost every bus and train to central London was filled to capacity. The police estimated that over one million people were thronging the

21 In Piccadilly Circus
Eros was set in a gilded
cage – part of London's
panorama of street
decorations.

22 In Oxford Street,
Selfridges store erected
this magnificent equestrian
statue of the Queen.

23   The Coronation became a theme in many advertisements.

processional route. Huge crowds waited outside Buckingham Palace. They had their reward. As the Queen and the Duke of Edinburgh left the Palace to spend the week-end at Royal Lodge, Windsor, thousands of cheering people surged forward to halt their car while the perspiring policemen pushed backwards and the police horses danced their delicate pirouettes among so many unwary toes.

Over 60,000 people an hour were passing through Parliament Square, pressing forward to the Abbey. The huge colourful emblems on the rising fronts of the Commonwealth stands were a focus of attention, before the multitudes moved on to see the Annexe and the Abbey.

We had not expected this great invasion of London so many days before the Coronation and we had arranged for a rehearsal of the Speaker's State Coach over its route to the Abbey. The two magnificent Whitbread horses, Royal and Sovereign, had to be made familiar with their task. They waited patiently in their red and gold harness until the police persuaded the huge crowds to give them carriage way. The big coach eventually rumbled sedately and safely out of Palace Yard towards the Abbey to provide another element in the holiday excitement.

The sun shone, the temperature soared and the crowds continued to grow. By late afternoon the Mall was a carpet of people, multicoloured by the women's bright summer dresses. We had opened the stands in the Mall and the footweary thousands sat there, eating their sandwiches and watching the other thousands passing slowly by.

There were unfamiliar figures among those passing crowds whose appearance aroused great interest and endless discussion. They were the men and women who had come from the far ends of the Commonwealth. There were, among that crowd, policemen from Fiji in their scalloped skirts under dazzling white tunics, tall chiefs in long flowing robes from many African territories, a group of the Royal Papuan Constabulary in shorts and sandals, Maori ratings from the New Zealand cruiser, the *Black Prince*, soldiers from Malaya, tall Pathans in pugrees and the small lithe Gurkhas. Mingling with the throngs which continued to press down the Mall were also slouch-hatted Australians and the soldiers from New Zealand, Ceylon, South Africa, Canada and Pakistan. The scarlet tunics and stiff-brimmed hats of the Royal Canadian Mounted Police were immediately recognisable, but the Pakistani bandsmen in their green tunics and tartan plaids must have been a puzzle to many as were the soldiers or police from the Bahamas, Barbados, Aden and the Leeward Islands. As they strolled by they presented an informal pageant of the peoples of the Commonwealth, the like of which would never again be seen in London once the Coronation was over.

Quarters for the troops and police in London had been a problem. The officers and men taking part in the procession or lining the route totalled 29,200 – 3,600 from the Royal Navy, 16,100 from the Army and 7,000 from the RAF. There were 2,000 from the Commonwealth and 500 from the Colonies. There were also 6,700 reserve and administrative troops and 1,000 officers and men of the Royal Military Police were brought in to assist the Metropolitan Police. Accommodation had also to be found for 7,000 police drawn from 75 provincial forces.

The wartime camps at Aldershot and around London were refurbished, the deep air raid shelter on Clapham Common was re-opened and the vast exhibition halls at Olympia and Earls Court were converted to mass dormitories and dining-rooms.

A city of 3,500 tents was erected in Kensington Gardens for the troops from Pakistan, Malaya, the Gurkhas and the police. Small boys deprived of their sailing water on the Pond found a fascinating consolation in watching the strange soldiers from overseas.

Every regiment and corps of the British Army was represented, each by 30 officers and other ranks including National Servicemen. The Home Guard was given the honour of leading the procession and were the only unit to wear battledress.

How many would be there on the day? The estimates rose and fell like an erratic barometer. Some felt that the televising of the ceremony would greatly reduce the number on the route – it was even feared that there might be gaps in the crowds. Others were sure that 2 June would bring the greatest crowds that London had ever seen. There appeared to be solid grounds for that opinion – every bed in every hotel in London – including many in attics and corridors – was booked. The Tourist Board had appealed to private families to open their doors to visitors and thousands had replied with offers of accommodation.

British Rail would run 6,500 special trains from the provinces in twenty-four hours, apart from their usual services, and at least 6,000 coaches would discharge their passengers outside the route from midnight onwards, in addition to the bus services of London Transport. The world's largest liners, already converging on Britain were booked to capacity; the airline bookings were the highest ever recorded. The airlines of twenty nations brought their passengers to Heathrow, Northolt and Prestwick.

The plans for the 2 June traffic and crowd control had to be brought forward when, ten days before the event, traffic in central London was brought to a standstill by the crowds which were pouring in by every means of transport. The provincial police suddenly found themselves on unfamiliar beats and the protective barriers along the pavements were placed into position along the route. There were eight miles of these low barriers. There would also be the 70 heavy barriers, each 9 feet high, guarding the Coronation Route from a too sudden influx of spectators. It was not necessary, however, to close these heavy barriers before the night of 1 June.

For the control of crowds in central London the route was divided into sections which were each known by distinctive colours. The Mall area was green, Trafalgar Square and Whitehall were red, Pall Mall and St James's Street were gold, Marble Arch and Oxford Street were orange and so on.

Tickets for the Government stands were printed to correspond with these colour sections. People with tickets for the green and red sections had to be in their places by 6 a.m., in the gold, cerise and yellow sections and also for Haymarket in the blue section by 7 a.m., and in the orange and other sections by 9 a.m.

The processional area was to be closed to through traffic from midnight on 1–2 June. All London Transport buses would terminate at sixteen special points on the perimeter. London Transport buses would run 44,000 journeys on 65 routes before 8.30 a.m. Four Tube stations were closed and traffic restrictions placed on six others. London Transport issued over 2 million free copies of guides with maps and colour codes of their plans.

As on other great public occasions a vast behind-the-scenes operation was organised for the protection and comfort of the crowds. Over 1,000 firemen with their engines and equipment were stationed within the processional area. Gas, electricity, water and telephone engineers took up their positions at midnight. Below the feet of the unsuspecting crowds the LCC engineers and sewermen would ensure that the vast and complex underground services were safely maintained.

There would be 8,500 Red Cross and St John's Ambulance men, nurses and doctors on duty operating from 130 posts. Ambulances were located at accessible points. The medical services were centred on Westminster Hospital to which the serious cases would be brought; there was a perimeter route for emergency use around the processional area.

Feeding the multitudes was a big problem for the Ministry and the catering firms which were appointed. Refreshment tents were set up behind the stands and other tented catering points put up in the Royal Parks; 30,000 catering staff were brought in.

Special facilities were laid on for fresh supplies to reach other cafés and restaurants before midnight. The union lifted its ban on milk deliveries before 7 a.m. and the milk floats with flags and their passes prominently displayed trundled on and off the route from 5 a.m. to the encouraging cheers of the crowds already on the pavements.

Before the Coronation my time from early morning until evening was a succession of meetings, interrupted by the compulsory attendance at the rehearsals in the Abbey. There was continued liaison with the Earl Marshal's office, Scotland Yard, London Transport and other bodies. I was rushing off to meetings at the Foreign Office and Commonwealth Relations Office to satisfy the need of their overseas posts for the latest information and for briefing material for High Commissioners and Ambassadors. It seemed that in every country in the world, outside of Russia and China, the representatives of Her Majesty were in pressing demand as speakers on the theme of the coming Coronation at functions of every kind. In the USA our Ambassador, Sir Roger Makins, was flying from city to city to keep his engagements. In most countries, too, our official representatives, usually with the British residents' associations, were organising celebrations for 2 June which would be attended by the Heads of State.

I was not surprised by this popularity of Her Majesty's representatives overseas. Every day I used to glance briefly at reports and photographs of the Coronation preparations which poured in sheaves on to my desk from all over the world. I am sure there has not been any other occasion in our history when, old wars and rivalries forgotten, the people and governments of so many lands turned to Britain with such interest and friendliness, with such respect for its traditions and with such warm good wishes for its continuing influence among the nations of the world.

A fever of excitement was everywhere; strange things began to happen. As I came away from the Victoria Monument the crowds rushed forward to cheer the arrival of the new Russian Ambassador at the Palace, the hammer and sickle flying boldly on the bonnet of his car. It was a time when the frost-bite of the Cold War was at its most severe. As Mr Malik looked out at the crowd it seemed to me that there was a look of perplexity on his heavy features. Were these British really cheering him?

More understandable was the sudden dash of the crowds towards a car bearing the pennant of the Warden of the Cinque Ports. The Prime Minister sat back in the car, hugely smiling and waving his traditional cigar at the crowds.

'Good old Winnie,' they shouted, with affectionate wartime memories.

I think the dancing in the streets started outside the public houses in the East End but the custom soon spread westwards. I saw Morris dancers roystering outside the Abbey and late one evening it seemed to me that even sober-suited civil servants were footing it outside the 'Shades' at the end of Whitehall. Trafalgar Square became the stage for African and Jamaican dancing, while the British crowds gathered round, clapping their hands to the rhythm, until they finally all joined into one chaotic sea of movement.

For me, however, the climax of these rejoicings was the scene in Piccadilly late on the evening of Sunday 31 May. I had come in for the final rehearsal of the route which began at 5 a.m. in the hope of avoiding the crowds. It was a vain hope since the crowds were already condensing like the dew almost everywhere. By 6 a.m. Parliament Square was packed with cars bumper to bumper with scarcely any movement. By 9 a.m. it was estimated that 40,000 people were outside the Palace and a great roar of cheering greeted the Queen and the Duke of Edinburgh when they drove out to attend the service, with the Queen Mother, at the Marlborough House Chapel.

The huge crowds took over London for the rest of the day. As I cleared my desk I could hear the sounds of London coming across the river like the droning of a vast hive of bees.

I had been asked to do a commentary for CBC on the decorations and scenes in London that evening, but it proved impossible to take the car of recording equipment along the route. About 11 p.m. the police had been forced to close Piccadilly to traffic and let the crowds take over. A huge circle of people joined hands and were dancing round and round the gilded Eros in one continuing revolving circle. They had spontaneously altered the words of Danny Kaye's popular song about Copenhagen. 'Wonderful, wonderful London Town' came the great swelling crescendo from thousands of voices. It was an unforgettable sight and sound.

The Prime Ministers of the Commonwealth had come for the Commonwealth Conference and among other things had formally approved the form of the Coronation ceremony. The Commonwealth Parliamentary Association gave a luncheon for the Queen in Westminster Hall. It was intended to be in the ancient tradition of the great Coronation Banquets but I felt that it was a very sober affair by those standards.

There had been a Garden Party in brilliant sunshine on the lawns of Buckingham Palace. One hundred nations were represented among the 4,000 guests. The remaining royal and other official guests were pouring into London. On Saturday 30 May the Duke of Edinburgh at Victoria welcomed nearly 200 guests – foreign princes, sheikhs, rajahs, Ministers of foreign governments and the representatives of a score of other countries who had crossed the channel in a specially chartered ferry, the *Maid of Orleans.*

On the same morning the Duke of Gloucester and the Duke of Kent were at Heathrow to receive Prince Bernhard of the Netherlands, who had piloted his own aircraft. Other arrivals included Crown Prince Olaf of Norway, Prince Axel of Denmark, Crown Prince Akihito of Japan, Prince Bertil of Sweden, Prince and Princess George of Greece, Prince

Chula of Thailand, the Crown Prince of Ethiopia and many other representatives of present or one-time ruling houses.

Some of the guests brought unusual offerings. El Glaoui, the Pasha of Marrakesh, brought the Queen a golden crown and the Mentri Berar of Perak brought an illuminated address of loyalty to the Queen which began – 'An address of sincerity and a gift of divers kinds from a heart of translucent purity which harbours neither doubt nor suspicion so long as the sun and the moon endure in the revolving vault of heaven.'

The whole of London was full of smiling people with their happy and excited children. The streets were transformed by the decorations, and the bright summer shirts and dresses and the gay uniforms and exotic robes and dresses of a hundred countries. The nights seemed to be filled with rejoicing – there was music in the streets and everywhere people were holding parties. Every ballroom in London was filled with the swirl of dancers in the 'Coronation Waltz'.

The Mousetrap had begun its record-breaking run at the Ambassadors Theatre, the topical *Young Elizabeth* had opened at the Criterion and Anna Neagle was appearing in the appropriately named *Glorious Days* at the Palace. At Covent Garden the huge production cast were rehearsing Benjamin Britten's new opera *Gloriana* based on the love story of Elizabeth I and Essex.

Sir William Walton composed a new Coronation March 'Orb and Sceptre' and the Arts Council commissioned ten composers and poets to write a collection of songs entitled a *Garland for the Queen*. The Coronation proved to be a tremendous stimulus to every form of creative activity, in every field of craftsmanship and the arts.

It was not only London which was experiencing this great surge of popular enthusiasm and rejoicing. The big cities and the little towns and villages were suddenly gay with decorations – people were out in the streets in the evening, they were getting together to organise every sort of festivity. The communal spirit of the war years was abroad everywhere again.

The newspapers and commentators were seeking to give the popular rejoicing a permanent basis. It was, they said, the beginning of a 'New Elizabethan Age'. Greatness and glory would be ours once again. I think that in those days we felt that in some way the dream might become a reality. The aspiration was given a great and sudden impetus on the very morning of the Coronation when it was unexpectedly announced that E. P. Hilary and Sherpa Tensing had planted the Union Jack – with the flags of Nepal and India – on the peak of the mighty Everest. *The Times* declared: 'Seldom since Francis Drake brought the *Golden Hind* into Plymouth Sound has a British explorer offered to his Sovereign such a tribute of glory as Colonel John Hunt and his men are able to lay at the feet of Queen Elizabeth for her Coronation Day.'

How greatly the world has since moved on, I realised when, writing these pages, I looked again at the invitation list for the Government's reception for the Commonwealth and other official guests at the National Gallery on Saturday evening 30 May. It was one of the few I had time to attend. As I walked through the crowds in Trafalgar Square the official guests' cars had been brought to a halt by the cheerful crowds who had the opportunity for a close-up inspection of the occupants.

The National Gallery was an effective venue. The 1,300 guests moved against the background of Constables, Rubens, Monets and other masterpieces of Western art, but the sartorial trappings of the West were far outshone by those of the Eastern and African guests. Jewels like stars glistened in the turbans of Indian rajahs, Malayan sultans wore richly coloured silks with pearl-handled knives in their waistbands, and the robes of the African chiefs ran the spectrum of colours from gold to black. There were the military uniforms of many countries, the dazzling white robes of the Arabian princes and everywhere there were the graceful and colourful dresses of the women.

There were also representatives of countries and territories whose names no longer even appear on the maps. It was a place, as I now know, filled with the glowing colours of a sunset.

On the night of 31 May tens of thousands of people moved into central London – this time to stay. The bright summer weather had gone, it was wet and cold. They camped in the parks, huddled beneath ground sheets and on benches, wherever they could be found. As the dawn broke they moved, still cheerful, to their positions along the route – the police had not allowed anyone to claim a place before the morning of 1 June.

After them thousands more poured in with gathering momentum. By mid-day the crowds had taken up all the best positions in Trafalgar Square through which the procession would pass three times. By 3 p.m. they were six deep along the Mall and every other front line position along the whole route had been taken. The Met. Office had been supplying us with three-hourly forecasts. The outlook for the huge waiting crowds during the night was appalling – heavy continuous rain with hail and thunder and rapidly falling temperatures.

When I trod my difficult way to the control room in Trafalgar Square I passed through the ranks of people huddled on airbeds or stools on the pavements, sheltering under improvised tents of waterproofs and rubber sheeting. They seemed to have lost none of their cheerfulness or their eager anticipation. As the heavy rain came down that night they went through the whole repertoire of British popular songs from 'John Peel' and 'Daisy Daisy' to 'Wonderful London Town'.

Inside the sheltered Abbey a small ceremony marked the end of its months of preparation. The Earl Marshal had been in and out of the Abbey almost every day for months, but on this evening he made a formal entrance through the great West Door. The Dean was waiting to receive him with the keys of the Abbey in his hand. The keys were formally passed to the Earl Marshal who now became responsible for the safety of the Queen in the Abbey, the building and everything within it. Late on Coronation evening he would formally return the keys to the Dean.

The great lights were shining down on the Coronation Theatre and the Sanctuary where the final preparations were being made. The gleaming plate and treasures of the Abbey were being placed on the High Altar and on the richly covered table below the Royal Gallery.

The ancient Chair of King Edward was positioned in front of the High Altar and presently four men came in bending beneath the weight of the Coronation Stone. With great care the Stone was slid into position beneath the seat of the Chair. Chair and Stone were again united and resting in their almost immemorial place.

Another event of that evening was very inconspicuous. The Dean had waited at the Cloister entrance in Dean's Yard until a small closed van arrived with the escort of a single police car. The Crown of St Edward, the Imperial State Crown and the Regalia had come from the vaults of the Goldsmiths' and Silversmiths' Company. A guard of eight Yeomen Warders formed the escort to the Jerusalem Chamber where the crowns and jewelled swords and sceptres were laid on the long table. The Yeomen Warders from the Tower were the traditional custodians of the Crown Jewels, but on this occasion they laid their tall partizans against the wall in the Jerusalem Chamber and strapped pistol holsters over their Tudor uniforms. Fifteen Special Branch men would also spend the night inside the Abbey. Outside the ring of security was tightly closed.

Over the centuries the Crown Jewels had rested in the Jerusalem Chamber on the night before the Coronation. It was a room which had already become historical in the Middle Ages – a fourteenth-century manuscript stated that even then it was there 'as of old time'. It was the room where, as Shakespeare has described, Henry IV, as was so strangely foretold, lay down to die and the young Hal had reached out an impetuous hand to seize the crown.

In that ancient chamber the Crown of St Edward was again awaiting the moment when it would be raised high above the head of another sovereign in the long succession of kings and queens who had come to be consecrated and crowned in the Abbey Church of St Peter.

24   The patient crowds settle down on the pavements along the Route, many for two successive nights.

below
25   Improvised shelter against the rain.

26   A midnight picnic during the long night's waiting.

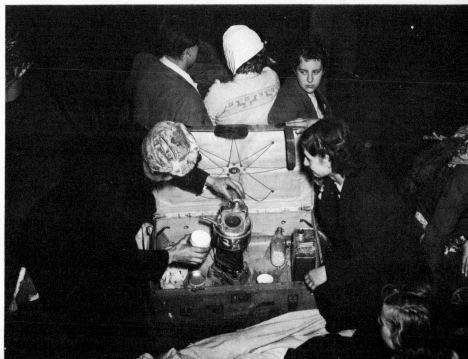

22 The Prelude to the Day

In the grey light of that wind-swept morning my car stopped at the police checkpoint at Lambeth Bridge. The officers inspected the coloured priority passes on the windscreen and waved us on. Before us the dark mass of the Victoria Tower stood out against a grey, cloudy sky. It was a cold, bleak beginning to an historic day.

We were stopped by a second security check below the long and unfamiliar bridge which had overnight spanned the road between St Stephen's Hall and the Abbey – a tangible link between Church and State which would also provide a convenient entry for peers and MPs. In Palace Yard the huge gilded coach of the Speaker was being prepared for its lumbering progress to the peers' entrance. Then the car turned into the strangely transformed precincts of Parliament Square to set us down at the entrance to Dean's Yard.

It would be many hours before I would get further sustenance so my wife and I went straight to the big refreshment tent. There was a very mixed crowd gathered round the coffee urns – Ministry security staff in their blue uniforms who had kept guard through the night on every entrance to the Abbey; Yeomen Warders in their Tudor doublets; uniformed officers of the Corps of Signals who would monitor every yard of the Processional Route and at Z hour give the signal to the guns at the Tower, Hyde Park and Windsor Great Park to fire at the exact moment of the crowning; police inspectors from their weary vigil in Parliament Square and CID officers who had less conspicuous duties in, above and even below the Abbey; a few of my Civil Service colleagues looking very unfamiliar in the knee breeches and silk hose of Court Dress, and a few workmen who were on standby for any structural emergency, including the tailor who was available to repair any sudden defects in the ancient ancestral robes which some people might wear on this occasion.

These were the 'technicians' of the Coronation, representative of the many thousands whose work behind the scenes would contribute so much to the security and success of the day.

There was time to swallow only a hasty cup of coffee before taking leave of my wife, who would later find her way to her seat in the Abbey, before I went out to the car which would take me around the periphery of the route.

I wanted to check the final arrangements at the control room for the BBC and the press stands in Trafalgar Square. They were plainly beyond my reach. The Square was a solid wall of waiting humanity. A tired police inspector, who had coped with all the problems of these vast crowds during the night, told me: 'If it is essential for you to get through, I will have my men open a way for you, but it will shuffle the crowd and people who have been at the front all night will lose their places.' 'No, leave it,' I said, 'I can get a report through the Coronation Exchange.'

As I crossed the road to the Mall, I looked up at the array of White Ensigns and the huge red and gold Royal Arms on the Admiralty Arch. The designer of those ensigns had surely meant them to shine at their best in wind and water!

I entered the Mall, and not even that grey morning could detract from the splendour of that triumphant route to the Palace. The four great but delicate arches holding aloft their golden lions and white unicorns seemed to have gathered a new magnificence by their contrast with the grey skies. Suspended from the arches, almost spanning the roadway, were the golden princess diadems surrounded by floating golden balls which the Minister, David Eccles, had described as 'drops of dew on threads of gossamer'. Now they were indeed splendid 'dewdrops', glistening in the rain. Linking the arches down the route were the long lines of standards, mounted with golden crowns and each hung with four scarlet banners bearing the Royal Monogram. When I looked at this splendid route on this wet and windy morning I was glad to know that all this splendour had been carefully designed by our chief architect, Ronald Bedford, to withstand even the weather stresses of the worst June morning for many years.

Behind all this panoply were the people. The solid ranks of spectators had reached back to the raised platforms which, in turn, could provide for an extra 24,000 standing people in addition to the thousands in the seated stands behind. The long lines of spectators were themselves a colourful complement to the official decorations. Gay raincoats glistened in the rain, and multi-coloured umbrellas blossomed like huge flowers down the long line of the Mall.

I stopped to speak to one of my officers who was stewarding a stand. Nearly every place was already occupied. He had no problems, everyone was wonderfully happy in spite of the weather. The public address system which would relay the Service from the Abbey had been successfully tested. He informed me that the beer in cartons – an innovation to prevent the dangers of broken glass – had been delivered to the refreshment places below and behind the stands. He added, hurriedly, that there was no connection between the arrival of the beer and the happy mood of the people, since it would not be on sale until mid-day.

A police sergeant came over to me – by his helmet badge a member of the provincial forces brought into London to ease the immense strain on the Metropolitan police. They were the days when strange constabularies walked the streets of London; Shropshire police were holding the pavements in Whitehall, Tynemouth held Bridge Street and men from Plymouth were keeping the kerbs around the Palace until the ceremonial troops had moved into their places.

He stamped his tired feet. 'I have never seen crowds like these, they were twelve deep by 3 a.m. and in spite of the weather as happy as sand fleas on Morecambe beach. Not one drunk or troublemaker among them all. Look at those two over there.' He pointed behind the stand where two forms were huddled under a groundsheet. 'There's no need to disturb them, they'll be up before the troops come marching by.'

He touched the Gold Staff which I carried as my visible passport. 'Will you be in the Abbey, sir?' 'Yes.' 'It's a great privilege for you, sir.' 'Indeed, it is.'

'Still, there'll be plenty to see here, too. I am luckier than the rest of the boys on my regular beat. I'll have something to remember for a lifetime,' he said cheerfully.

In a corner of the stand one of the artists commissioned by David Eccles to portray the scenes along the Coronation Route was not so cheerful. His easel was covered in protective brown paper. 'The rain is making the paint run – it will be a genuine water colour. I'm doing sketches; in spite of the weather the colours here are fantastic.'

As I returned to the roadway and walked towards the Palace the rain stopped and a hopeful streak of blue sky appeared between the clouds. The umbrellas began to come down and a faint cheer rippled along the pavements. There were already lights in the Palace windows. The night Royal Standard flew over the Palace and according to custom would not be replaced by the larger day Standard until 6 a.m.

The base of the Victoria Monument was already surrounded by a lively throng of young people representing the youth organisations of Britain – Scouts, Cubs, Guides, Brownies, the Boys Brigade and scores of other organisations. The Memorial, as always on State occasions, was a site eagerly sought for by the BBC, press, film cameramen and photographers. We had constructed a stand over its broad plinth for 250 of the broadcasting and news interests of many countries. As I climbed the stairs to the entrance they looked down over the rim of the stand, a more dismal gathering than any I had seen that day! They were concerned that if the State Coach left the Palace in the rain they would not get 'one of the great pictures of the day' – the Queen leaving for her Coronation. The only reassurance I could really give them was that the coach windows had been treated to shed raindrops. The BBC engineers were in a more cheerful mood; they had repeatedly checked their sound and vision links and were satisfied that their big cameras with their new 40-inch telephoto lens would still give them high-quality pictures.

The principal TV commentator at this point was Chester Wilmot. This veteran war correspondent was coolly poised for an occasion which many of his other BBC colleagues regarded as a great ordeal. The Ministry Press Officer at this stand, C. C. Dodds, had had some moments of trial. Not the least of these were the problems of detecting and removing the interlopers swarming up from the youth organisations below.

It was time to return to the Abbey. I walked to where the car had come round to wait for me. A few minutes later we were driving into the great quadrilateral of stands which had taken over Parliament Square.

The whole of this area around the front of the Abbey had been laid out to represent the realms and territories of which the Queen was Head, and the stands had been reserved for the thousands of people from the Commonwealth and Colonies. Facing the Abbey, the blue undersides of the stands' roofs sloped upwards to reveal the bright colours of the Arms of the Commonwealth countries. Below the stands were massed hundreds of red rhododendrons in full bloom, and on higher ledges above were some of the flowers which had been flown in as floral tributes from many lands. I wondered how, on this intemperate day, the lotus and temple flowers from Ceylon and the 200 exotic orchids from Singapore were surviving the ordeal of our climate.

The State Coach conveying Her Majesty the Queen & HRH The Duke of Edinburgh

The State procession of the Queen (9)

27   Paintings of the Coronation scenes were commissioned by the Ministry; sketch by Feliks Topolski of the State Coach passing by.

As I left my car before the entrance to Dean's Yard again, I paused to look up at the strange heraldic figures of the Queen's Beasts guarding the Annexe with, as David Eccles had said 'expressions of ferocious loyalty on their aristocratic faces'.

Only four months previously I had seen these fantastic figures taking shape, with their creator, James Woodford, clambering around the huge mounds of embryonic clay from which the final casts were made. Now they seemed as solid as the Abbey itself, staring down at me from the distant annals of British history – a truly appropriate prelude to a ceremony which, too, had its origins in distant and immemorial times.

I passed through the rigid security checks, deposited my damp overcoat and stepped into another world.

23 The Queen is Crowned

This was indeed another world in which the dry pages of history had suddenly blazoned into a splendid and tangible life. The Vestibule of the Abbey was already filling with the personalities who would form the Royal Procession. The spacious room was radiant with light and glowing with colours. Opposite the West Door was the huge wall of frosted glass, engraved with emblems, which seemed to hold a light which was not present in the day outside. The same rich texture of light was held in the gold and ivory fabrics which draped the walls. In the ceiling the golden stars seemed to shed their own glittering points of light over the scene below.

It was an incomparable setting for the brilliant colours of the robes and uniforms of those who had already gathered there. Beside the Regalia Table were the scarlet Tudor figures of the Yeomen of the Guard. Their black velvet hats were overtopped by the shining gilt helmets and white swan feather plumes of three Gentlemen at Arms who were looking at the magnificent gold tissue frontals of the Table, which still awaited the priceless burden of the Regalia.

The Officers of Arms were moving on their final arrangements. In their scarlet, blue and gold tabards embroidered with the Royal Arms – velvet for Kings of Arms, satin for Heralds, brocade for Pursuivants – they were proceeding with a ritual which their predecessors had performed through the centuries. Beneath their tabards they were wearing the white breeches and white silk stockings of their Coronation dress instead of the black undergarments of other state occasions.

The focal point of these comings and goings was the figure in the dark overcoat, with the collar slightly upturned and his hands deep in his coat pockets. It was the Earl Marshal himself, the master of this splendid gathering, standing in an attitude of almost detached informality. Later in the day I would see him magnificently transformed in his scarlet coat richly embroidered in gold, with white knee breeches and stockings beneath the grandeur of the Robe of State.

The room was busily filling with all the colours of the Orders of Chivalry – scarlet, blue, green and pearl grey. A Knight of the Garter who would help to hold the canopy was moving majestically in his blue mantle with the Badge of the Garter gleaming, and the blue and gold Garter below his knee. In one corner was a companionable gathering of young pages in their long waistcoats, white breeches and lace cravats, their coats ranging through all the colours of the liveries of the peers whose coronets they would carry – blue, white, yellow, maroon and brown, but not scarlet – a colour reserved on this day for the Royal Pages alone. One page was breathing heavily on his peer's coronet and thoughtfully polishing it on his sleeve. There was also a sprinkling of chaplains in scarlet cassocks, black silk scarves and scarlet mantles.

It was a scene which only a few hundred privileged people would see, and I turned away reluctantly to get on with my duties. The BBC control room at the East End of the Abbey was a crowded mass of the most advanced and complex equipment ever assembled for a single broadcast. The engineers had been testing their circuits, hour after hour, testing to the 'fall back' circuits and the emergency radio transmitter link between the roof of the Abbey and Broadcasting House. The only anxiety was that the wind was creating a resonance like thunder on the 'effects' microphones outside the Abbey. I did not tell them that the Met. Office had forecast genuine thunder at times.

I climbed the steep stairways to the Triforium, or upper gallery, of the Abbey. At the East End, over the High Altar and looking directly down on the Theatre, was the structure we had built for the two vital TV cameras, and commentary positions for the BBC, the French radio and the French Canadian broadcasting service. It had been a tight squeeze to fit the men and the equipment into that limited space, and it was the tightest squeeze of all for the somewhat portly Richard Dimbleby. He was already in his 'box' conning over a thick bundle of notes.

Richard Dimbleby had prepared for this day with the thoroughness of a man facing his greatest ordeal. At the Ministry we had taken him through every detail of the previous Coronation arrangements in this century; the Earl Marshal and the Archbishop of Canterbury had unsparingly given him of their time and knowledge. He had been present at all the main rehearsals. He carried a heavy responsibility. He had to guide the millions of viewers through a highly complex and solemn ceremony without creating any sense of intrusion; he had to follow the timing so perfectly that his voice would never for a second overlap the voice of the Archbishop or even the Queen herself. All this he did perform with perfect dignity and timing.

He looked up from his notes and saw me. I asked him if all was well. He replied, 'I don't think there are any technical problems. The cameramen are happy, but I will only be content when this day is over and I know that everything has gone as it should.'

A police launch had collected him from his yacht, the *Vadel*, lying near Westminster Pier and he had been at his position since 5.30 a.m. John Snagge and Howard Marshall, the commentators for sound radio, were also in their positions conning over their 'red books' of the Coronation Service.

When I came down to my final position north-east of the Sanctuary I found a group of men close to despair. An enclosed sound-proofed position had been built here behind the Sanctuary tombs for the colour and black and white film cameras as well as one TV camera. This could, therefore, give perfect coverage points for nearly the whole of the ceremony. Small glass panes were let into the walls opposite each camera position, and during the night the dust from the ancient stones had filtered down to obscure the glass. There was no prospect of filming through that thick veil. The colour films, which during the past months had caused so many problems, would not be seen by the millions throughout the world who were intended to see them.

Below the camera positions were seated three rows of bishops, and their lordships were already in their places. I borrowed the beautiful white silk handkerchief I saw peeping from the pocket of my assistant Gold Staff Officer, Flying Officer the Hon. Luke White, and went down the stairs and round the north-east pillar to confront the serried ranks of bishops in their Convocation robes. As I explained the problem, the astonishment in their faces changed to amusement. The handkerchief was passed back and one by one the back row of bishops rose in their places to clean the panes of glass above them. Their lordships did a splendid job of window cleaning! I put this incident on record since, without their ecclesiastical assistance, much that was hidden would not have been made plain. Certainly without their co-operation the magnificent films, like that produced by Castleton Knight of Rank–Gaumont, would never have been seen by the world. Thank you, my lords!

In the meantime Luke White had been checking the positions of the police cadets under our control. The police cadets provided an important service within and around the Abbey during the day. He told me they were all in position. I picked up my telephone and reported to Sir James Gault in Warrior's Chapel that I had completed my first tour of duty and all seemed well. 'Let us hope it stays that way,' he replied, and added the warning, 'The Abbey doors will close in twenty minutes.'

For the first time during that long morning I could turn and look into the Abbey itself. It was a place transformed. During the past weeks of the final preparations I had grown used to the high tiers of gold- or blue-covered seats rising high up the ancient walls. Now nearly every place below the Theatre was taken and the glowing waves of colours flowed between and into the North and South Transepts. In the South Transept, behind the three vacant chairs of the Royal Dukes, the peers not taking part in the ceremony or walking in the processions were massed in their Coronation robes of crimson velvet with capes of miniver. The seating went by precedence – the Dukes occupying the front row with their white shoulder capes crossed by four rows of black ermine bars; behind were the Marquesses entitled to three and a half rows of ermine bars and so through the rows of Earls and Viscounts until the final row of Barons with a mere two rows of bars. In their splendours of this single day the Peers of the Realm alone had come by Royal Summons. Among them were many peers whose ancestors in their successive generations had come to the crowning of a sovereign in this same Abbey. There were, indeed, also the descendants of some who had plucked the crown from more than one king's head.

Behind them in the South Transept, and much more remote, were the far less colourful ranks of the commons – pushed back as it were into the ancient position from which they had through the centuries struggled forward to their present front position of power. But not, so it seemed, for today.

Opposite the peers, in the North Transept, across the golden carpet of the Theatre were the ranks of peeresses, their capes a snowfield of white ermine above the red velvet of their robes; long white gloves above the elbow and the bright sparkling of diamonds on their throats and in their hair. For peeresses below the rank of Countess, Norman Hartnell had designed the option of a new Coronation Robe, still with the traditional red velvet and ermine but which, in the modern mode, opened elegantly to reveal the fine

Brussels lace, embroidered silks and satins of their dresses. At the moment of the crowning, instead of coronets these peeresses would put on a crimson Cape of State. This was probably the first major change in the peeresses' Coronation robes for 250 years.

I began checking the names of the peeresses against my seating list; and it seemed like a roll-call of the names in British history – the Duchesses of Argyll, Buccleuch, Beaufort, Grafton, Marlborough, Northumberland, the Marchionesses of Anglesey, Abergavenny, Cambridge, Lansdowne, Queensbury – the names along the rows were printed in the pages of history.

Above me on the right were the Judges of the Realm, crimson-robed and wearing full-bottomed wigs. There was a grave solemnity about this gathering of the majesty of the law. They looked the most formidable array of men present on this occasion.

Over the South Transept on its west side there was a compact gathering of Admirals, Generals, Privy Councillors and members of the Coronation Committee – the glitter of epaulettes, the blue and scarlet of full dress uniforms contrasting with the black damask of the Privy Councillors. The seats in the Choir still awaited their occupants.

My eyes returned to the empty Theatre before me. The bright radiance of the fifty great lights far overhead in the dark roof fell on the golden carpet and the scarlet damask covering of the Throne on its five steps. The Theatre seemed to be filled with the golden radiance of a summer day. Nearer to the Altar, raised on its golden lions and holding the Stone of Destiny, was King Edward's Chair.

Beyond the Chair and below the Royal Gallery, draped with golden tissue bearing the Royal Arms, the golden plate of the Abbey blazed on its table. To the left was the scarlet Chair of Estate and the Faldstool, and rising above it all was the High Altar with the splendid embroidered frontal which every sovereign presents to the Abbey on their coronation.

Then the first chord of ceremony was struck. The deep restrained notes of the Abbey organ began softly to play the strains of Purcell, appropriately for he was once organist here and himself responsible for a coronation ceremony. There was a quiet air of expectancy, a stiffening of attention, the day was about to begin. I looked up at the top of the Choir screen and saw the golden uniforms of the State Trumpeters; the 400 choristers were filing to their positions behind the organ on either side of the nave. The coming hours would be filled with melodious and triumphant sound.

The white light on my control telephone came on and I lifted the receiver. It was a doctor at the Medical Centre in the Precinct to tell me they had been treating an elderly and distinguished journalist who now wanted to get to his place. 'How ill was he?'

'He's feeling much better. I think it was just a matter of last night celebrating the occasion too much and too soon.'

'Can he climb the steep steps to the Triforium?'

'I think he's determined enough. He'll do it on his hands and knees if necessary – and survive to write the tale.'

I sent a Gold Staff Officer to help my old acquaintance on his way.

The police cadet at no. 9 entrance was having difficulty in convincing a staff officer that he had every right to be there. Someone hurrying belatedly to his place had dropped an overcoat at the bottom of the stairs. Mr Sizer, the Ministry Engineer, controlling the big complex system of loud speaker reproduction inside the Abbey and the relays to the official stands wanted me to check the quality of sound at my position.

A few moments later came the biggest shock of the day. The BBC control room had reported that there had been a complete failure of sound at the television switching centre of Broadcasting House. A power link had failed.

It was a moment of black dismay. I thought of all our months of arduous planning with de Lotbiniere and his staff, the scores of points we had arranged for cameras in almost impossible situations, the tremendous massing of technical resources, and the millions of ordinary people waiting by their television sets, and poor Richard Dimbleby, up in his eyrie, after all his travail, suddenly stricken dumb.

There was nothing I could do to help the agonised engineers at Broadcasting House, but I had a duty to perform. It had been arranged that Jean Metcalfe at Buckingham Palace would include in her commentary the key phrase 'the coach moves' as a pre-arranged signal to the procession marshals in the event of a failure in their own communications. I had a sudden picture of the State Coach with its escort of Household Cavalry starting down the Mall with five companies of Foot-guards failing to close up in time. Through the Coronation exchange I spoke to the Signals Officer in the Abbey. He had already heard the news. 'Bad luck for the BBC but we've got our own circuit open to the signal unit on the Victoria Memorial. I think we're safe,' he said. He paused and added quickly, 'Hold on.' He came back to tell me that the BBC engineers had found the faulty lead and that Sylvia Peters was ready to appear on the screen audibly to announce the Coronation broadcast 'on this greatest day of television history'.

I put down the telephone with a feeling of immense relief. The BBC had almost failed to make the beginning of its 'greatest day'.

When I was able to look out into the Abbey again the members of the Royal Family not in the Queen's Procession had taken their places in the Royal Gallery, and the Procession of the Royal and other Representatives of Foreign States was being led into its place in the Choir by Bluemantle and Rouge Croix Pursuivants. First came the phalanx of princes – the Crown Prince of Norway, Prince George of Greece, Prince Axel of Denmark and Prince Albert of Liège; walking behind them was the sturdy figure of the American General Marshall and alongside him in the best republican tradition, Georges Bidault of France in black evening dress; and here, too, crossing the frontiers of the Cold War was Yakob Alexandrovitch Malik of the Soviet Union. It was a long procession of the representatives of seventy states, wearing every kind of ceremonial dress and glittering decoration – from the cool white sweeping garments of the Emirs of Saudi Arabia and Iraq to the florid splendour of His Royal Highness Prince Chula Chakrabongse of Thailand. They were quickly seated in their places on both sides of the Choir, where the Speaker of the House of Commons with his Mace – here covered with a green cloth – before him and the Cabinet members were already in their places.

The roll of the processional music was swelling to herald the arrival of the Rulers of States under the Queen's Protection – a small brilliant procession led by Rouge Dragon and Portcullis Pursuivants – the Sultans of Perak, Lahej, Brunei, Kelantan, Selangor and

28   The Peers arrive at the Abbey in the rain.

Zanzibar, rich, so it seemed, with all the jewels of the Orient. Behind these potentates, walking alone, was the tall figure of Queen Salote of Tonga, with red egret feathers in her hair. Later that day she was to capture all hearts by her cheerful endurance in the pouring rain.

Now all attention turned to the Sanctuary where the Dean and Prebendaries had arrived from the Jerusalem Chamber with the Regalia. They began their slow movement down the Choir and Nave as the choir began the Tallis five-part litany. A sacred part of the ceremony had begun.

As the clergy reached the Vestibule and the last response of the litany died away the processional music mounted again as the Pursuivants led in the Procession of the Princes and Princesses of the Blood Royal – the Princess Royal, the Duchesses of Gloucester and Kent with their sons and Princess Alexandra.

Through the arch of the Choir Screen I could see a ripple of movement as the people in the Nave rose to receive the Procession of the Queen Mother. The brilliant tabards of the Somerset and Windsor Heralds were followed by the young Princess Margaret. Then the stately pacing of four Heralds – Richmond, York, Chester and Lancaster – preceded the Queen Mother, coming to the crowning of her daughter in the place where she had been crowned sixteen years before. For nearly everyone there it was a poignant moment full of recollections of the dark war years and many burdens so graciously borne. She was wearing the Blue Riband of the Garter over a white satin gown embroidered in gold and silver. As she passed men bowed and women curtsied, the ranks of the peeresses seemed to sink in a graceful and co-ordinated movement. She passed slowly to the steps of the Royal Gallery, paused for her Mistress of the Robes to gather up her long train and glanced for a moment at the empty scarlet Throne.

A few moments later I was told that the State Coach had left the Palace at 10.26. I knew that in the Vestibule the Lord Great Chamberlain was ready to deliver the Regalia to their bearers, and that the others taking part in the procession would be standing in their carefully chosen and rehearsed positions.

The Queen's Company Colour was already posted at the entrance to the Choir and through the arch I could see the Abbey Beadle, who would lead the procession, standing in his place. The feeling of expectancy was increased by the swiftly gathering tempo of organ and orchestra.

Not even the swelling tide of music or the thick Abbey walls could blot out the sound from without which was coming with gathering force, like rolling waves, towards us – the deep pulsing sound of thousands of people cheering. The Queen had arrived at the Abbey.

At precisely 11.09 the Beadle, Mr G. F. Calvert, took the first step forward and the procession began to move down the Nave and under the high arch of the Choir Screen. The Canons of the Abbey in their scarlet cassocks and red mantles struck the first notes of brilliant colour against the dark carved oak of the Choir stalls, preceding the Dean of Westminster in the red velvet cope worn at the coronation of Charles II; the Cross of Westminster was borne high as though to insist that all the secular splendour to follow was still part of a ceremony which could only be consecrated by the Church itself.

29 and 30 (overleaf)   The Queen arrives at the Abbey.
The State Coach comes to a stop before the Royal Entrance.

30   The Queen pauses at the entrance while Maids of Honour gather up her long train. The
Duke of Edinburgh keeps a watch on the proceedings.

A long vibrating roll of drums informed us that the officers leading the Orders of Chivalry were passing from the Vestibule into the Abbey – a sound which paled into insignificance compared with the trumpets which heralded the Queen's arrival at the West Door. The sudden silver stridency of the trumpets clamoured through the Abbey, peal rising above peal until the ears could hardly contain the sound.

As the last echoes died away, the choir began the first phrases of Parry's setting of the anthem 'I was glad when they said unto me, we will go into the House of the Lord', which had now been sung at this moment at four coronations.

The six Pursuivants carrying their batons, walking three abreast, were passing into the Choir and behind them flowed a procession whose form in general is at least as old as the coronation of Richard I in 1189. Here now came the Orders of Knighthood – the rose-pink satin mantle lined with pearl grey silk of the Order of the British Empire, the dark blue silk edged with red satin of the Royal Victorian Order, the crimson satin of the Bath and the first blue mantle of the Garter.

The Barons of the Cinque Ports in their scarlet cloaks were waiting at the entrance to the Choir to receive the Standards with the emblems of the Commonwealth, carried by their High Commissioners. There was a moment when the long procession might have faltered, but the firm hands of the Cinque Ports prevented any hitch.

The Standards of the quarterings of the Royal Arms were passing into the Choir and behind came the Royal Standard borne by Viscount Montgomery of Alamein in Garter mantle over his Field Marshal's uniform. How totally different from the once familiar beret and battledress!

Here now came the first of the Regalia on their scarlet cushions – the Ring, the Armills, the Sword for the Offering, carried for the Keeper of the Jewel House by Lord Hardinge of Penshurst and preceded by two Pursuivants came the Knights of the Garter who were to hold the canopy for the Anointing.

The seven Prime Ministers of the Commonwealth were walking two abreast – some of them made familiar to us by war or civil conflict – Dudley Senanayake of Ceylon, Mohammed Ali of Pakistan, Jawaharlal Nehru of India, Daniel Malan of South Africa, Sidney Holland of New Zealand, Robert Menzies of Australia and Louis St Laurent of Canada. And here, in solitary state, the cynosure of all eyes was the Prime Minister, Sir Winston Churchill, wearing his new Mantle of the Garter over the uniform of Lord Warden of the Cinque Ports. As he glanced from side to side it was evident that he was savouring this splendid moment with the deep appreciation of a man who had lived, as well as written, history.

The Cross of York preceded its Archbishop, who was followed by the Lord High Chancellor in his immense full-bottomed wig and robe of black damask trimmed with gold. Behind him came his Purse Bearer with the tasselled Purse which contains – now only theoretically – the matrices of the Great Seal of England. Then the High Cross of Canterbury and the Archbishop, the Most Reverend Geoffrey Fisher, with his attendant chaplains. On him lay the full weight of today's ecclesiastical ceremony.

The Heralds and the Lyon King of Arms filed through the entrance and the Duke of Edinburgh came into sight, wearing an Admiral's uniform below his Garter mantle. On each side of him were four Gentlemen at Arms, overtopping him with their high white plumes and ceremonial axes. His position in front of the Regalia had been decided by the precedent of the Queen's Consort, Prince George of Denmark, at the coronation of Queen Anne in 1702.

Here were coming some of the glittering splendours of the Regalia, St Edward's Staff, the Sceptre with the Cross, the Golden Spurs, the Third Sword, Curtana and the Second Sword; the Kings of Arms carrying their crowns, the Lord Mayor of London in his crimson robe crossed with gold, carrying the Crystal Sceptre of the City which is borne only at a coronation.

Now the Earl Marshal, marvellously transformed from the sober-suited figure of the past months, walking beside the Great Sword of State which the Marquess of Salisbury was holding in both hands before him. Between the Rod with the Dove and the Orb, the Lord High Steward was carrying St Edward's Crown.

Then, again to remind us that this was in its final essence a sacred hallowing, came three bishops carrying the Paten, the Bible and the Chalice.

With almost unbelievably perfect timing the voices of the choir suddenly subsided, the Queen appeared at the Choir entrance, and the clear voices of the Westminster school-boys rang out triumphantly into the silence. 'Vivat Regina! Vivat Regina Elizabetha! Vivat! Vivat!' Sound and vision were joined in a moment of compelling impact.

It was a moment, like others that day, which it is difficult to describe without falling into the facile phrases of adulation. It is necessary to recall the atmosphere of rising emotion in the Abbey among people for many of whom this was 'the greatest day of their lives', and the almost hypnotic concentration with which they had been following the splendour of the procession. Garter King of Arms in simple words and capital letters had set down the appearance of Her Majesty at that moment. It read: 'The QUEEN in Her Royal Robes of Crimson Velvet, hemmed with ermine and bordered with gold lace; wearing the Collar of the Garter; on her head a Diadem of Precious Stones.'

The words convey her splendour but leave out so much – a slender and lovely young woman in a magnificent gown covered in thousands of seed pearls set in silver. Her white satin bodice and skirt created a radiance which outshone all the magnificence which had gone before. It was only as she continued to move forward that one began to notice the moving hem of her gown which was embroidered with the oak leaves of England, the maple leaf of Canada and the other Commonwealth emblems set with precious stones around the Tudor rose. Her long 20-foot train was supported by the six silver-gowned Maids of Honour. Young, regal and magnificent, the Queen had come to her crowning.

The Lords of Parliament carrying the Regalia were now reaching the Theatre, each one to be greeted by the combined thunder of orchestra, organ and all available trumpets. The Abbey was echoing with waves of sound of almost barbaric intensity.

Twelve minutes after entering the West Door, the Queen arrived at the Theatre, passed the waiting Throne and faced the Altar. The Archbishop of Canterbury bowed to her. Then she went to her Chair of Estate below the Royal Gallery and knelt at her Faldstool in private prayer.

During this interval the pieces of the Regalia were handed one by one to the Archbishop who passed them to the Dean of Westminster to lay on the Altar. These symbols of temporal power had passed symbolically into the keeping of the Church.

The Archbishop of Canterbury, thus given the authority of Church and State, mitred and carrying his Cross, came slowly down from the Altar and moved to the East side of the Theatre. The four Great Officers of State came to stand with him. At the same time the Queen was moving forward to stand by King Edward's Chair; her Maids of Honour spread her train out behind her, a vivid crimson streak on the golden carpet. It was the ancient moment of Consent and Recognition.

The deep firm voice of the Archbishop rang out into the silence:

'Sirs, I here present unto you Queen Elizabeth, your undoubted Queen, wherefore all you who are come this day to do your homage and service. Are you willing to do the same?'

There was a second of silence, as if the Abbey was gathering its breath, before the great shout of 'God Save Queen Elizabeth' swept down the aisles.

As the echoes died, the trumpets began their long peals of silver sound, and the Queen gently acknowledged the acclamation of her people.

The Archbishop, supported by the Great Officers, moved in turn to the south, west and north sides of the Theatre, the Queen turning to face each quarter, and each time the thunder of voices seemed to grow in volume and the trumpet notes rose still higher in almost savage intensity.

Those few clamorous moments of the Recognition had suddenly changed the whole atmosphere in the Abbey. There had been an act of participation. A rich and splendid spectacle had now become charged with a common emotion which was as intense as it is difficult to describe. Maybe something was stirring in our ancestral memories – Saxon kings lifted with acclamation on their shields; Norman kings despite the hereditary principle insisting on the security of their 'election'; the Tudor Henry VIII making sure of the positive words that he was 'while the rightful and undoubted inheriteur by the laws of God and man' he was none the less at that ceremony to be 'elected, chosen and required by all three estates of this lande to take upon him the said crown and royal dignitie'. It was a moment with a very long and significant history.

The Queen had now returned to her Chair of Estate; on each side of her were the Bishops of Durham and Bath and Wells who have held the privilege, ever since the coronation of Richard Coeur de Lion, of 'supporting' the sovereign on this occasion; on her right were the Officers of State with the Swords, and on her left the shimmering tableau of her Maids of Honour.

The Archbishop had now to seal the compact between the Church, the State and the Sovereign. Standing before the Queen he began to administer the Coronation Oath, saying:

'Madam, is your Majesty willing to take the Oath?'

In a clear purposeful voice, which the hidden microphones carried to every part of the Abbey, the Queen replied.

'I am willing.'

The Archbishop began to administer the Oath, asking her if she would 'solemnly

31   The Queen in the Chair of Estate at beginning of the ceremony. On her left are Officers of Arms, the Lord Mayor of London and the Maids of Honour. The Bishops of Bath and Wells and of Durham are on each side of her Chair. Behind in the Royal Gallery are the Queen Mother, Princess Margaret and other members of the Royal Family.

promise and swear to govern the peoples of the United Kingdom, the Commonwealth and her Possessions and Territories according to their respective laws and customs.'

'I solemnly promise so to do.'

The Archbishop asked, 'Will you to your power cause Law and Justice in Mercy, to be executed in all your judgments.'

'I will.'

The Archbishop now came to the part of the Oath in which the many distant centuries of conflict between Church and Sovereign are still enshrined including the strong abiding influence of the Reformation.

'Will you to the utmost of your power maintain in the United Kingdom the Protestant Reformed Religion established by Law. Will you maintain and preserve inviolably the settlement of the Church of England, and the doctrine, worship, discipline and government thereof, as by law established in England.'

Thus Geoffrey Fisher, speaking in the voice of Cranmer and going on to add the words which still retained a distant echo of the ancient Canon Courts and long-settled ecclesiastical disputes in a far older form of the Service.

'And will you preserve unto the Bishops and Clergy of England, and to the Church there committed to their charge, all rights and privileges, as by law do or shall appertain to them or any of them?'

'All this I promise to do.'

The Queen rose from her Chair and, with the Sword of State going before her, went to kneel at the Altar and with her hand resting on the Bible open at the Gospel of St John, she affirmed again: 'The things which I have here before promised, I will perform and keep. So help me God.' She held the Levantine leather-bound Bible to her lips and signed the engrossed copy of the Oath on its piece of vellum which would later be added to the Coronation Roll deposited in the records of the Court of Chancery.

When the Queen was again seated in her Chair of Estate, there came another innovation at this Coronation ceremony. Since the Anglican Communion Service had not yet begun, it was possible for the Moderator of the General Assembly of the Church of Scotland to take part in the ceremony. In the black austerity of his Geneva gown, amid so much splendour, he went to receive the Bible from the Dean and moved with the Archbishop to stand before the Queen. The Archbishop invited her to accept the Bible, 'as the most valuable thing this world affords'. The deep vibrant Scottish voice of the Moderator proclaimed: 'Here is Wisdom; this is the royal Law; these are the lively Oracles of God.'

During the centuries the coronation has been enclosed in the most sacred service of the Church – first the Mass and later the post-Reformation service of the Holy Communion.

The Archbishop in his magnificent cope was standing before the Altar, while the choir sang the beautiful words of the Introit taken from the Special Mass for the King in the fourteenth-century *Liber Regalis*.

'Behold, O God our Defender: and look upon the face of thine Anointed. For one day in thy courts is better than a thousand.'

The words which the strong voice of the Archbishop next began to say had themselves endured for nearly 1,000 years since they were also used for the coronation service of

King Edgar in 973. He prayed as the Queen knelt with bowed head, in the ancient words that 'thy servant Elizabeth, our Queen . . . may so wisely govern, that in her time thy Church may be in safety, and Christian devotion may continue in peace. . . .'

The Epistle and Gospel which followed were also an ancient part of the Service, with the injunction to 'Fear God. Honour the King,' and to 'Render therefore unto Caesar the things which are Caesar's.' The words had the familiarity of many Sunday mornings, polished so smooth with usage that they usually passed almost imperceptibly past the ear; but in that place they had a significance as though they were being heard for the first time.

There was a brief pause before the great choir and orchestra began Vaughan Williams's composition of the Nicene Creed, every word of that old profession of Christian faith being carried with perfect clarity by the massed voices of the choir.

The approach to the great sacramental moment of the ceremony now began with the Archbishop intoning the opening words of the 'Veni, Creator, Spiritus' – the great hymn which has for centuries been the prelude to the consecration of bishops and kings in Western Europe, 'Come, Holy Ghost, our souls inspire'.

The Archbishop had gone up to the Altar to lay his hands on the Ampulla, which held the oil for the Anointing. He began the ancient prayer invoking the sevenfold gifts of the Holy Spirit:

'O Lord and heavenly Father, the exalter of the humble and the strength of thy
chosen, who by Anointing with Oil didst of old make and consecrate kings, priests
and prophets, to teach and govern thy people Israel: Bless and sanctify thy chosen
servant Elizabeth, who by our office and ministry is now to be anointed with this Oil
and consecrated Queen. . . .'

The prayer ended and the Queen raised her head and rose to her feet as the voices of the choir surged into the fiery splendour of Handel's 'Zadok the Priest' composed for the coronation of George III: 'Zadok the priest and Nathan the prophet anointed Solomon king; and all the people rejoiced and said: God save the king, Long live the king, May the king live for ever. . . .'

After nearly three thousand years the rite of the priest and the prophet of Israel could still make their imprint on a ceremony in a very distant place and time.

'And all the people rejoiced,' insisted the choir, filling the Abbey with jubilant and repetitive sound, 'rejoiced . . . rejoiced, and all the people rejoiced.'

As the great volume of sound was rising to the final cascade of 'Amens', the Queen had moved forward from her Faldstool. The Mistress of the Robes made a small gesture with her hand and the six Maids of Honour bent down to lift the long train of the Royal Robe.

A strange transformation was now about to begin. On her arrival in the Theatre the Orb and the Sceptre, the emblems of regal dignity and authority, had been given into the keeping of the Church. Now even the appearance of temporal splendour had to be put aside. The Queen raised her hands to her jewelled diadem and passed it to the Mistress of the Robes. The Lord Great Chamberlain, as all his predecessors had also done, came forward to assist in removing the Royal Robe; its train was folded back from rank to rank by the Maids of Honour until it was a crimson pile of velvet in the arms of the Groom of the Robes. The Collar of the Garter was taken away and the Queen's beautiful embroidered dress was covered by a severely plain white garment. This was a moment which many people were to recall even more vividly than the act of crowning itself. There, surrounded by so much colour and magnificence, was a slender young girl, her hands clasped before her in an attitude of quiet submission, her hair unadorned, standing alone in her simple white dress.

There was a great flowing of movement around the Theatre as the participants moved to their places for the next act of the service. The jewels in the Sword of State flashed as Lord Salisbury came forward. The Queen turned and moved to her place in the time-worn Chair of King Edward. Against the dark oak of that ancient Chair she looked strangely set apart from the magnificence around her. The Chair was only a few feet from where I was standing and I could see the quiet withdrawn look on the Queen's face.

The white light came on my receiver, and I heard that the young Prince Charles was arriving in the Royal Box. I wrote the information on a pad and passed it to a messenger behind me. In a few moments every cameraman was waiting for the boy who had come to see his mother crowned.

His nurse, Helen Lightbody, brought him into the Royal Box. He was wearing a white shirt and white trousers and his hair had been smoothed down until it shone. He ran along the front of the gallery, his head barely above the balustrade, until he reached the place where the smiling Queen Mother was holding out her hand to him. On the other side his aunt, Princess Margaret, leaned down to greet him. There was a whispered word from his grandmother, then he gripped the top of the balustrade with both hands and gazed in wide-eyed fascination at the scene before him.

In the meantime the Officers of Arms had carried forward a magnificent canopy of cloth of gold supported on four long silver staves, and Garter King of Arms had summoned the four knights of the Order from their places in the South Transept. The Dukes of Wellington and of Portland, Viscount Allendale and Earl Fortescue came forward in their blue velvet mantles to take hold of the staves. The canopy moved over the Chair and the Queen was concealed from view.

The bishops assistant also moved as though to form with their copes their own screen of protection from each side.

The Dean of Westminster came slowly down from the Altar carrying the little eagle-winged Ampulla and the old anointing Spoon. At that moment I gave the signal to stop the film cameras and turn away the TV cameras.

The Dean poured the oil from the beak of the Ampulla, dripping it carefully into the twin bowls of the Spoon. The Archbishop took up the oil on his fingers. Then he turned and went beneath the canopy to the Queen.

We heard the solemn words of consecration:

'Be thy Hands anointed with holy Oil.
    'Be thy Breast anointed with holy Oil.

32 All Splendour Put Aside. The Queen in the Coronation Chair for her anointing. The Knights of the Garter hold the splendid canopy which conceals this sacred moment of the ceremony from general view.

'Be thy Head anointed with holy Oil: as kings, priests and prophets were anointed.

'And as Solomon was anointed king by Zadok the priest and Nathan the prophet, so be thou anointed, blessed and consecrated Queen over the Peoples, whom the Lord thy God hath given thee to rule and govern. . . .'

The Archbishop stood back as the canopy was moved away, and the Queen knelt at the Faldstool placed in front of the Chair. As the Archbishop raised his hand to bless the newly consecrated Queen I knew that he must have felt that the most sacred act of 'this great solemnity' had now been completed. There was a deep fervour in his voice as he uttered the words with which St Dunstan had invoked the blessing on the anointed Edgar, the first King of All England, and the distant ancestor of the woman before him:

'by his holy Anointing pour down upon your Head and Heart the blessing of the Holy Ghost, and prosper the works of your Hands: that . . . you may govern and preserve the Peoples committed to your charge in wealth, peace and godliness. . . .'

When the Queen had returned again to the Chair there was another pattern of movement in the Theatre as the clergy and peers took up their positions for the Investiture.

The time for humility was over. The Queen had received the recognition of her people, she had taken the Oath, she had been consecrated. She could now receive the emblems of her regal authority and put on the robes which only the anointed sovereign may lawfully wear.

The Queen stood up to receive the first vestment of royalty. The Dean of Westminster was holding the white linen garment, the Colobium Sindonis, and helped by the Mistress of the Robes, he placed over the Queen's shoulders the 'muslin undergarment' such as had once been worn at their coronations by the Emperors of Byzantium. The glory of Byzantium was recaptured again in the garment of shining gold with wide flowing sleeves which the Queen next raised her arms to receive. The Supertunica was fastened at the waist by a golden girdle. When the Queen moved back to the Chair, all simplicity had been put aside; she was a figure of burnished and majestic gold.

The Golden Spurs were brought to her. She touched them with her hands in token acceptance and sent them back to the Altar.

The ordeal of the Marquess of Salisbury, the bearer of the Great Sword of State, was nearly over. This heavy sword is carried upright in the presence of the Sovereign on great ceremonial occasions like the State Opening of Parliament and the Coronation. Lord Salisbury had been holding this large sword, weighing over 8 lb and 4 feet high, steadfastly upright with a two-handed grasp on the hilt since the moment before the Queen arrived at the Abbey. It was a heavy burden for an elderly peer.

He now delivered the sword to the Lord Chamberlain of the Household. I saw him rubbing his cramped fingers before the Sword for the Offering was placed in his hands. This beautiful sword, weighing less than 3 lb, would have been attached to the girdle of a king but is not so worn by a Queen Regnant.

Lord Salisbury carried this slender sword to the Archbishop while a profusion of lights seemed to run along the diamonds, rubies, sapphires and emeralds on the scabbard.

The Archbishop laid it upon the Altar, praying in words adapted from the *Liber Regalis* that the Queen might use it 'as the Minister of God for the terror and punishment of evildoers, and for the protection and encouragement of those that do well. . .'.

The Archbishop came down again from the Altar carrying the sword, paused while the Archbishop of York and the Bishops of London and Winchester gathered around him before they moved together to the Queen. The sword was placed upright in her hands, with the admonition which the Church had often spoken to Kings when entrusting them with the power of the sword:

'With this Sword do justice, stop the growth of iniquity, protect the Holy Church of God, help and defend widows and orphans, restore the things that are gone to decay, maintain the things that are restored, punish and reform what is amiss, and confirm what is in good order. . . .'

There now came another of those moments when the golden dreamlike tenor of the ceremony leaped into a sudden personal vividness. The Queen had risen from her seat and was walking towards the Altar with the Jewelled Sword lying upon the palms of her outstretched hands. As she passed I heard the dry whisper of her heavy golden robe. Her eyes were turned down to the scabbard giving her face a look of intense concentration. Her bare head was in strange contrast with the regal glory of her golden robe.

The Sword for the Offering was laid on the Altar and while the Queen returned to King Edward's Chair, the Marquess of Salisbury approached the Archbishop carrying an embroidered bag closely tied at its neck. It contained one hundred shillings, the immemorial price for the 'redemption' of the sword. In return Lord Salisbury received the sword again from the Dean and drew it from its scabbard. In the words of the rubric he would 'carry it naked before her Majesty during the rest of the solemnity'. He moved to his position on the right of the Queen. Another ancient ritual had been completed.

The 'hundred shillings' freshly minted would be among the lifelong treasures of the clergy and officers of Westminster Abbey.

The Dean came carrying the Armills, restored after much liturgical confusion, for the first time since the coronation of the first Elizabeth. The golden Bracelets, the gift of the Commonwealth, were gently closed on the Queen's wrists as the 'symbols of sincerity and wisdom' and 'pledges of that bond which unites you with your Peoples'.

The Groom of the Robes, coming from St Edward's Chapel behind the Altar, handed to the Dean the long and heavily embroidered length of the Stole Royal. It was placed around the Queen's neck and gently tied to her arms above the elbow.

The Dean now took the Pallium, or the Robe Royal, and held it before him by where the shoulders would be. In the North Transept a peeress gave a swift stifled gasp. The lapse was understandable. Among all the resplendent colours of robes, mantles, copes, vestments and tabards there had been nothing to equal the shining glory of this beautiful garment. It was a mantle of pure cloth of gold, embroidered with Tudor roses, thistles, leeks and shamrocks and showing clearly the golden shapes of the imperial eagles.

The Archbishop spoke now to the resplendent Queen:

'Receive this Imperial Robe, and the Lord your God endue you with knowledge and wisdom, with majesty and with power from on high: the Lord clothe you with the robe of righteousness, and with the garments of salvation.'

One by one the jewelled pieces of the Regalia were brought down from the Altar. 'Receive this Orb set under the Cross,' said the Archbishop placing the golden globe in her right hand, 'and remember that the whole world is subject to the Power and Empire of Christ our Redeemer.'

The Ring, set with a sapphire with a ruby cross, was placed upon the fourth finger of the Queen's right hand. 'Receive the Ring of kingly dignity, and the seal of Catholic Faith.'

Lord Woolton, summoned by the Somerset Herald, came to discharge the former office in serjeanty of the Manor of Worksop, kneeling to present a Glove for the Queen's right hand. It was an act of ancient significance symbolising the abolition of Danegeld, reminding the kings thereafter to have a gentle hand in taxation. Lord Woolton had been ill and there had been some anxiety when he had performed his part at the rehearsal in May. Now the little ceremony of feudal tenure was faultlessly performed by one of the very latest in the ranks of the peerage.

Those almost universal symbols of royal authority, the Sceptres, were brought down from the Altar. The two Sceptres were always given at the same time as a sign that justice and mercy should always go together, as the words of the Archbishop now made plain. 'Receive the Royal Sceptre, the ensign of kingly power and justice.'

The huge Star of Africa, the most perfect diamond in the world, flashed its brilliant fires as the Queen held the Sceptre upright in her right hand.

The Sceptre with the Dove was placed in the Queen's left hand. 'Receive the Rod of Equity and Mercy,' the Archbishop said to his Sovereign. 'So execute justice that you forget not mercy.' As the Rod passed to the Queen the light gleamed on the white enamel of the dove with outstretched wings, the badge of Edward the Confessor.

The Investiture with the Regalia was now complete. The Archbishop stood back from the Chair and there was a long moment when no one spoke or moved. The silence in the Abbey was intense. The Queen was sitting stiffly upright in the old high-backed Chair, a figure of shining gold with the jewelled Sceptres in her hands. At that moment we saw her as no one would ever see her again in her lifetime. She was remote from any familiar conception of royalty – the purple robe and the crown of regal dignity.

The still figure in strange golden vestments seemed to have receded into a time far remote from our own. She was like an image in a hieratic ikon, a page from an old richly illustrated manuscript, or a golden statue from the distant past.

There were very few in the Abbey who could see the Queen at this moment of her transformation. The high back of King Edward's Chair cut off the view from the congregation behind. Even the Duke of Edinburgh, leaning forward from his seat with the two Royal Dukes of Gloucester and Kent, could not have seen his wife at that stage. Yet twenty million viewers outside the Abbey had been able to follow the Investiture with a detail which was denied even to all the peers of ancient lineage in the South Transept.

33   The Investiture with the Regalia. The Archbishop places the Orb in the Queen's hand.

34 After the Queen was invested with the Sword she carried it back to the Altar to the Dean.
It was 'redeemed' for one hundred shillings by the Marquess of Salisbury.

X   The Abbey Altar on Coronation morning, with the magnificent Abbey treasures.

XI   The State Coach passes
Admiralty Arch on the way to the
Abbey.

XII   The Chair of Estate, now in
Buckingham Palace.

That brief pause of hushed attention was ended by the pursuivants. At their signal the pages carrying the coronets of their peers came into the Theatre. Their lively colours of blue, green, white and yellow made a touch of youthful pageantry among the rich golds and scarlets which had dominated the scene. They passed over their coronets, bowed to their Peers and withdrew. There was a sound in the Abbey like the rustling of leaves as the Peers and Peeresses in the transepts took up their coronets in readiness for the act which was now being prepared.

The Archbishop was standing at the Altar; before him lay St Edward's Crown. He raised it in his hands so that the gold and jewelled circle could be plainly seen. As he set it down again his words restored a practice of the medieval centuries, the Blessing of the Crown:

'Bless we beseech thee this Crown, and so sanctify thy servant Elizabeth upon whose head this day thou dost place it for a sign of royal majesty, that she may be filled by thine abundant grace with all princely virtues.'

As the Archbishop came down again from the Altar the other bishops assistant moved beside him so that it seemed that the whole authority and dignity of the Church was around him as he approached the Queen.

Everyone was watching the Dean of Westminster as he placed the Crown on a scarlet cushion and came slowly and very carefully down from the Altar. As he approached the Archbishop I saw the Dean look down to make sure that the two tiny gold stars in the velvet lining which marked the front of the Crown were in the correct position. On this occasion an Archbishop would not have to fumble with the Crown to find the front.

With the Crown between his hands the Archbishop came up to the Chair and stood on its supporting step. He seemed to tower above the Queen, his robes almost enfolding the slender golden figure before him.

We saw the uplifted Crown, the cope falling back from his arms; a second's pause and then the slow descent of the Crown on to the Queen's head. The Queen was looking straight into the Archbishop's face; I saw a momentary tremor of her lips. It was done!

The peers and Kings of Arms were putting on their coronets and heraldic crowns. The Lord Chancellor was fumbling with his coronet on his heavy full-bottomed wig and then a pandemonium of sound filled the Abbey.

The clamant shouts of 'God Save the Queen' mingled with the fierce fanfares of the trumpets. Like distant chords in the tumult was the clamour of the bells in the north-west tower of the Abbey. Also far beyond our hearing in that storm of sound, in accordance with ancient custom 'by signal given, the great guns of the Tower were being shot off'.

As the great tumult in the Abbey faded into an almost reluctant silence, the Archbishop spoke again to the Queen in the form of words which had been used at this moment since 973:

'God crown you with a crown of glory and righteousness, that having a right faith and manifold fruit of good works, you may obtain the crown of an everlasting kingdom by the gift of Him whose kingdom endureth for ever.'

35   The Moment of the
Crowning. The Archbishop
raises St Edward's Crown high
over the Queen's head.

As he finished speaking the choir began the anthem which has endured as part of the ceremony for ten centuries – setting the seal of music on the acclamation with the 'Confortare' of King Edgar's coronation. 'Be strong and of good courage,' came the eloquent injunction, 'keep the commandments of the Lord thy God, and walk in his ways.'

The Archbishop was standing, mitred and with the Cross of Canterbury in his hand, to pronounce the splendid words of the Benediction:

'The Lord give you faithful Parliaments and quiet Realms; sure defence against all enemies; fruitful lands and a prosperous industry; wise counsellors and upright magistrates; leaders of integrity in learning and labour; a devout, learned, and useful clergy; honest, peaceable and dutiful citizens.'

Then he turned to the congregation, praying that all the Peoples of the Commonwealth during this reign may 'continually enjoy peace, plenty and prosperity'.

It was at this point that young Prince Charles, who had been watching the events in the Theatre with obvious spellbound attention, turned impetuously to the Queen Mother. She gently put down his gesturing hands and Princess Margaret leaned down to him with a quietening finger laid to her lips. His wonder and excitement were plain to see. When I looked again some time later he had gone. He must have been a very bewildered and perplexed small boy.

The time had come for the Queen to 'take seisin of her dominion'. The bearers of the swords moved from their positions on the right of the Chair of Estate to form guard behind the Throne, while the lords grouped around King Edward's Chair came also to place themselves around the Throne, so that there was a peer of each degree on each of the steps of the Throne.

The Queen got up from King Edward's Chair and for the first time since the Recognition she turned to face the congregation beyond the Theatre. Beneath the heavy gold crown her face was small, pale and very composed. The ends of the two sceptres touched the shimmering fabric of her Robe as she moved the few paces to the Throne. Very slowly, her head held rigidly still, she mounted the five steps and as she turned the hands of the bishops and peers reached out to 'lift' her into the symbolic possession of her kingdom.

'Stand firm and hold fast from henceforth the seat and state of royal and imperial dignity,' said the Archbishop to the enthroned Queen in words her ancestors had heard as they each came to their crowning.

'And the Lord God Almighty, whose ministers we are, and the stewards of his mysteries, establish your Throne in righteousness, that it may stand fast for evermore.'

A young boy in the white and red livery of the Earl Marshal came into the Theatre carrying a scarlet-covered kneeling stool. He made his obeisance, climbed the steps and placed the stool before the Queen's feet. Then with well-rehearsed precision he retreated backwards to his position at the left of the steps where he would hold a scarlet cushion on which the peers could place their coronets as they went to perform their Homage. Master Duncan Davidson, page to the Earl Marshal, had done his part to perfection.

36   Prince Charles sees his mother crowned.

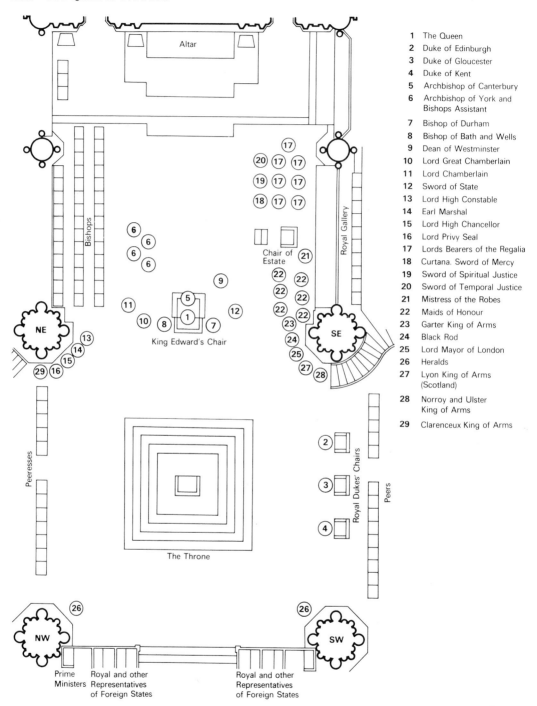

37   The Crowning. Positions in the Theatre, based on one of the many detailed plans prepared by the College of Arms.

Key to diagram:

1   The Queen
2   Duke of Edinburgh
3   Duke of Gloucester
4   Duke of Kent
5   Archbishop of Canterbury
6   Archbishop of York and Bishops Assistant
7   Bishop of Durham
8   Bishop of Bath and Wells
9   Dean of Westminster
10   Lord Great Chamberlain
11   Lord Chamberlain
12   Sword of State
13   Lord High Constable
14   Earl Marshal
15   Lord High Chancellor
16   Lord Privy Seal
17   Lords Bearers of the Regalia
18   Curtana. Sword of Mercy
19   Sword of Spiritual Justice
20   Sword of Temporal Justice
21   Mistress of the Robes
22   Maids of Honour
23   Garter King of Arms
24   Black Rod
25   Lord Mayor of London
26   Heralds
27   Lyon King of Arms (Scotland)
28   Norroy and Ulster King of Arms
29   Clarenceux King of Arms

The Queen now passed the two Sceptres to the lords who had borne them and removed the Glove so that her hands were free for the Homage.

The Homage was an act which came from the very heart of feudal England. The words coldly read, could seem to be without any real meaning to the age in which they would now be repeated and the act itself might seem to have the posture of humility strange to modern eyes. Yet at that moment, encompassed by the intense feeling with which they were surrounded, both the words and the act had a relevance far beyond their time. In that place, the ancient words could still have their significance and meaning for the day on which they were spoken, as though they proclaimed, even after ten centuries, that allegiance and service were still an enduring part of the fabric of any stable society.

The Archbishop of Canterbury, the authority of his ministration now put aside, came first to the Throne to do his fealty as a subject of his Sovereign. He knelt before her as she had previously knelt before him and placed his hands between hers. All the bishops, kneeling in their places, repeated the words after him, substituting only the names of their diocese:

'I Geoffrey, Archbishop of Canterbury, will be faithful and true, and faith and truth will bear unto you, our Sovereign Lady, Queen of this Realm and Defender of the Faith, and unto your heirs and successors according to law. So help me God.'

The Duke of Edinburgh had come from his place in the South Transept. This tall, fair-haired young man paused at the foot of the steps to lift his shoulders as though to relieve the cumbersome weight of his robes. He laid his coronet on the page's cushion and went up to kneel at the feet of his wife and his Queen. Only once before in English history, in 1702 when Prince George of Denmark had done Homage to Queen Anne, had a husband done Homage to his wife.

As the Duke placed his hands between hers, the Queen looked down at his upturned face. There was a faint smile on her lips. It was a strange interlude to be enacted between husband and wife, who were also liegeman and sovereign:

'I Philip, Duke of Edinburgh, do become your liege man of life and limb, and of earthly worship; and faith and truth I will bear unto you, to live and die, against all manner of folks. So help me God.'

He rose to his feet, leaned forward to touch the Crown and as he bent down to kiss the Queen's cheek, the crimson folds of his robes seemed to enfold the slender golden figure on the Throne.

Gloucester, the next of the Royal Dukes, came forward to do his homage followed by the young Duke of Kent, whose hands were trembling as he reached them out towards the Queen. She leaned forward slightly to take his hands firmly and reassuringly between her own.

The man responsible for the smooth and stately progress of the ceremony took off his coronet and climbed the steps to the Throne. The Duke of Norfolk, premier Duke of the Realm, knelt to do his Homage, while over in the South Transept the Dukes on the first row of seats were also kneeling in their places to repeat, after their titles, the words of the

38 The Homage. Clothed in golden Royal Robes the Queen has moved from the Coronation Chair to the Throne where she will receive the Fealty of the Archbishops and Bishops and the Homage of the Peers.

39 The Duke of Edinburgh kisses the Queen's cheek after his Homage.

Homage. He rose to touch the Crown and kissed the Queen's right hand.

After him in their order came the senior in each rank of the peerage – the Marquess of Huntley, the Earl of Shrewsbury, Viscount Arbuthnot and Baron Mowbray, while the peers of the same degree knelt in their places to repeat the words.

The voices of the peers doing Homage were captured above the choral music of Redford, Orlando Gibbons and Healy Willan by the microphone hidden for that purpose beneath the Throne. As Baron Mowbray came slowly backward from the Homage, silence fell briefly on the Abbey. The ceremony of the Coronation was over. The Queen had been crowned as Alfred was crowned, anointed as Edgar had been anointed, had been sworn as the Lion Hearted had once been sworn and had received the Homage in the words and form in which the Lords of the Council had knelt to do their Homage to the first Queen Elizabeth. I think that all of us there who looked towards the young Queen Elizabeth, crowned and golden, felt that something very important, very old and sacred, had again been consummated in that place.

Then the drums began their rapid beating, the trumpets struck their fierce notes from the old walls and a great shout rose again in the Abbey.

'God save Queen Elizabeth.
'Long live Queen Elizabeth.
'May the Queen live for ever.'

As the shouts of acclamation echoed and died away, the Archbishop of Canterbury turned and went back to the Altar. From the orchestra came a swift chord followed by the deep notes of the organ playing the opening bars of the 'Old Hundredth', 'All people that on earth do dwell'.

For the first time at a coronation the people were able to join in the singing of a hymn which was a part of the Service. The response came from full hearts and voices. They were without musical direction so everyone sang through all the verses, overwhelming a trumpet descant in one verse and ignoring the absence of organ support in another, as they wholeheartedly obeyed the injunction to 'sing to the Lord with cheerful voice'.

In the meantime the Queen had descended from the Throne and with the attending bishops and lords came to a stand before the Altar. She handed the Sceptres to the Lord Great Chamberlain and took off her Crown.

The Queen offered the Bread and Wine, which were laid upon the Altar, and she then made the ancient oblation of a newly crowned monarch, offering a Pall, or Altar Cloth, and a 'wedge of gold of a pound's weight'.

The Queen went to her Faldstool, set before the Altar, as a King of Arms came preceding the Duke of Edinburgh. They knelt side by side as the Archbishop made the only reference to the Duke in the ceremony, when he prayed that God might multiply his blessings 'upon this thy servant Philip who with all humble devotion offers himself for thy service in the dignity to which thou hast called him', and blessed him saying, 'Almighty God to whom belongeth all power and dignity, prosper you in your honour and grant you therein long to continue. . . .'

During the prayers and acts of Communion the whole character of the ceremony seemed to have changed from magnificence to a humble and private devotion. In keeping with this feeling the film and TV cameras were once more turned away from the beginning of the Prayer of Consecration until the Queen had again returned to her Throne.

After the Communion she had moved across the Theatre again wearing the Crown and carrying the two Sceptres. She was the only sovereign in modern times who had sustained the heavy Crown of St Edward from the crowning to the end of the ceremony except during the Communion – even her father had exchanged that heavy burden for the much lighter Imperial State Crown at this point of the Service.

The 'Gloria' sung, in the words of the musical direction, 'allegro vivace ma con maesta' was followed by the voice of the Archbishop, as vibrant and strong as at the beginning, saying the familiar words of dismissal.

Then the splendid ceremonial music of the 'Te Deum' composed by William Walton filled the Abbey again with the sounds of trumpets, organ, orchestra and voices.

'O Lord save thy people: and bless thine heritage.
'Govern them: and lift them up for ever.'

The words of a hymn, as old as Western Christendom, heard by King Edgar long ago and repeated here through all the centuries of turmoil and change.

The Queen sat motionless in the high Throne Chair. The two Sceptres were held rigidly in her hands. Her face seemed without expression beneath the heavy Crown of St Edward. There were few in the Abbey who would ever again see a newly enthroned sovereign in the splendour of the Coronation.

Then the Swords began to move from the side of the Throne and with the Archbishop going before her and the supporting bishops on each side the Queen passed from our sight through the door on the south side of the Sanctuary into St Edward's Chapel.

In the Chapel during the Recess, St Edward's Crown and the Regalia would be taken from her, and she would be arrayed in a Robe of Purple Velvet – it was the first time in her reign that she would wear the purple velvet of a crowned and consecrated monarch.

In the meantime the return procession was being assembled in the Theatre between the choir stalls. People were being ushered into their positions by pursuivants and officers. There was a brief time when all the splendid reds, blues, crimson and gold mingled in multi-coloured confusion before the Officers of State, peers, knights of orders, bishops and heralds were marshalled in their places. Winston Churchill, however, remained in a certain splendid isolation between the choir stalls. He stood apart from the other Prime Ministers of the Commonwealth, fingering the splendid George of his Garter Order and surveying this historic scene, of which no doubt he justly felt he was a not insignificant part. He moved into place as the return procession began to retrace the journey back to the West Door and the Vestibule.

As the first chords of the National Anthem resounded deeply from the organ pipes the Queen appeared through the arched doorway from St Edward's Chapel. Here was once more the familiar appearance of royalty. Her face was no longer overburdened by the heavy Crown and she had put aside the rich golden vestments. She was wearing the diamond-encrusted brilliance of the Imperial State Crown. The Sceptre with the Cross

was in her right hand and the Orb in the left. The long train of her purple and gold-trimmed robe was borne by the six Maids of Honour.

The forward processional movement was briefly halted as the Queen was passing her Throne Chair. I saw her glance towards it. Then the procession moved on again and all the splendid colours of copes, robes, mantles and tabards were moving away from the Theatre, passing with the young Queen and the day into our history.

40   The Return Procession. Wearing the Imperial Crown and carrying the Orb and the Sceptre the Queen passing down the Abbey to the West Door.

24   The End of the Day

The Abbey was full of hungry and weary guests, all eager to be gone. The place seemed to hum with impatience. In times past the guests had often either rushed to seize souvenirs from the Theatre or stampeded to the exits in their eagerness to get to the Coronation Banquet in Westminster Hall. There had been fights, torn robes and lost coronets.

Time had brought experience. The 'egress' had been carefully planned and tested at the final rehearsal. As the Queen's Procession moved from Choir to Nave the long silken ropes were being stretched across to control the timing and direction of the ways to the ten exits from the Abbey. As each block was reported clear the next one began to move on the command of the CGSO, Major-General R. G. Fielden, in Samaria. In a little over one hour the Abbey had been cleared of its guests, who left, unfortunately, many tokens of their presence behind them.

At the end of my own duties I reported to Sir James Gault in Warrior's Chapel. There had been few incidents. A prominent Civil Servant had to receive medical attention and one of the elderly peers in the Theatre had just managed to stay the course.

Late that evening the television cameras, still in place, would look again at the silent and deserted Abbey. In two days' time the great church would be opened to the public in its Coronation setting and for the first time in many centuries a Mystery Play would be performed in the Abbey.

As I crossed again to the North Transept the cleaners were already busy. The hours of waiting had not been passed in fasting and contemplation. Sacks were being filled with sandwich wrappings, paper bags and the napkins which had been used to protect the dresses and robes. There were jars which had held the savoury specialities from Fortnums and Harrods. Many of the guests had fortified themselves during the waiting hours – under the chairs the cleaners were finding scores of miniature, quarter and even half-sized bottles of spirits. It seemed that the peeresses had preferred gin or brandy while the peers had a strong predilection for whiskey.

There were a few examples of sheer vandalism. A sharp knife had cut away the Royal Cipher from the back of a peer's chair and a piece of blue cloth had been cut from a Queensway frontal in the nave. These depredations were astonishing but small compared to the damage and looting in times past.

The final vacuum cleaning later in the day would be very carefully done. At every coronation precious stones from coronets, necklaces and other jewellery had fallen unobserved from their settings. Among the finds on this occasion was a diamond necklace of great value which remained unclaimed for six weeks.

In the Annexe the Queen and her husband with other members of the Royal Family had retired to their rooms for a brief respite after the long ceremony, where a picnic-type luncheon of smoked salmon, foie gras, cheese and biscuits would be served. One of my colleagues was full of his account of how the Queen had nearly lost her luncheon – the footmen from the Palace arriving at the Abbey with the food hampers did not have the passes which were the strict condition of entry. The royal servants had remained protesting outside until all the necessary checks had been made.

This talk of luncheon reminded me of my own long period of abstinence and I was about to leave for one of the luncheon points when I heard my name on the loudspeakers calling me to the telephone.

It was the steward on the big press and TV stand at the Queen Victoria Monument. The arrangements for getting photo and film material away from that crucial point had been halted on the order of a Guards major who was not allowing anyone to 'cross the lines' of the troops around Buckingham Palace. He was obviously not familiar with the arrangements which I had made with the London District Command. I telephoned the Signal Unit in the Abbey but they could not suggest any way of reaching the recalcitrant major. I extracted the brown folder of 'Orders for Troops lining the Route' from the cabinet of files we had prepared for every contingency.

It was easy to see how a hasty reading of the orders could lead to misunderstanding. Para. 31(a) stated that 'all officers lining the Route, no less than the police, are responsible for keeping the Route clear.' Another paragraph qualified this instruction so far as the area around the Palace was concerned and pointed to the 'instructions issued separately in the Appendix'. I asked for one of the emergency cars from the Church House Garage to collect me at Horseferry House.

After the warmth and brightness of the Abbey I walked through the cold and depressing downpour of the worst June day I could remember. The wind carried the sound of music and I knew that the head of the long procession was already on the move. The car took me by Tothill Street and Petty France to the road block at Buckingham Gate. A police inspector passed me through to a Guards sergeant who looked at me thoughtfully. 'The major is a right scorcher', he told me as he indicated where I could find him. The major lowered down at me from under his tall bearskin. Reluctantly he looked at the instructions on which the rain was steadily falling. Reluctantly he conceded there had been a misunderstanding. The ways of communication would be opened again.

I crossed the lines of troops with the rain dripping on their polished toecaps to inform the steward. The rain was sweeping like a grey mist around the rising tiers of concentric stands which encircled the Monument. The long telephoto lens of the TV camera, shrouded in canvas, pointed like a howitzer down the Mall. The public address system which had relayed the service from the Abbey suddenly began to vibrate with the music of a military band. The head of the procession was entering Trafalgar Square.

'Get these packages away', I told the steward and watched the police cadets running like hares across the grey rainswept space around the Memorial. The photographers were taking the lens caps off their cameras and the journalists had come round to the tiers facing the Mall. The packed thousands in the Mall seemed to stir with expectancy. The

troops were passing their waterproof capes behind their lines and the ripples of command came briskly towards us as the troops were called to attention. The long route now had a fringe of stiff scarlet tunics.

The sound from the loudspeakers faded out to be replaced by the distant but direct music of the military bands, and the remote and hollow sound of cheering. I saw the car that nobody bothered to notice – the signal car which moved several hundred yards in front of the procession.

Then a moment later the roar of the crowd seemed to break through the Admiralty arches and come rolling down the Mall towards us as an officer of the War Office riding ahead of four troopers of the Household Cavalry brought the Procession into view led by the four military bands of the IV Hussars, Royal Scots Fusiliers and the Durham and the Gloucester Regiments.

We shall never again see together in one place the first contingents which came marching towards us under the golden crowns of the four great arches. Their uniforms were as diverse as the territories from which they had come – the Solomon Islands, North Borneo, Sarawak, Malaya, Bermuda, Trinidad, the Leeward Islands, Somaliland, Sierra Leone, Malta, Cyprus, West Africa, Singapore – men from the frontiers and island outposts of an Empire marching on one more occasion as forces of the British Crown. There were delighted smiles on their faces as the welcoming roar of the crowd surged around them.

Behind the Colonial contingents came the forces of the Commonwealth – the small brisk men of Ceylon, the turbanned troops of Pakistan, the tan uniforms of South Africa, slouch-hatted Australians, the 'Kiwi' troops of New Zealand and the Canadian detachments, with the scarlet tunics and wide brimmed hats of the Royal Canadian Mounted Police receiving a special roar of recognition and welcome.

The strangest sight I saw among those marching men were the Papua New Guinea troops, leading the Australian contingent, swinging along in their drenched blue skirts and blouses, their cheerful faces glistening with the rain.

Marching with the Commonwealth contingents were the detachments of their Naval and Air forces.

Four more military bands were leading the long blue lines of the first detachment of the British Isles, 2,000 men and women from all the RAF commands at home and overseas – Fighter, Bomber and Coastal Commands, the RAF Regiment, the Volunteer Reserve, the Women's Royal Air Force and all those specialist services which kept the men and the machines flying.

There was a glimpse of wartime battledress as the Home Guard – not yet known as 'Dad's Army' – came down the Mall leading the British Army contingents. Behind them were the detachments of the Territorial Army wearing the unfamiliar dark blue of the Army new no. 1 dress, with the coloured regimental stripes on the trousers as well as on the epaulettes of the officers.

41   The Departure from the Abbey.

There was a splendid skirling of pipes and rolling of drums as the pipe bands of the Irish and Scottish regiments, kilts swinging and tartan trews striding, came down the Mall with the pipers from Pakistan and Nepal to add their own higher notes to the fierce sounds of the Gaelic pipers.

They were followed by the Regular Infantry from the seventy-five regiments of the British Army. Breaking into the uniform blue of the marching columns came the contingent from the Brigade of Gurkhas, receiving their own great roar of welcoming recognition.

The marching lines coming down the route changed to a lighter blue as the contingents of the Royal Navy came into sight, including the white helmets of the Royal Marines. The colour of the marching line began to change again as the red tunics of the first detachment of the five companies of Foot Guards came through the Arch. As they approached, the front of the Palace was throwing back the fiercely rolling beat of the Corps of Drums of the Irish and Welsh Guards.

Drawing their guns and riding six abreast, the King's Troop of the Royal Horse Artillery divided to pass through Admiralty Arch, re-forming again as though they had never broken ranks.

The regular lines of marching men were broken by the appearance of the four carriages of the Colonial rulers with their escorts of mounted Military Police. I saw the Sultan of Perak in his brilliant blue robes leaning forward to view the waving and cheering crowds. It was, however, the fourth carriage which brought the thundering approval of the waiting crowds. In the only coach which had not drawn its protective hood against the rain, her dark hair streaked down her cheeks, her robe saturated with moisture, was the huge smiling Queen Salote Toupou of Tonga. All around me the photographers were pointing their cameras, some of them shouting in a shared affection with the cheering crowds. I am afraid that no one noticed the ruefully smiling, and equally wet, Sultan of Kelantan who was sharing the carriage with the Queen of a Pacific island who had completely captured the enthusiasm of Coronation London.

With that burst of cheering the crowd seemed for a while to have lost the capacity for further expression. The Clarence coaches of the Commonwealth Prime Ministers came sedately towards us. The crowds waiting to see Sir Winston Churchill were disappointed. His carriage had been forced to halt by the risk of a collision with another carriage. Thus, losing his place, Churchill had driven direct to Downing Street. The Marshals of the RAF, the chaplains, the surgeons, the Army Staff and the Admirals on horseback, I am afraid, got little recognition because the attention of everyone was now straining down the Mall for the climax of the day.

There was a gleam of scarlet beneath the Arch which heralded the arrival of the Yeomen of the Guard, followed by the rare appearance of the Queen's Bargemaster and twelve Watermen in their black jockey caps, scarlet tunics and breeches.

With a flash of silver trumpets and a flail of drumsticks the mounted band of the Royal Horse Guards came towards us and beyond the tossing plumes of the Household Cavalry we could see the roof of the State Coach with the golden crown upheld by three gilded cupids. The great roar of acclamation came rolling down towards us. This was the brief,

42   Commonwealth and Colonial troops in the procession.

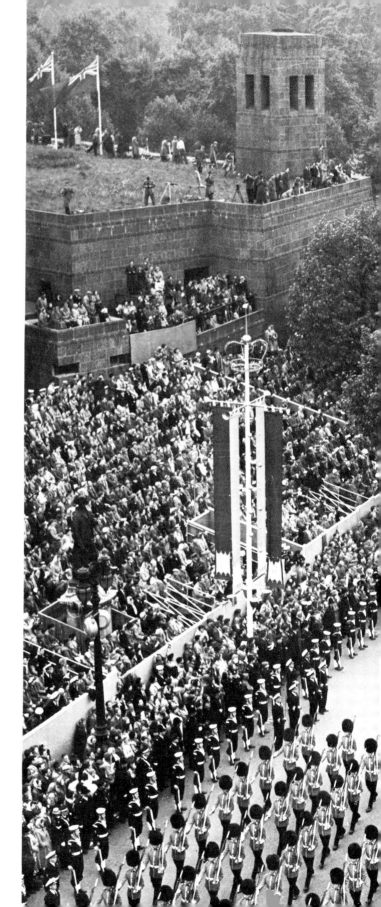

43   Guards and other British troops in the procession.

44   The Queen of Tonga in her open carriage, smiling in the rain.

culminating and rewarding moment for all the hours of waiting and cheerful endurance in the cold and rain. Many of the people on the pavements, who now seemed all throats and waving arms, had been there for two nights and a day. All those hours were redeemed, so it seemed, by this passing glimpse of a radiant young woman, wearing a crown of fairy-tale splendour, who waved and smiled and laughed to the thousands who had waited so long to acclaim her with 'heart and mind' and with a popular fervour with which few sovereigns have ever been received on their Coronation Day.

As I got this glimpse of the Queen passing by, I felt grateful to the obstructive Guards major who had brought me there. I now had two vivid and lasting pictures in my mind. I had seen her grave composure and dedication during the long ceremony in the Abbey and I had now seen the animated young Queen responding with laughing pleasure to the crowds who greeted her. It was like having seen both sides of a golden coin.

The moment passed. The Golden Coach with its Sovereign's Escort turned into the Palace gates and was lost to our view. The pressmen had moved over to the Palace side of the enclosure and were looking up at the Royal Standard flying in the northerly wind and at the balcony draped in crimson with gold fringes and tassels.

When would the Queen appear, I was asked? I knew it would not be for some time.

45 The Golden Coach passes by. The moment for which over a million people had patiently
waited.

Apart from a brief respite, there were a series of posed photographs of the Queen, the
Duke and other family groups. I looked down the Mall where the crowds were already
bulging into the road against the arm-locked resistance of the police. The police were
expediting the rate at which the disabled ex-servicemen were taken from their places in
front of the Palace. I suggested that all film and photographic material should be immediately got away before the crowds hemmed us in.

   I went to the stand telephone for more definite news. I knew that the procession had
reached the Palace well behind schedule. I learned that the rain had swept away the
careful sanding as fast as it had been laid down. When the horses began to slip the
marshals had slowed the pace of the procession. Policemen and troops at some points,
like the gentle slope in St James's Street, had to heave on the wheels of coaches and
carriages to assist the horses. Six soldiers had been injured by fixed bayonets when their
rear rank had slipped in the wet.

   What was the position of the RAF flypast over the Palace? While the Queen was in
the Abbey an aircraft had flown a weather reconnaissance and reported that unless the
low cloud lifted a flight over London in tight formation could be hazardous. The weather
had improved, however, and aircraft from Wattisham, Horsham St Faith and other stations

46 The glimpse of the radiant young Queen. Few noticed the bracket beneath her hand which supported the Orb.

XIII   The Recognition. Before the ceremony begins the Queen and the other participants turn to face the congregation while the Archbishop moves forward to speak to the people 'with a loud voice', saying, 'Sirs, I here present unto you Queen Elizabeth, your undoubted Queen.'

XIV   The Return to the Palace. The Queen in the State Coach comes to the long journey's end.

were already airborne and the RAF controller, Air Vice-Marshal Lord Bandon, on the roof of Buckingham Palace, had decided to bring them in. They would not, however, be flying in the tight formation which had been originally proposed.

When I looked down again, the triple Guards of Honour had been withdrawn and the lines of police were still struggling to hold the crowds. The cadets down below suddenly dodged under the policemen's arms and raced for the Palace railings. The police lines bulged, broke and were swept away as the avalanche of people came pouring down the Mall to reach the Palace. The huge amphitheatre around the Monument was filled with heads, umbrellas and waving flags.

I knew that the Queen's appearance on the balcony would coincide with the flypast. I passed on the information.

At 5.40 the windows on the balcony were seen to be opening and a great roar came from the crowds which mounted to its crescendo as the Queen appeared still crowned and wearing the Royal Robes. Behind her came the Duke of Edinburgh with Prince Charles and Princess Anne, the six Maids of Honour and the Queen Mother with Princess Margaret to form a tableau of the Royal Family.

The metallic thunder of the approaching aircraft almost drowned the acclamation of the crowd as the first wing of Meteors came over, their black arrow-head shapes trailing the misty clouds from their wing tips. The sky seemed filled with the sleek shapes of jet fighters in the salute order of 7 wings each of 24 aircraft. Down below the huge amphitheatre seemed to turn a fuzzy white as thousands of faces were lifted to the sky for the minute of the flypast. Then like a lid closing, every face turned to the balcony again.

I edged my way eventually through the crowds hemming us in and had a friendly buffeting from the crowds pouring down the Mall. The crowds outside the Palace would stay there until midnight; they would see the Queen at 9.45 on the balcony turn on the 'lights of London', sending the lights cascading down the Mall, lighting the huge cipher on the Admiralty Arch, turning the fountains in Trafalgar Square into liquid silver, until all the floodlights from the National Gallery to the Tower of London had been turned on. Six times the clamant demand of the crowd would bring the Queen on to the balcony.

The big buffet in Westminster Hall had been swept clean of food, but the Royal Gallery in the House of Lords had a friendly colleague in charge. I had a deep relaxing armchair, a huge plate of sandwiches and a big jug of coffee.

The peers still in the House had left their robes and mantles in the cloakrooms and some had exchanged their fine feathers for sober suits; a few were still in service uniforms and there were even a few hybrids like the peer who retained his white breeches below a thick polo-necked pullover.

There were duties and spectacles to keep me in London but the mainspring of my day seemed to have run down. So much of sight, sound and feeling had been crowded into the hours.

Later that evening I had to go back to the Abbey again. The familiar Ministry custodians were back on the doors. The Crowns and Regalia had gone from the Abbey – for the length of another lifetime. Only a few of the lamps were lit in the high vault above the Sanctuary so that they formed narrow pyramids of light in the surrounding darkness. As I stood by

47   The Queen on the balcony of
Buckingham Palace after the return from
the Abbey with the Duke of Edinburgh,
Prince Charles, Princess Anne, the
Queen Mother, and other members of
the Royal Family.

48   The Balcony Scene – a closer view.

the Choir Screen to look towards the Theatre it was like gazing down a narrow perspective, not only of distance but also of time. All the golden splendour of the ceremony, the brilliance of colour, the triumphant music, the pealing trumpets and the shouts of acclamation seemed already to have become part of a distant past, scenes which had already receded into the depths of memory.

I turned away to go to the Ministry's office, where the BBC had provided a link to the radio programme for our own and Abbey staff. There were a few colleagues, a black-gowned Abbey custodian and a CID officer waiting there. We listened to the Coronation broadcast – 'Long Live the Queen!' One by one the Prime Ministers and others in the many accents of the Commonwealth, paid their tributes of loyalty. Then we heard the familiar voice of Winston Churchill with its recollection of other and far less happy times. The old statesman spoke with emotion.

'We have had a day which the oldest are proud to have lived to see and which the youngest will remember all their lives. It is my duty and my honour to lead you to its culmination.

'You have heard the Prime Ministers of the Empire and Commonwealth pay their moving tributes on behalf of the famous States and races for which they speak. The splendours of this second of June glow in our minds.

'Now as night falls you will hear the voice of our Sovereign herself crowned in our history and enthroned for ever in our hearts.'

In a voice which rang with fervour the old Prime Minister proclaimed, 'The Queen.'

The Queen's voice was clear and firm, showing no trace of weariness after her long and arduous day. There were moments when it was touched by a deep undercurrent of emotion as she spoke.

'Throughout this memorable day I have been uplifted and sustained by the knowledge that your thoughts and prayers were with me. I have been aware all the time that my peoples, spread far and wide throughout every continent and ocean in the world were united to support me in the task to which I have now been dedicated with such solemnity.

'The ceremonies you have seen today are ancient and some of their origins are veiled in the mists of the past. But their spirit and their meaning shine through the ages, never perhaps, more brightly than now.

'I have in sincerity pledged my self to your service, as so many of you are pledged to mine. Throughout all my life and with all my heart I shall strive to be worthy of your trust.'

The Queen spoke of the support of her husband, 'Who shares all my ideals and my affection for you. I have in my parents an example which I will follow with certainty and confidence.

'There is also this. I have behind me, not only the splendid traditions and annals of more than a thousand years, but the living strength and majesty of the Commonwealth, of societies old and new, of lands and races different in history and origin but all, by God's will, united in spirit and in aim.

'Therefore, I am sure that this, my Coronation, is not a symbol of power and a splendour that are gone but a declaration of our hopes for the future and for the years, I may, by

50   The Coronation Celebrations. One of the thousands of street parties in cities and towns throughout Britain and many parts of the Commonwealth.

49   Coronation Night. Vast crowds move towards the Palace beneath the floodlit arches. London was a city of light, music and dancing in the streets.

CORONATION *OF HER MAJESTY*
QUEEN ELIZABETH II

By Command of The Queen

the Earl Marshal is directed to invite

to be present at the Abbey Church of
Westminster on the 2nd day of June 1953

Norfolk.

Earl Marshal

51   The Coronation Invitation. Coronation invitation cards have always been the treasured souvenirs of those who received them. Those for George IV and Queen Victoria were heavy with crowns and heraldic decorations. The card for Queen Elizabeth II was of a more elegant design.

The designer was Miss Joan Hassall, RE, and Mr S. B. Stead, the official Artist and Scribe of the Stationery Office was responsible for the lettering.

Two qualities were sought in the design – dignity for the great occasion and grace for the Queen herself. These have been expressed by Miss Hassall by combining the formal splendour of the Royal Coat of Arms with free-flowing arabesques of flowers associated with the Commonwealth countries. No particular order of precedence is indicated in the arrangement of the flowers, and to mark this the two sides are not identical. The British oak leaf appears several times among the flowers of the garland as a reminder that the symbolism of the oak is common to British people. A part of the Regalia has been introduced into the design as being appropriate to the occasion, with the Sceptre and Rod integrated into and embraced by the Commonwealth flowers, while the Crown dominates the central group containing the Orb, the Ampulla with its Spoon, and two of the Swords.

The flowers which appear are the rose, which is associated with England; the thistle, Scotland; the leek, Wales; the shamrock, Northern Ireland; the maple leaf, Canada; the wattle, Australia; the fern, New Zealand; the protea, South Africa; the lotus, India; cotton, jute and wheat, Pakistan; and another lotus, Ceylon.

The card, which was printed in very dark blue on white, was $8\frac{3}{4}$ in. by $10\frac{1}{2}$ in.

52   The Queen and the Duke of Edinburgh on their return from the Abbey.

53   A Coronation Day picture for the Royal Family Album.

God's grace and mercy, be given to reign and serve as your Queen.

'As this day draws to its close, I know that my abiding memory of it will be, not only the solemnity and beauty of the ceremony, but the inspiration of your loyalty and affection. I thank you all from a full heart. God bless you all.'

Although I had almost been satiated with spectacle I went back to the Palace of Westminster; the Serjeant at Arms, Sir Charles Howard, had sent me an invitation to view from the terrace the great firework *feu de joie* which was going to burst over the Thames. A wide area of the South Bank had been used to set up the display, the cost being shared by the Ministry and the LCC. There was a cold wind on the terrace but the sight was worth waiting for. The crash of forty-one maroons firing the Royal Salute was the prelude to the night sky lighting up with a huge pyrotechnic portrait of the Queen in sparkling colours, followed by one of the Duke of Edinburgh, Prince Charles and Princess Anne. From then on the skies were filled with rising and falling cascades of colour, gigantic catherine wheels 100 feet across and a waterfall of silver light pouring down along the 900 feet of the waterfront. The huge crowds on the Embankment and along Westminster Bridge roared their approval.

It was the night when floodlit London danced in the ballrooms and in the streets until dawn. I did not stay to see it. As I sank back gratefully into my car I could see the bonfire blazing as we passed Hyde Park. It was one of a thousand bonfires which had been lit that night. From Cornwall to John o' Groats the fires were being lit in parks and village greens, on hills and mountain peaks, along the Cotswold and Malvern Hills, on the North and South Downs, along the Pennines, on the mountains of Wales and on the craggy top of Ben Nevis. Many of them were on sites where they had blazed their messages of war and danger and of the coming and the passings of kings and queens for over a thousand years.

When I arrived home my children came rushing to tell me of the spectacles and excitement of their own day. My two young sons had seen the procession from seats in the Mall. My daughter, too young for the journey, had watched the events on television with her grandmother, surrounded by her friends and our neighbours.

At last, weary with the excitements of a day they would always remember, they were ready for bed. As my little daughter kissed me good night, she said, 'Why have you got that funny stick and why are you wearing that funny dress?'

She was right. It was time to put away my Gold Staff and to take off my garment for the day. My suit was still very much like that worn by civil servants when Charles II had come to his coronation. Pepys had witnessed that event and recorded it. He had sneaked into the Abbey and cajoled his way into the great stand in the North Transept of the Abbey and sat with the greatest pleasure for seven hours storing in his retentive mind that magnificent spectacle below him. I took down my copy of his Diary and at the end of that long day I read what another servant of the Crown had written on that occasion.

'Now', he wrote, 'after all this I can say that besides the pleasure of the sight of these glorious things, I may now shut my eyes against any other objects, nor for the future trouble myself to see things of state and show, as being sure never to see the like again in this world.'

The Return Journey
Order of the Procession
from the Abbey to Buckingham Palace

THE COLONIES

7 The Officer Commanding the Colonial Contingents, Lt-Col. G. N. Ross, the Gordon Highlanders (attached Royal West African Frontier Force).

8 Detachments from the armed police forces of Cyprus, Solomon Islands, Trinidad, Bahamas, Windward Islands, North Borneo, Sarawak, and Malaya.

9 Air Force detachments from Hong Kong, Malaya and Aden Protectorate.

10 Detachments from armed forces of Barbados, Bermuda, British Guiana, British Honduras, Leeward Islands, Falkland Islands, Singapore, Hong Kong, Malta, Gibraltar, Jamaica, Malaya, Fiji, Kenya, Somaliland, East Africa, Northern Rhodesia, and West Africa.

11 Naval detachments from Sierra Leone, Mauritius, Malaya, Hong Kong and East Africa.

THE COMMONWEALTH

12–18 Officers commanding and detachments from armed forces of Southern Rhodesia, Ceylon, Pakistan, South Africa, New Zealand, Australia and Canada (including Canadian Mounted Police).

THE UNITED KINGDOM

19 Representing bands of the Royal Army Medical Corps, Royal 22e Regiment, Canadian Army, No. 1 Regional Band, Royal Air Force, No. 2 Regional Band, Royal Air Force.

The Royal Air Force

20–24 The Air Officer Commanding and detachments from 17 RAF Groups, including Royal Air Force Volunteer Reserve, Royal Auxiliary Air Force, Women's Royal Air Force, and Princess Mary's Royal Air Force Nursing Service.

The Army

25 The Home Guard and the University Training Corps detachment.

26 Representing bands of the Royal Air Force College, Royal Air Force Regiment, Royal Army Ordnance Corps, and Royal Army Service Corps.

27 The Royal Military Academy and the Honourable Artillery Company.

28 Women's Royal Army Corps and Queen Alexandra's Royal Army Nursing Corps.

Other Corps

29 The Officer Commanding and detachments of Other Corps of the Army (represented by the Royal Army Medical Corps).

The Infantry Contingent

30 The Officer Commanding the Infantry Contingent.

The Territorial Army

31 Detachments from 92 battalions of the Territorial Army plus 21st Special Air Service Regiment and 16th Independent Parachute Company.

The Brigade of Gurkhas

32 The Officer Commanding and detachments from Gurkha Regiments.

33 Bands of 1st Battalion the Rifle Brigade and 1st Battalion the Duke of Cornwall's Light Infantry and detachments from 10 Pipe Bands and Massed Pipe Bands of the Brigade of Gurkhas.

The Regular Army

34 Detachments from 75 Infantry Battalions, plus 1st Independent Parachute Company and the Glider Pilot Regiment.

35 The Officers Commanding and detachments from the Royal Corps of Signals, Royal Engineers and Royal Artillery.

36 The Officers Commanding and the Yeomanry and Territorial Army and Regular Army Armoured Corps Contingents.
37 Detachment of Royal Horse Artillery.
38 The Officer Commanding the Household Cavalry Contingent and detachments from the Armoured Car Regiment of the Royal Horse Guards (The Blues) and the Life Guards.
39 Four bands including the Band of the Royal Marines (Plymouth Group).

The Royal Navy

40–42 The Officer Commanding the Naval Contingent and detachments including Royal Marines, Women's Royal Naval Service and Seamen.

The Household Brigade

The First Detachment of Foot-guards
43 The Officer Commanding, a staff officer, and 5 companies of Guards.
44 Bands of the Welsh and Irish Guards and Corps of Drums of 1st Battalions Welsh and Irish Guards.

The Second Detachment of Foot-guards
45 The Officer Commanding, a staff officer and 5 companies of Guards.
46 The Officer Commanding and the King's Troop, Royal Horse Artillery.

CARRIAGE PROCESSION AND ESCORTS, SENIOR OFFICERS AND PERSONAL STAFF

The Carriages of Colonial Rulers

47 1st carriage: HH the Sultan of Lahej; HH the Sultan of Selangor accompanied by HH the Tengku Ampuan.
48 2nd carriage: HH the Sultan of Brunei; HH the Sultan of Johore accompanied by HH the Sultana.
49 3rd carriage: HH the Sultan of Perak; HH the Sultan of Zanzibar accompanied by HH the Sultana.
50 4th carriage: HH the Sultan of Kelantan; HM the Queen of Tonga.
All escorted by Mounted Military Police.

The Carriages of Prime Ministers

51 1st carriage: the Prime Minister of Northern Ireland, the Rt Hon. Viscount Brookeborough, CBE, MC, accompanied by the Viscountess Brookeborough; the Prime Minister of Southern Rhodesia, the Rt Hon. Sir Godfrey Huggins, PC, KCMG, CH, accompanied by Lady Huggins.
Northern Irish and Southern Rhodesian Mounted Escort.
52 2nd carriage: the Prime Minister of Ceylon, the Hon. Dudley Senanayake.
Ceylon Mounted Escort.
53 3rd carriage: the Prime Minister of Pakistan, the Hon. Mohammed Ali, accompanied by the Begum Mohammed Ali.
Pakistan Mounted Escort.
54 4th carriage: the Prime Minister of India, the Hon. Jawaharlal Nehru, accompanied by Mrs Indira Gandhi.
55 5th carriage: the Prime Minister of the Union of South Africa, Doctor the Hon. D. F. Malan, accompanied by Mrs Malan.
South African Mounted Escort.
56 6th carriage: the Prime Minister of New Zealand, the Rt Hon. S. G. Holland, PC, CH, accompanied by Mrs Holland.
New Zealand Mounted Escort.
57 7th carriage: the Prime Minister of the Commonwealth of Australia, the Rt Hon. R. G. Menzies, PC, CH, QC, accompanied by Mrs Menzies.
Australian Mounted Escort.
58 8th carriage: the Prime Minister of Canada, the Rt Hon. L. S. St Laurent, PC, QC, accompanied by Mrs St Laurent.
Canadian Mounted Escort.
59 9th carriage: the Prime Minister of the United Kingdom, the Rt Hon. Sir Winston S. Churchill, KG, PC, OM, CH, TD, accompanied by Lady Churchill.
Escort of 4th Queen's Own Hussars.

THE CARRIAGES OF THE PRINCES AND PRINCESSES OF THE BLOOD ROYAL

60 First Division, Non-commissioned Officers' Escort, Household Cavalry.
61 1st carriage: the Lady Patricia Ramsay; Her Royal Highness Princess Alice, Countess of Athlone; Major-General the Earl of Athlone; Her Royal Highness Princess Marie Louise.
62 2nd carriage: the Duchess of Kent; the Duke of Kent; Princess Alexandra of Kent; Prince Michael of Kent.
63 3rd carriage: the Princess Royal; the Duchess of Gloucester; Prince Richard of Gloucester.
64 Second Division, Non-commissioned Officers' Escort, Household Cavalry.

THE CARRIAGE PROCESSION OF
HM QUEEN ELIZABETH THE QUEEN MOTHER

65 State landau conveying suite.
66 First Division, Captains' Escort, Household Cavalry.
67 The Irish State Coach, conveying Her Majesty Queen Elizabeth the Queen Mother and Her Royal Highness Princess Margaret.
68 Second Division, Captains' Escort, Household Cavalry, with Standard.
69 QHP, QHS, QHDS, Chaplains, Honorary Chaplains and Aides-de-Camp, Royal Air Force.
70 QHP, QHS, QHDS, Chaplains, Honorary Chaplains and Aides-de-Camp, Army.
71 QHP, QHS, QHDS, Chaplains, Honorary Chaplains and Aides-de-Camp, Naval and Royal Marines.
72 Band of the Grenadier Guards, Corps of Drums 1st Battalion Grenadier Guards.
73 Air Ministry Staff.
74 War Office Staff.
75 Admiralty Staff.
76 Senior Officers of the armed forces of the Commonwealth.
77 Deputy Supreme Commander (Air), Air Officers Commanding-in-Chief and Inspector General.
78 General Officers Commanding-in-Chief and General Officer Commanding Northern Ireland District.
79 Flag Officers Commanding-in-Chief, Home Commands.
80 Air Aide-de-Camp and Aides-de-Camp General.

MARSHALS OF THE ROYAL AIR FORCE

81 1st carriage: Sir John C. Slessor, GCB, DSO, MC; Sir Arthur Harris, Bart, GCB, OBE, AFC; the Lord Douglas of Kirtleside, GCB, MC, DFC; the Lord Tedder, GCB.
82 2nd carriage: the Viscount Portal of Hungerford, KG, GCB, OM, DSO, MC; Sir Edward L. Ellington, GCB, CMG, CBE; Sir John M. Salmond, GCB, CMG, CVO, DSO.
83 3rd carriage: the Viscount Trenchard, GCB, OM, GCVO, DSO; the Lord Wilson of Libya, GCB, GBE, DSO.

FIELD MARSHALS

84 Sir Claude J. Auchinleck, GCB, GCIE, CSI, DSO, OBE; the Earl Alexander of Tunis, KG, GCB, GCMG, CSI, DSO, MC; the Lord Ironside, GCB, CMG, DSO; the Viscount Montgomery of Alamein, KG, GCB, DSO.

ADMIRALS OF THE FLEET

85 Sir A. John Power, GCB, GBE, CVO; Sir Algernon U. Willis, GCB, KBE, DSO; Sir John H. D. Cunningham, GCB, MVO, DL.
87 Air Council – Air Members.
88 Army Council – Military Members.
89 Board of Admiralty – Sea Lords.
90 Chiefs of Staff – United Kingdom: General Sir John Harding, GCB, CBE, DSO, MC, ADC; Admiral Sir Rhoderick McGrigor, GCB, DSO; Air Chief Marshal Sir William Dickson, GCB, KBE, DSO, AFC.

THE PROCESSION OF HM THE QUEEN

91 The Queen's Escort of Officers from the Colonial Contingents.
92 The Queen's Escort of Officers from the Commonwealth Contingents.
93 The Yeomen of the Guard.
94 The Queen's Bargemaster and 12 Watermen.
95 Mounted Band of the Royal Horse Guards (The Blues).
96 First Division of the Sovereign's Escort.
97 Three two-horsed state carriages conveying suite.
98 Second Division of the Sovereign's Escort.
99 ADC to the Deputy Commander to the Field Marshal Commanding Coronation Troops: Captain G. R. M. Sewell, Grenadier Guards; ADC to the Field Marshal Commanding Coronation Troops: Captain A. I. Castle, Royal Horse Artillery.
100 Deputy Commander to the Field Marshal Commanding Coronation Troops: Major-General J. A. Gascoigne, CB, DSO; Commissioner of Police of the Metropolis: Sir Harold Scott, KCB, KBE.
101 The Field Officer of the Escort: Lieutenant-Colonel W. H. Gerard Leigh, the Life Guards; the Field Officer Commanding the Escort, Lieutenant-Colonel D. de C. Smiley, MVO, OBE, MC, Royal Horse Guards.
102 The State Coach conveying HER MAJESTY THE QUEEN and HIS ROYAL HIGHNESS THE DUKE OF EDINBURGH.
103 The Standard.
104 The Master of the Horse: the Duke of Beaufort, KG; the Lord High Constable and Field Marshal Commanding Coronation Troops: Field Marshal the Viscount Alanbrooke, KG, GCB, OM, DSO.

105   The Captain, the Yeomen of the Guard:
the Earl of Onslow, MC, TD; the Gold-Stick-
in-Waiting: Major-General Sir Richard
Howard-Vyse, KCMG, DSO.

106   The Field Officer in Brigade Waiting:
Colonel T. F. C. Winnington, MBE, Grenadier
Guards; the Silver-Stick-in-Waiting:
Colonel E. J. S. Ward, MVO, MC, the Life
Guards.

107   Personal Aides-de-Camp to the Queen:
General His Royal Highness the Duke of
Gloucester, KG, KT, KP, PC, GCB, GCMG,
GCVO; Admiral the Earl Mountbatten of
Burma, KG, PC, GCSI, GCIE, GCVO, KCB, DSO.

108   Principal Services Aides-de-Camp:
General Sir Frank E. W. Simpson, KCB, KBE,
DSO; Admiral Sir John Edelston, KCB, CBE.

109   Equerries to the Queen: Lieutenant-General
Sir Frederick A. M. Browning, KBE, CB, DSO;
Major Sir Michael Adeane, KCVO, CB;
Colonel Sir Dermot McM. Kavanagh, KCVO;
Captain Viscount Althorp.

110   Brigade Major Household Brigade:
Major A. M. H. Gregory-Hood, MC, Grenadier
Guards; Chief of Staff to the Field Marshal
Commanding Coronation Troops:
Brigadier W. M. Sale, CVO, OBE.

111   Adjutant in Brigade Waiting: Major F. J. C.
Bowes-Lyon, MC, Grenadier Guards; Silver
Stick Adjutant: Major J. K. Doxford, Royal
Horse Guards.

112   Royal Grooms.

113   Third Division of the Sovereign's Escort.

114   Fourth Division of the Sovereign's Escort.

Sources and Bibliography

The public documentation of the Coronation of Queen Elizabeth II is undoubtedly the most complete of any in history. From the Accession in February 1952 to the Coronation on 2 June 1953 the newspapers, magazines and professional and technical periodicals followed every step of the preparations, which were also recorded on films, newsreels, radio and BBC TV and by the media of many countries round the world. There is abundant information for future researchers and historians.

This information came from the Ministry of Works, the Service Departments, the Earl Marshal's office, the Church Information Service, Westminster Abbey, as well as from the other firms, contractors and craftsmen and artists who were involved and from organisations like the Council of Industrial Design on Coronation Souvenirs, the Royal School of Needlework, the British Travel and Holiday Association, the Coronation Accommodation Committee, London Transport, British Railways, the London County Council and the organisations of street traders such as those of Regent Street and Oxford Street in London. Every provincial and local paper had copious accounts of their preparations and events.

The Ministry provided a continuous flow of information by press conferences, facility visits to the centres of preparations and from October 1952 an almost weekly series of background notes and general press statements.

The official publications on the Coronation Service

The Coronation of Her Majesty Queen Elizabeth II. The Form and Order of the Service. (This was issued in several formats.)

The Coronation of Her Majesty Queen Elizabeth II. The Ceremonial. (This omitted the prayers and anthems and concentrated on the Earl Marshal's directions for the lay ceremony.)

Both were published by Order in Council.

Approved Souvenir Programme, The King George Jubilee Trust, London 1953. (Details of the Processions, the Route and the Form and Order of the Service.)

The Music . . . to be Performed at the Coronation of Her Majesty Queen Elizabeth II, Novello, 1953.

Edward C. Ratcliff, Ely Professor of Divinity in the University of Cambridge, was a member of the Archbishop of Canterbury's Liturgical Committee on the Service. His book, *The Coronation Service of Queen Elizabeth II* (SPCK, 1953), was my guide on liturgical matters.

Where personal recollections and descriptions are concerned I have relied on my own diaries and notes made at the time.

The Coronation History and Liturgy

Beauchamp, Lord, ed., *Liber Regalis*, Roxburghe Club, London, 1870.

Bridge, Sir Frederick, *An account of the Music performed at Coronation of Edward VII*, Novello, 1901.

Burke, *Historical Records of the Coronation of . . . Edward VII*, Harrison, 1901.

Eeles, F. C., *The English Coronation Service*, Mowbray, 1902.

Jones, William, *Crowns and Coronations*, Chatto & Windus, 1883.

Legg, J. Wickham, ed., *Missale ad usum Ecclesiae Westmonasteriensis*, Henry Bradshaw Society, 1891.

Legg, J. Wickham, ed., *Three Coronation Orders*, Henry Bradshaw Society, 1900.

Legg, J. Wickham, *The Coronation Order of James I*, Robinson, 1902.

Legg, L. G. Wickham, *English Coronation Records*, Constable, 1901.

Macleane, Douglas, *The Great Solemnity*, George Allen, 1911.

Perkins, Jocelyn, *The Crowning of the Sovereign*, Methuen, 1937 and 1953.

Ratcliff, E. C., *The English Coronation Service*, SPCK, Skeffington, 1936.

Ratcliff, E. C., *The Coronation Service of Queen Elizabeth II*, SPCK, Cambridge University Press, 1953.

Schramm, P. E., *History of the English Coronation*, London, 1937.

Taylor, Anthony, *The Glory of the Regality*, Payne & Foss, 1820.

Twining, E. F., *The English Coronation Service*, Simpkin Marshal, 1937.

Walker, Sir Edward, *Preparations for Coronation of . . . Charles II*, London, 1820.

Woolley, R. M., *Coronation Rites*, Handbooks for Liturgical Study, Cambridge, 1915.

Reference was also made to chroniclers such as Bede, the Anglo-Saxon Chronicles, William of Malmsbury, Henry of Huntingdon, Matthew Paris, Froissart, Roger Hovedon, down to the contemporary accounts in the *Annual Register* and the letters of Horace Walpole.

The official papers for many coronations, including those for 1953, are in the Public Records Office.

Westminster Abbey

Carpenter, E., ed., *A House of Kings*, John Baker, 1966.

Noppen, J. G., *Royal Westminster and the Coronation*, Country Life, 1937.

Stanley, Dean A. S., *Memorials of Westminster Abbey*, John Murray, 1886.

Westlake, H. F., *Westminster Abbey*, Philip Alan, 1927.

The Regalia

Holmes, Martin and Sitwell, Maj.-Gen. H. D. W., *The English Regalia*, HMSO, 1972.

Ministry of Works, *The Crown Jewels*, Official Guide, HMSO, 1953.

Sitwell, Maj.-Gen. H. D. W., *The Crown Jewels*, Dropmore Press, 1953.

Younghusband, Maj.-Gen. G., *The Crown Jewels of England*, Cassell, 1919.

Younghusband, Maj.-Gen. G., *The Jewel House*, Herbert Jenkins, 1921.

The Court of Claims

Woollaston, Sir G. W., *The Court of Claims*, Harrison, 1903.

The Coronation Chair

Ministry of Works, *The Coronation Chair*, HMSO, eds of 1953 and 1957.

General

Catalogue of Paintings and Drawings of the Coronation Commissioned by the Ministry of Works, Ministry of Works, 1953.

The Coronation and the BBC, BBC Publications, 1953.

Hook, W. F., *Lives of the Archbishops of Canterbury*, 10 vols, Richard Bentley, 1860.

Stubbs, William, *The Constitutional History of England*, Clarendon Press, 1896.

Turner, E. S., *The Court of St James*, Michael Joseph, 1960.

Wade, E. S. C. and Bradley, A. W., *Constitutional Law*, Longmans, 1965.

White, A. B., *The Making of the English Constitution*, Putnams, 1908.

The Year that Made the Day, BBC Publications, 1953.

Index

Page numbers in italic refer to photographs.

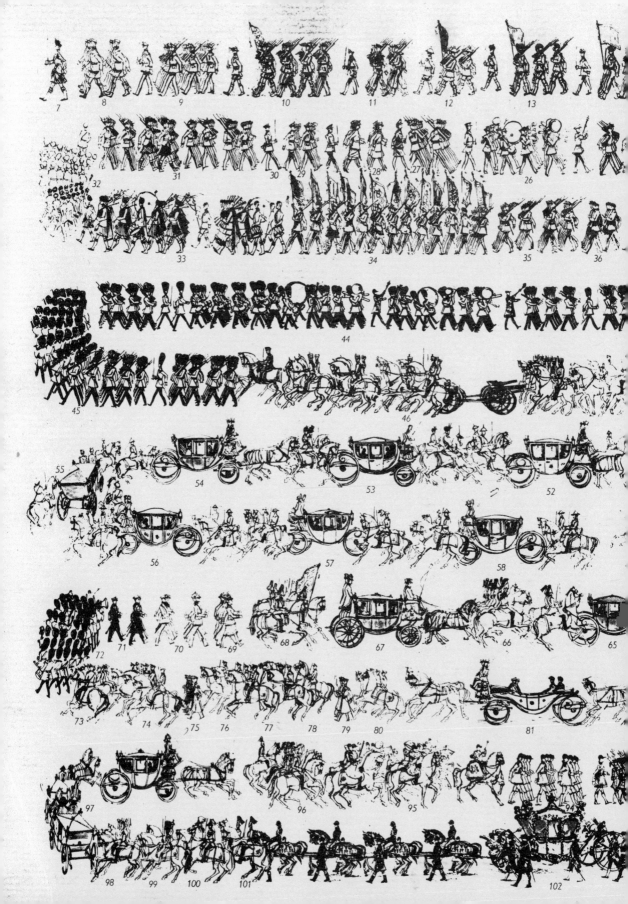